STATIC AND DYNAMIC APPLIED GENERAL EQUILIBRIUM TAX AND TRADE POLICY MODELS OF THE UK ECONOMY

STATIC AND DYNAMIC APPLIED GENERAL EQUILIBRIUM TAX AND TRADE POLICY MODELS OF THE UK ECONOMY

Keshab Bhattarai
Lecturer in Economics
The University of Hull, United Kingdom

SERIALS PUBLICATIONS
NEW DELHI (INDIA)

First Published - 2008

ISBN: 978-81-8387-138-9

Published by

SERIALS PUBLICATIONS
4830/24, Prahlad Street, Ansari Road
Darya Ganj, New Delhi-110002 (India)
Phone : 23245225. Fax : 91-11-23272135
E-mail: serials@satyam.net.in

CONTENTS

PART - III
Global General Equilibrium Trade Model
From UK Perspective

FOREWORD

Applied general equilibrium models have been in use for policy analysis over past 30 years. These models are used to simulate a model economy with various tax, trade and growth policy issues. It includes a static multisectoral and multi-asset model, a dynamic multisectoral model and a global trade model from the UK perspective.

Applied general equilibrium models take the Walrasian-Arrow-Debreu general equilibrium theory and solve it for an actual economy to analyse the efficiency and redistribution effects of taxes, trade and growth policies. Harberger (1959) showed the deadweight loss of taxes to be proportionate to the square of the tax rates. Shoven and Whalley (1972, 1977, 1984) developed calibration and computation techniques for an applied multi sectoral general equilibrium models using Scarf (1960) algorithm. Since then a large number of computable general equilibrium (CGE) models have been built and applied to analyze policy issues both of developed and developing economies (Ballard-Fullerton-Shoven-Whalley (BFSW(1985)), Taylor (1990), Robinson (1991), Shoven and Whalley (1992), Mercinier and Srinivasan (1994), Piggott and Whalley (1985)). These early models were essentially static and good for comparative static analysis. Advances in computational technology in 1990s (GAMS/MPSGE/PATH (Rutherford (1995), Dirkse and Ferris (1996))) has made it also possible to compute transitional effects of policy changes with more disaggregated dynamic general equilibrium models (Rutherford (1995) and Bhattarai (1997)). These dynamic models have more realistic institutional and sectoral dimensions for policy analyses on long-run growth, investment, savings, and capital than those found in one sector perfect foresight models as discussed by Ramsey (1929), Auerbach and Kotlikoff (1987) Perroni (1995).

I dedicate this book to millions of people in the UK and the US who have inspirec me on this work. I am particularly thankful to Professor John Whalley who selected me to work for the ESRC sponsored dynamic general equilibrium modelling of tax and trade policy issues in the UK economy at the University of Warwick in early 1996. I take full responsibility for all errors and omissions.

PART - I

STATIC MULTI-CAPITAL ASSET GENERAL EQUILIBRIUM TAX MODEL OF THE UK ECONOMY

1

INTRODUCTION

This book will contain three main parts. The first part will discuss a static tax multisectoral and multi-asset applied general equililibrium tax model and its application to the UK economy. We briefly discuss the specification of preferences and technology and market clearing conditions in Chapter Two. Implementation of the model with real UK data is discussed in Chapters Three and Four and the main results of implementation of this model are reported in Chapter 5.

The second part will contain an illustration of a dynamic multisectoral applied general equililibrium tax model and its application of evaluate efficiency and growth impacts of capital, labour and other indirect taxes in the UK economy. A more elaborate specification of dynamic general equilibrium models is shown in chapter two. The calibration technique with dataset and elasticities are discussed in chapter three. Results on dynamic efficiency effects and growth paths of capital, investment, output and employment are presented in chapter four. Specification of the dynamic model will be provided in Chapter 7 and calibration and results will be discussed in Chapter 8.

The third part will contain a global economy model from the UK perspective. The Chapter 9 contains specification and implementation of the global trade model. An eleven region multisectoral global trade model with a global trade analysis project (GTAP) dataset where UK is specified as a separate region is presented in chapter eight.

Chapter 10 will include overall summary and conclusion of the book.

Appendices will contain base year data tables and main codes of the model.

Though some of these research findings may have appeared in the form of working papers this book provides a comprehensive presentation of these models in one place. Most of the research activities undertaken under an ESRC research project in the Universities of Warwick (1996-1999) and Hull (since 1999).

STATIC MULTISECTORAL AND MULTI-ASSET GENERAL EQUILIBRIUM MODEL

First part of the book sets out the specification, calibration, replication and application of a 16 sector static general equilibrium tax policy model of the UK economy using a benchmark data set for the year 1995. To our knowledge this is the first attempt, after Piggott and Whalley (1985), to use a large scale GE tax policy model of the UK economy. This model uses data assembled by the Economics Unit of the Inland Revenue and aims to evaluate the efficiency effects of equal yield tax reforms in the UK economy using the year 1995 as its benchmark. The sectoral classification as well as the tax structure built into the model reflects the modelling interests of the Unit. Activity on this multisectoral tax model was undertaken jointly with the Economics Unit of the Inland Revenue. We include capital tax rates from the P-Tax[1] programme, which is now fully incorporated in GAMS code along with the core model. The benchmark 1995 data set is taken from the revised Input-Output table of the UK for the year 1995. Appendix 1 discusses the derivation of the data using Input-Output Balances and other data from the ONS in more detail.

The basic ingredients of the model are the same as those found in standard GE models of an Arrow-Debreu economy (Arrow and Hahn (1971)). Households maximise utility subject to their budget constraints. Their consumption and labour supply decisions influence producers' decisions, aimed at maximising profits subject to technology constraints. This model fulfils all of the standard equilibrium conditions that are characteristics of an applied general equilibrium model in the tradition of the BFSW model (Ballard, Fullerton, Shoven and Whalley (1985)). These equilibrium conditions imply that the markets for goods, labour and capital clear, firms receive zero profits in equilibrium, income is equal to expenditure for households, investors and government, and the value of exports equals the value of imports. The government collects direct and indirect taxes from households on their income and consumption, production and capital income taxes from corporations, and import duties from traders. It spends revenue on public consumption or redistributes it as transfers to households.

The GE tax model considered here includes five types of taxes existing in the UK in 1995. These taxes were: 1) capital income tax applied to five different categories of capital assets –buildings, plant and machinery with short and long life, vehicles and dwellings[2]; 2) tax on labour income (on labour; capital component is included in capital income taxes; 3) indirect taxes on public and private consumption and investment; 4) indirect taxes on use of intermediate inputs, and 5) tariffs on imports. We calibrate the model to the 1995 data set and ensure consistency of our code by replicating the benchmark data as a model solution.

The tax rates used in the model reflect the tax regime in the UK in 1995. Specifically, capital tax rates are differentiated by asset and sector; tax rates on income from building services and housing services are generally between 40 and 50 per cent, while the tax rate on dwellings is assumed to be zero. Similarly income from vehicles is taxed at between 15 and 21 per cent, while tax rates on plant and machinery of short life range from 12 per cent to 16 per cent across sectors. Besides capital income taxes the model uses a 38 per cent marginal income tax rate on household labour income.

VAT rates on intermediate and final demands are applied after other indirect taxes. Tariffs and subsidies are imposed on the basic price of commodities. Other levies and duties are applied to prices gross of tariffs and subsidies. Finally the VAT rates are applied on prices gross of all other taxes. Substantial difference exist in aggregated indirect tax rates on public and private consumption and investment, and on intermediate inputs. Generally indirect taxes on consumption are higher than those rates on investment or government consumption. Tariff rates vary between 0 and 4 per cent in the data set.

The model has mainly been used for equal yield capital income tax policy reforms, analyzed with the model after replicating the benchmark data. For each tax policy scenario, we compute changes in total money metric aggregate welfare by summing up money metric equivalent variations for households, investors and government. The money metric equivalent variations measure the amount of money to which the changes in the new equilibrium relative to the benchmark equilibrium are equivalent. A positive equivalent variation represents a gain compared to the old equilibrium and a negative equivalent variation represents a loss. We compute changes in the money metric equivalent variation measure in response to tax changes in the UK relative to GDP for various alternative tax policies. We check the robustness of the model results by computing the sensitivity of the EV/GDP ratio to relevant substitution elasticities.

The major advantage of a large scale multi-sectoral general equilibrium tax model, such as the present one, lies in its ability to provide answers relating to the impact of tax changes at a specific level of desegregation, such as individual sectors or households, readers should be aware that there are some clear weaknesses of large scale general equilibrium models.

We use the model to assess the impacts of three different taxes included in the model: capital income taxes, indirect taxes[3], household income taxes and tariffs.

The major findings of the model are the following:

1. We show welfare gains when capital income tax rates existing in 1995 are replaced by a uniform yield preserving 26.5 per cent rate across sectors and assets for a low labour supply elasticity. In the central case, we find a gain of 0.035 per cent of UK GDP (£217 million). The gain is 0.0223 per cent of UK GDP (£140 million) in the case of unit elasticity specification. These results are reasonably robust with respect to high and low labour supply elasticities.
2. The efficiency gain from replacing existing taxes by uniform capital income tax rates in the no equal yield capital tax reform case was about 0.28 per cent of UK GDP.

3. The computed efficiency gain from replacing capital income tax by yield preserving lump-sum taxes was 0.3 per cent of UK GDP.
4. We check the robustness of the welfare results by means of sensitivity analysis. The welfare impacts of moving to a yield preserving capital income tax from a set of existing taxes is positive and almost linear in the values of substitution elasticities among assets (s_k) for a particular set of elasticities of substitution between labour and capital assets (s_v). Similarly, it is also linear in the values of substitution elasticities between capital and labour for any particular value of substitution elasticities among capital assets. When both s_v and s_k are very high, each assuming a value of 5.0, the welfare impact of switching to a uniform tax rate was about 0.11 per cent of UK GDP, which amounts to nearly £729 million.
5. Changes in the relative prices of capital assets across sectors compared to the benchmark following a yield preserving capital income tax reform lead to a reallocation of capital assets across sectors. An equal yield uniform tax reform reduces inter-sectoral and inter-asset differences in the relative user cost of capital in the counterfactual scenarios. Consequently we see a significant reallocation, up to a 20 per cent increase or up to a 10 per cent reduction in the use of capital assets in a low labour supply elasticity case and changes between –5 and 5 per cent in the use of labour resources across sectors, occurring in comparison to the base year. Both capital and labour reallocation effects are robust with respect to the labour supply elasticity.
6. When capital inputs become relatively cheaper than labour inputs, producers tend to substitute capital for labour; this happens in the agriculture, finance, public administration, and education sectors. Capital becomes relatively expensive in manufacturing sectors, after a uniform tax reform. We see substitution of capital by labour in these sectors. The effect of the reduction in capital assets is however not completely compensated for by increased use of labour. Therefore the output level decreases in most of the manufacturing sectors though not by as much as would have been warranted by the reduction in the use of capital in these sectors.
7. The effects of tax changes differ in an open capital market treatment compared to a closed capital market. We open the capital market by fixing the net of tax return at the benchmark level, assuming the UK to be a small open economy compared to the global market. The gap between the sum of endowments of capital assets and use of these assets is met by inflows and outflows of assets in the open capital market. The stock of individual assets across sectors may change from -15 to 30 per cent of the base year stocks. When the existing capital income taxes are replaced by uniform yield preserving capital income taxes, we find inflows of capital for which the user cost of capital has reduced, and outflows of

assets, such as short and long lived plant and machinery and vehicles, for which the user cost has increased. The capital asset reallocation patterns in response to a move to uniform capital income tax rates from the existing differential tax rates in the open capital market case are very different than in the closed capital market case. The pure effect of opening up the capital market ranges from 0.03 per cent of base year capital stock in the education sector to 5.6 per cent in the engineering sector.

8. We compute the marginal excess burden (MEB) of taxes in the UK by dividing the change in welfare resulting from a change in the tax rate used to raise additional revenue using a given tax instrument by the net change in government revenue. We find that the MEB varies according to the tax instruments in use. For the low labour supply elasticity case, the MEB ranges from 35 pence in the case of capital income taxes to 54 pence per pound of additional revenue from production taxes. The effects of other taxes lie between these two MEB numbers. If MEB figures reflect the degree of distortion for the tax instrument used to raise the additional revenue, production taxes in intermediate goods and indirect tax on investment goods seem to be the most distortionary tax instruments in the UK economy. MEB figures are higher for higher values of labour supply elasticities compared to corresponding numbers for lower labour supply elasticities. These MEB figures are comparable to estimates available elsewhere in the literature (BFSW(1985)).

THE DYNAMIC MULTISECTORAL GENERAL EQUILIBRIUM MODEL

The second part of the book illustrates a multicultural dynamic general equilibrium tax model of the UK economy benchmarked to the steady state with a 1995 data set received from the Inland Revenue. In the model an infinitely lived household allocates wealth between consumption and savings to maximize lifetime utility; investors allocate investment among production sectors based on their profitability; the government uses revenue collected from direct and indirect taxes to purchase goods and services for public consumption and transfer income to the households. Prices in each period adjust until the markets for goods, capital, and labour clear. Compared to the static model, long-run capital stocks are endogenous and tax-induced changes in the net-of-tax return affects sector specific capital accumulation. In the short run the return to assets may differ across sectors in transition, leading to greater amounts of investment in some sectors and shutdown of investment in some other sectors, but the return on capital assets is equalized across all sectors in the long run.

We use this model to evaluate dynamic efficiency effects and growth path impacts of equal yield tax reforms. When distortionary capital income tax rates, ranging from 24 to 48 per cent in the base year, are replaced by a uniform capital income tax rate of 25 per cent rate, the dynamic efficiency gain is about 0.77 per cent of the base year GDP. Some sectors, such as agriculture, where the capital input cost has been reduced relatively in the counterfactual scenario by lower capital income tax rates, experience an expansion. Other sectors (such as engineering), where the capital income tax has not reduced that much in the counterfactual scenario relative to the benchmark, experience slower growth. Reducing labour income tax from 24 per cent in the benchmark year to 15 per cent results in a welfare loss of up to 2.05 per cent of the base year GDP, mainly because more distortionary taxes have to be increased to make up for lost revenues. Replacing differential tax rates on production by a uniform 5 per cent rate across sectors results in a welfare gain of 1.4 per cent of the base year GDP. Similarly, replacing differentiated household consumption tax rates by a uniform 5 per cent rate generates a welfare gain of 0.6 per cent of GDP. We find similar welfare gains for a reform in government consumption taxes and tariffs. The private sector's ability to anticipate reform affects transitional effects as well as the dynamic efficiency effects of reform, raising them in some cases and lowering them in others. Simulation results appear to be robust with respect to changes in the degree of international openness of capital markets.

Although the specification of economic relationships in each period is very similar to that of the static version of the model, simulation results can be expected to differ between the two models, mainly for the following three reasons: (i) long-run capital stocks are endogenous in the dynamic model, resulting in an elastic long-run capital supply response; as a result, any tax-induced changes in the net-of-tax return to capital, which would be fully borne by capital in the static model, are dampened in the dynamic model by supply responses; (ii) sectoral effects during the transition to a new balanced-growth path are affected by the sector-specificity of capital assets; although in the long run the return to investment must be equalised across sectors, which is equivalent to a static specification with sectorally mobile capital, in the short run the return to assets may differ across sectors, leading to the shutdown of investment in some sectors; (iii) in the open capital market case, there is a further possibility of inflows and outflows of capital stock in the economy which results in the rate of return being pegged to the world rate of return.

A GLOBAL TRADE MODEL FROM THE UK PERSPECTIVE

This part of the book will reports on a 11 region 15 sector global trade model which includes the UK as one of the regions. Model results show that a global elimination of tariffs, export taxes and subsidies raises the volume of global trade. Gains from the global free trade are 1.3 per cent of the global GDP, roughly about 325 billion dollars in 1995. In absolute terms Japan gains the most (91 billion dollars) followed by Europe (67 billion dollars) and the USA (54 billion dollars). UK gains about 11 billion dollars (6.8 billion pounds) from multilateral trade liberalisation. These gains are significantly higher than gains reported from unilateral liberalisation obtained from a small open economy model. Gains from free trade as a share of GDP are much higher for emerging countries such as China than for other regions in the model.

I dedicate this book to millions of people in the UK and the US who have inspired on this work. I am particularly thankful to Professor John Whalley who selected to work for this project.

NOTES

1. This program uses a method originally set out in King and Fullerton (1984) to determine marginal tax rates on capital investment.
2. The tax on dwellings is not computed and is approximately set at zero. This asset is not an input in production function for other sectors.
3. Indirect taxes compose of import duties, subsidies, duties and levies and value added taxes. The taxes have distinct input values in the model and could be analysed separately.

2

MODEL STRUCTURE

Applied general equilibrium models for tax policy analysis have been in use for almost four decades, starting with Harberger's (1959) two sector model for analysis of the effect of tax on capital income. More elaborate general equilibrium models were implemented following Scarf's algorithm (see Shoven and Whalley (1972, 1977, 1984) for a review of early models). The Ballard-Fullerton-Shoven-Whalley (BFSW(1985)) model of the U.S. economy is a good example of a large scale model for tax policy analysis (19 industries, 15 consumer goods, households with a series of income ranges). It includes all the existing taxes in the U.S. economy and uses a sequenced equilibrium approach to study dynamic behaviour in the economy. There has been a subsequent increase in the use of GE models for tax and trade policy analysis in the spirit of the BFSW models (for a detailed review see Taylor (1990), Robinson (1991), Shoven and Whalley (1992), Mercinier and Srinivasan (1994)). In the case of the UK economy, Piggott and Whalley (1985) present a 33 sector standard tax/subsidy model calibrated to a 1973 data set.

The general equilibrium tax model discussed in this report falls among these large scale small open economy models. It captures the circular flow of output, income and expenditure in the goods and factor markets in the UK economy for the benchmark year 1995. Households, endowed with labour and capital, supply factors of production to firms, which use these inputs in producing goods and services. As suppliers of factor inputs, households get remuneration according to the marginal contribution of factor services in production. Income earned from work and/or supplying capital services is then either spent on consumption of domestic or foreign products, or saved for future consumption. Firms use sales revenue from products sold at market places to pay for the inputs used in the production process.

Both households and firms make optimal choices given their budget or cost constraints. Solutions to the model are given by equality between the demand for and supply of goods. These demand and supply functions for each product are derived from optimizing behaviour by households and firms. In addition, governments and investors are other agents in the model. The government collects revenue, and spends it either for public consumption or to make transfers to households. Investors use aggregate savings from households and the government to purchase investment goods. It is an open economy model, with the value of imports for intermediate use and final demand paid for by export earnings.

Factors are mobile across sectors in this model. Therefore in equilibrium each factor receives the same net of tax remuneration across sectors. Factor services will flow to a sector with a higher marginal revenue product from one with a lower marginal revenue product until the net of tax remuneration is equal across sectors. Demand for and supply of goods and factors readjust until all excess demands and excess supplies are eliminated through changes in prices. The forces of perfectly competitive markets guide the allocation of resources in the economy. Such an economy, however, is distorted by taxes and transfers. How big is the effect of such a distortion is often not very clear. In this report we focus on quantifying the efficiency effects of distortionary capital and labour income taxes, other indirect taxes on intermediate and final demands which existed in the UK in 1995.

Before producing a detailed specification of the model, it is pertinent to consider some limitations of the model. The major advantage of a large scale multi-sectoral general equilibrium tax model lies in its ability to provide answers relating to the impact of tax changes at very specific levels of disaggregation, such as individual sectors or households. Most of the micro or macro models in the literature are not able to address many sectoral issues that are important for policy makers. However, readers should be aware that there are some disadvantages of large scale general equilibrium models. These models are quite often labelled as black boxes because of the very complex structure of the model in which it is difficult to trace out the detailed consequences of a certain experiment. Large scale models generate a long list of output to a set of lengthy input.

In addition to these black box arguments there are other shortcomings in the current model. Firstly, this is a full employment model. Therefore, this model cannot provide answers to issues relating to unemployment in the labour market and capacity under-utilization in capital markets. Secondly, the model assumes perfect competition in both commodity and factor markets where each economic agent has perfect information about the world and has no impact on market activities. Thus we cannot study issues relating to market power. Third, at the moment the model includes only one representative household along with government and investors in the economy. Thus, though the model is useful for analysing the efficiency effects of tax changes, it is not capable of providing information about intra-household income distribution. Fourth, this is a static model and useful only for comparative static analysis between two equilibria. It cannot say anything about the intertemporal adjustment from one equilibrium to the next.

Each of these limitations needs to be borne in mind while interpreting model results. The model results need to be challenged until they are in concordance with economic logic and intuition. Long experience with these models becomes important in accessing the most plausible results from the model. Each of the limitations cited above can be relaxed in a more clearly specified general equilibrium model. We can learn from some exercises being carried out in neighbouring countries. The MIMIC model developed and used in the CPB Netherlands and the DREAM and MOBIDK models developed in Denmark contain elaborate specifications of unemployment. These models show that it is possible to study unemployment or under-utilisation of capital assets in the general equilibrium framework. It is also possible to incorporate a non-competitive market structure in a well specified GE model as in the MOBIDK model. For those interested in income distribution issues, this model could be extended to a multiple households model by incorporating data from a family expenditure survey and matching them with the structure of the economy as found in the Input-Output Tables. A simple numerical example with multiple households and sectors with a number of tax instruments is provided in Appendix 2 of this report. Intertemporal adjustment in quantities and prices can be studied by adding a time dimension to the current model, as we do in a companion report. Fine tuning all these limitations is, however, a time consuming task with many hurdles on the data front.

HOUSEHOLD PREFERENCES, DEMAND STRUCTURE AND TECHNOLOGY

Utility of a representative household in the UK model is given by a CES function of leisure and composite consumption. The optimal amount of leisure is the part of the time endowment not spent at work which is consistent with the household's utility maximization decision.

The structure of the nested utility function used in the model is represented in Figure 1. At the top level of this nest, utility is a function of leisure and composite consumption. The composite consumption good is made of 16 sub-composite goods as shown in the second level of the nest. Each sub-composite good is a nested function of domestic and imported goods. Like household consumption demand, investment and government consumption demand also comprise domestic and imported sources. More detail on products is given in the input output tables in the next section and domestic and import use matrices in Graham Siddorn's tables and notes in Appendix 1.

The major distortions in final demand are indirect taxes. These taxes are applied differently to household consumption, investment, and government consumption of goods supplied either from domestic sectors or by imports. Labour income taxes influence the labour-leisure choice in the utility function. Section Four contains more discussion about the structure of the UK tax system and its representation in the model.

The production structure used in this model is quite elaborate, as is shown in Figure 2. At the bottom of the figure the composite capital stock is aggregated from five different capital assets - long - lived plant and machinery, short lived plant and machinery, vehicles, buildings and dwellings. Note that dwelling asset is an input only in the housing sector.Composite capital and one type of labour are inputs in value added for the 16 sectors in this model. Then this value added is aggregated with domestic and imported intermediate inputs from 16 sectors in producing gross output for each sector. The gross output is either sold in domestic markets or exported to the rest of the world.

Here again, taxes and subsidies apply to each stage of these production nests. Capital income taxes are imposed on income from capital assets. In Section Four of this report, we outline how they are derived from cost of capital formulae from a calculator called P-Tax, that have been in use in the Economics Unit of the Inland Revenue. We also include a labour income tax on the wages received by the household sector.

The user cost of inputs is gross of taxes in the model. There are production taxes on the use of domestic and imported intermediate inputs. The production tax represents taxes such as excise duties, VAT on intermediate inputs and tariffs on the use of imported intermediate inputs. These various production taxes/ subsidies distort input and output prices and cause the allocation of resources across sectors to differ between tax and no tax equilibria.

Demands

As represented in Figure 1, a single household maximises utility, which is described by a nest of CES functions defined over composite consumption and leisure, subject to a budget constraint including a composite price for the commodity and leisure. The composite commodity demand is derived from these for sub-composite goods ($i = 1,..., N$). Each of these sub composites is obtained from domestic and imported sources.

At the top of the nest the utility function is written as

$$U = \left(\alpha C^{\rho} + \beta\ L^{\rho}\right)^{\frac{1}{\rho}} \tag{2.1}$$

where U is the utility of household, C is the consumption of the composite good, L is the leisure taken by the household, a is the share of full income of household spent on consumption of the composite good, β is the share of full income spent on leisure, and r is the elasticity parameter in the utility function; the elasticity of substitution between goods (and leisure) being equal to $\sigma = \dfrac{1}{1-\rho}$ (Varian (1992)).

The household receives income from capital and labour endowments, and transfers from the government, paying taxes on household and capital income. The disposable income of a household is given by

$$H = \sum_{j} \sum_{i} r_j (1 - t_{j,i}) \theta_{j,i} \overline{K}_j + (1 - t_l^h) w\overline{L} + TR \tag{2.2}$$

where H is the income, $\theta_{j,i}$ is the share of type j asset used in sector i, $\overline{K}_j$ is the endowment of capital type j for the household, $\overline{L}$ is the endowment of

Figure 1
Nesting Structure in utility functions used in the UK model

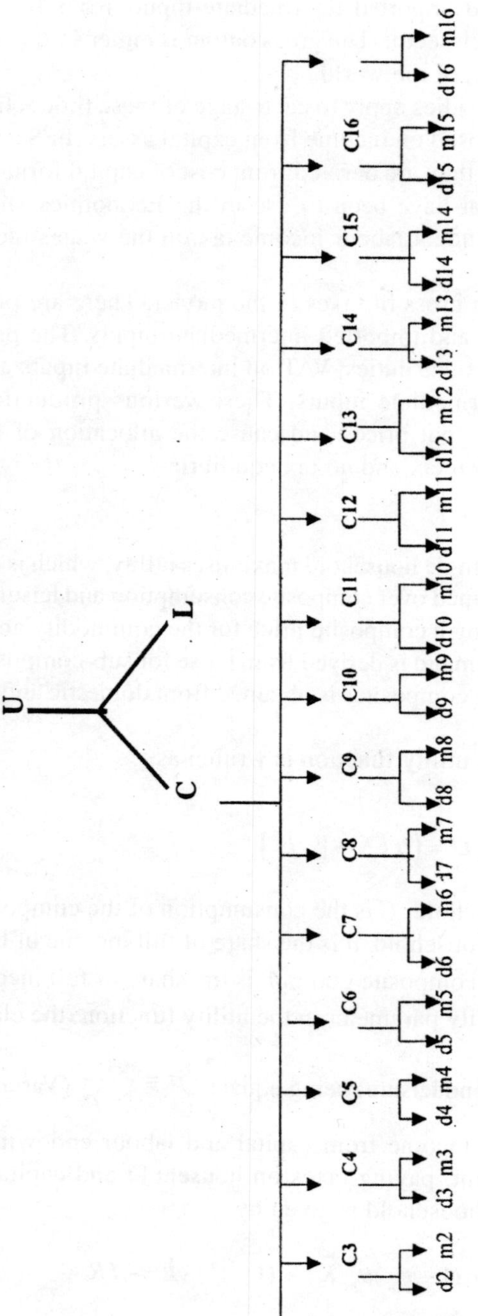

Notation: U = Utility
C = Composite consumption good
L = Leisure
C1..C16 = Sectoral composite
d1..d16 = domestic supply for consumption
m1..m16 = imports for consumption

Figure 2

Nesting Structure in production used in the UK tax model

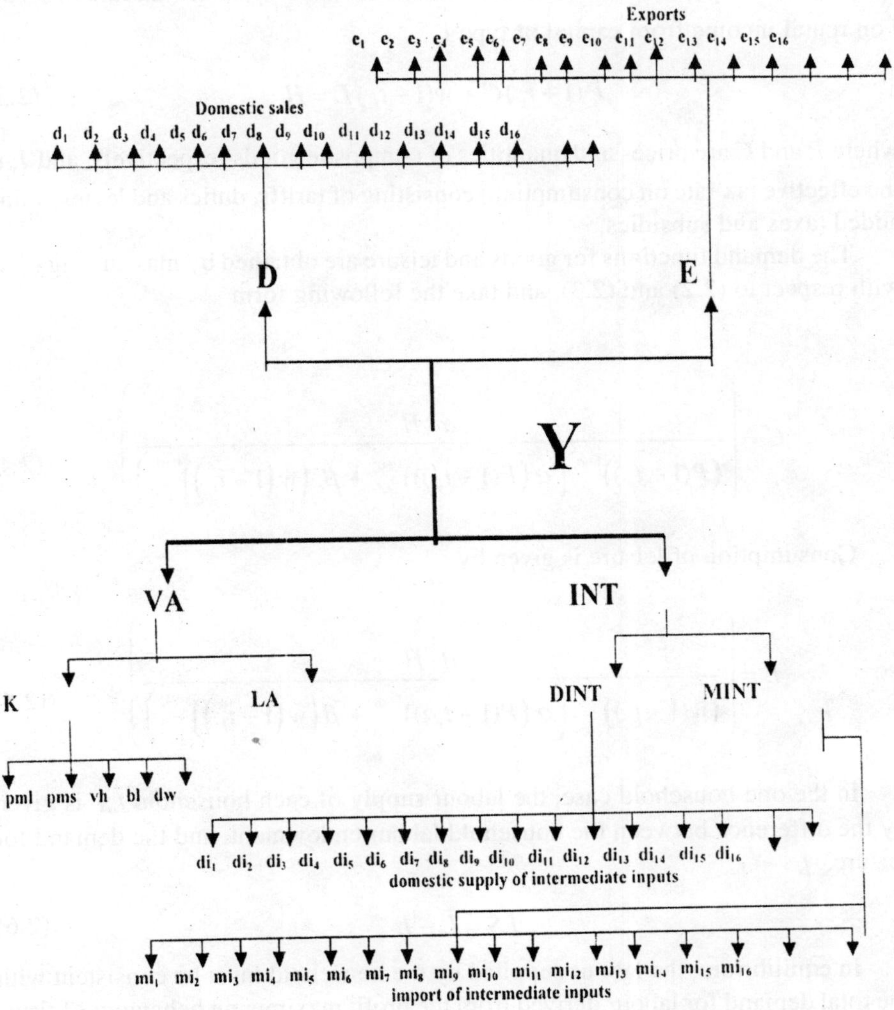

Notations: Y = output

Pml = plant and machinery long life

INT = intermediate inputs

E = Exports

vh = vehicles

MINT = Import of intermediate inputs

LA = labour

$di_1..di_{16}$ = domestic intermediate inputs

$mi_{1..}\ mi_{16}$ = imported intermediate inputs

VA = value added

D = domestic sales

Pls = plant and machinery short life

DINT = domestic intermediate inputs

K = Composite capital

bl = buildings

dw = dwellings

$e_{1..}e_{16}$ = exports

$d_1..d_{16}$ = domestic sale

labour, TR are the transfers received, r is the rental rate of capital by type j, w is the wage rate, t_l is the tax rate on labour income[1], and $t_{j,i}$ is the tax rate in sector i on rental income from capital of type j.

$$P(1+t_v)C + w(1-t_l)L = H \tag{2.3}$$

where P and C are prices and quantities of composite goods respectively, and t_v is the effective tax rate on consumption; consisting of tariffs, duties and levies, value added taxes and subsidies.

The demand functions for goods and leisure are obtained by maximising (2.1) with respect to (2.2) and (2.3), and take the following form

$$C = \left(\frac{\alpha\ H}{(P(1+t_v))^{1-\sigma}\left(\alpha\left(P(1+t_v)\right)\right)^{1-\sigma} + \beta\left(w\left(1-t_l\right)\right)^{1-\sigma}\right)} \right) \tag{2.4}$$

Consumption of leisure is given by

$$L = \left(\frac{\beta\ H}{(w(1-t_l))^{1-\sigma}\left(\alpha\left(P(1+t_v)\right)\right)^{1-\sigma} + \beta\left(w\left(1-t_l\right)\right)^{1-\sigma}\right)} \right) \tag{2.5}$$

In the one household case, the labour supply of each household LS is given by the difference between the household labour endowment, and the demand for leisure, L.

$$LS = \bar{L} - L \tag{2.6}$$

In equilibrium, the labour supplied by the household must be consistent with the total demand for labour derived from the profit maximising behaviour of firms (as set out in the following section).

Composite consumption covers N sub-composite goods in the model,

$$C = \psi\left(\sum_i \delta_i^c CC_i^{\frac{\sigma-1}{\sigma}}\right)^{\frac{\sigma}{\sigma-1}} \tag{2.7}$$

where CC_i is the ith good composite of domestic and imported consumption goods, ψ is the unit parameter of the CES composite function and δ_i^c is the share of the consumption good. The overall value of composite consumption should satisfy:

$$P \cdot C = \sum_i P_i \cdot CC_i \quad \text{for } i = 1..N \tag{2.8}$$

International Trade

The term p is the price of composite consumption net of indirect taxes, and CC_i is composite consumption good of both domestic and import of the *i*th good. The total supply, A_i, for each sector is produced using domestic and imported goods, and is given by a CES Armington function. It is given by

$$A_i = \Phi\left((1-\delta_i^m) D_i^{\frac{\sigma_m - 1}{\sigma_m}} + \delta_i^m M_i^{\frac{\sigma_m - 1}{\sigma_m}}\right)^{\frac{\sigma_m}{\sigma_m - 1}} \tag{2.9}$$

where A_i is the CES aggregate of domestic supplies D_i and import supplies $M_{i.}$ δ_i^d is the share of domestic supplies for good *i*, and δ_i^m is the share of imports in good *i*, σ_m is the elasticity of substitution in the aggregate supply function, and Φ is the shift parameter of the aggregate supply function. Overall market clearing in the product market implies that

$$A_i = CC_i + G_i + I_i \tag{2.10}$$

where G_i and I_i represent composite consumption by the government and investment respectively (discussed below). In value terms,

$$PA_i \, A_i = PD_i \, D_i + PM_i \, M_i \tag{2.11}$$

where D_i and M_i are domestic and import supplies at prices PD_i and PM_i respectively, and PA_i is the price of total supply in sector *i*.

In the above equation, domestic supply, D_i, is the part of the output sold in the domestic market. The rest of domestic output is sold abroad, and given by the product transformation function.

$$Y_i = \Theta\left((1-\delta_i^e) D_i^{\frac{\sigma_y - 1}{\sigma_y}} + \delta_i^e E_i^{\frac{\sigma_y - 1}{\sigma_y}}\right)^{\frac{\sigma_y}{\sigma_y - 1}} \tag{2.12}$$

where E_i is exports, is domestic supplies, σ_y is the elasticity of substitution in total supplies, δ_i^e is the share of exports, and Θ is the shift parameter in the production function. The total value of gross domestic product is composed of value of domestic sales and exports.

$$PY_i \ Y_i = PD_i \ Y_i + PE_i \ E_i \tag{2.13}$$

The value of exports is equal to the value of imports in equilibrium.

$$\sum_i PE_i E_i = \sum_i PM_i M_i \tag{2.14}$$

where PE_i and PM_i are the world prices of exported and imported commodities in terms of the numeraire. These import and export prices could be different than the domestic prices because of differentiation between domestic and foreign products in this model. Gross of export tax or tariff prices of domestic commodities tends to be close to the world prices as the elasticity of transformation between domestic sales and exports and elasticity of substitution between domestic supplies and import reach to the infinity.

Production

Producers use labour and capital in each of N sectors to yield value added. This also is given by CES functions.

$$VA_i = \Omega_i \left((1-\delta_i)(K_i)^{\gamma_i} + \delta_i (LS_i)^{\gamma_i}\right)^{\frac{1}{\gamma_i}} \tag{2.15}$$

where VA_i is the gross value added of sector i, Ω_i is a shift parameter in the production function, K_i and LS_i are the amounts of capital and labour used in sector i, δ_i is the share parameter of labour in the CES function, and γ_i is the CES factor substitution parameter.

The gross output of each sector Y_i contains value added, VA_i and intermediate inputs. We allow substitution between domestic and imported intermediate inputs, and between value added and intermediate inputs.

$$PY_i Y_i = PV_i . VA_i + \sum_j PA_i \ (1+t^d_{i,j}) DI_{i,j} + \sum_j PM_i (1+t^m_{i,j}) MI_{i,j} \tag{2.16}$$

where $DI_{i,j}$ is the demand for domestic intermediate input and $MI_{i,j}$ is demand for imported intermediate inputs, PV_i is the composite price of value added, and VA_i is the value added component of gross output, $t^d_{i,j}$ and $t^m_{i,j}$ are taxes on intermediate demands.

At any set of prices, producers in each sector maximise profits subject to their technology constraint

$$\Pi_i = PY_i \ Y_i - wL_i - \sum_{j,i} r_j K_{j,i} - \sum_j PA_j (1+t^m_{i,j}) MI_{j,i} - \sum_j PA_j (1+t^d_{i,j}) DI_{j,i} \tag{2.17}$$

where Π_i is the profit of sector i. In equilibrium, factor demands by sectors are determined where the value of the marginal product of factors equal factor prices, and there are no positive profits for producers.

TREATMENT OF THE PUBLIC SECTOR

Government Budget

The government collects revenue from taxes on capital and labour income and value-added taxes on final demand, production taxes on intermediate inputs, and tariffs on imports. All tax revenues collected are either used to purchase public goods or transferred to households in lump sum form; ie.

$$G + TR = \sum_j \sum_i t^k_{j,i} r_j K_{j,i} + \sum_i t^{vc}_i P_i CC_i + \sum_i t^{vg}_i P_i G_i + \sum_i t^{vk}_i P_i I_i$$

$$+ \sum_i t_l wLS + \sum_i t^m_i M_i + \sum_j \sum_i PA_j t^m_{i,j} MI_{j,i_i} + \sum_j \sum_i PA_j t^d_{i,j} DI_{j,i_i} \quad (2.18)$$

where G is public consumption, and $t^k_{j,i}$ is the tax rate on capital income from asset j used in sector i. These rates are taken from P-Tax formulae. There are four different indirect taxes in the model: tariffs, duties and levies, VAT and subsidies. t^{vc}_l is the effective *ad valorem* tax rate on final consumption of households, t^{vg}_i is effective indirect tax rate on public consumption and t^{vk}_i is effective tax rate on investment. t_l is the tax rate on labour income, and t^m_i is the tariff on imports, and are taxes on intermediate demands.

These taxes, particularly when they are levied at different rates on different sectors and households, have distortionary impacts on the allocation of resources in the economy. These are captured by the model. The value of government consumption is given by:

$$G = \sum_i PA_i GD_i + \sum_i PA_i GM_i \quad (2.19)$$

where GD_i is government consumption of domestic goods and GM_i is government consumption of imported goods.

MODEL CLOSURES AND SAVINGS AND INVESTMENT

Total investment demand I equals the use of investment goods from domestic and imported sources.

$$I = \sum_i PA_i ID_i + \sum_i PA_i IM_i \quad (2.20)$$

where ID_i is investment demand for domestic good i, and IM_i is investment demand for imported good i. The savings-investment identity closes this model where I is the gross of indirect taxes.

We have taken a closed capital market view until so far. This essentially means the allocation of assets across sectors sums up to the domestic endowments of assets which implies:

$$\overline{K}_j = \sum_i K_{i,j} \qquad j=1,..5 \tag{2.21}$$

where $\overline{K}_j$ is the endowment of *j*th type of asset and $K_{i,j}$ allocation of type *j* asset in sector *i*. Reallocation occurs until the rental rate of capital is same across all sectors.

The closed capital market assumption is not realistic for the UK economy, where capital freely moves according to domestic and foreign rate of returns. More realistically

$$\overline{K}_j + FK_j = \sum_i K_{i,j} \tag{2.22}$$

where FK_j represents net inflow or outflow of asset type *j*. The inflow and outflow of capital asset depends upon the gap between the rental rate in the UK and the Rest of the World.

$$r_j^{UK} \geq r_j^w \Rightarrow FK_j \geq 0 \tag{2.23}$$

$$r_j^{UK} \leq r_j^w \Rightarrow FK_j \leq 0 \tag{2.24}$$

where r_j^{UK} is the net of tax return in asset *j* in the UK and r_j^w is the net return in the world market. Thus the amount of inflow or outflow depends upon the gap between the domestic and world rental rate of capital. Capital asset movement occurs until this gap is eliminated.

We consider an open capital market scenario in the UK model by fixing the net tax return on capital assets at the return at the world market, which we assume to equal unity. Major implication of this structure is that investors use domestic assets until the net of tax return on those assets are higher or equal to the return from the assets borrowed from abroad. Free inflows and outflows are allowed to make returns on assets from the domestic and world market to be the same by changes in the marginal productivity of capital.

It should be noted that analysis of capital mobility in a small open economy models is not yet quit satisfactorily developed in the applied general equilibrium literature. Goulder-Shoven-Whalley (1983) introduce foreign capital in the US tax model by assuming that foreigners are endowed with five times more than the US capital assets, implicit assumption being that the US economy forms 20 percent of the global economy. If we accept this reasoning then small open economy model of the UK may roughly assume a foreigner endowed with 25 times more of capital assets than the UK households (considering UK GDP to be 4 percent of the Global GDP). Then the UK producer could use two types of asset *j*, domestic and foreign, in producing good *i* in the current model. They could use foreign asset if the return in those assets is higher than those in the domestic assets or they could sell assets to foreigners if they are ready to pay interest rates higher than prevailing in the UK. The amount of inflow and outflow will be determined by equality between the domestic and foreign interest rates. For simplicity in absence of an explicit modelling of the production, foreigners are simply assumed to consume capital assets they posses in equilibrium.

More realistic analysis of inflow and outflow of capital assets requires a model structure where the UK economy forms a part of the global economy. We report a global economy model from the UK perspective in our separate document using the GTAP data set where inflow and outflow of capital assets to the UK from other countries and from the UK to other countries guarantees same rates of return on capital assets globally with assumption of perfect capital mobility across economies.

MODEL EQUILIBRIUM CONDITIONS AND CLOSURE

In this model a competitive equilibrium is given by prices of consumption goods, P_i; the rental rate of capital assets r_j; a wage rate for labour, w; levels of gross output, Y_i (gross of intermediate use); capital use, K_i; and sectoral use of labour, L_i; imports M_i, exports X_i, intermediate inputs $INT_{i,j}$, investment I_i, government consumption G_i, private consumption C_i, such that,

(i) The markets for goods and services, labour and capital clear; and

(ii) budget constraints of households, the government and investors are satisfied.

More specifically, the market clearing condition for the goods market is given by

$$Y_i = \mathrm{F}_i^d + \sum_{j=1}^{N} a_{ij}^d Y_j \tag{2.25}$$

where $F_i^d = C_i^d + I_i^d + G_i^d + E_i^d$ is a decomposition of final demand into household consumption, investment, and government consumption, $\sum_j a_{ij}^d Y_j$ is total intermediate demand, and $a_{i.j}^d$ is sector *i* input per unit of sector *j* output.

$$M_i = F_i^m + \sum_{j=1}^{N} a_{ij}^m Y_j \tag{2.26}$$

where $F_i^m = C_i^m + I_i^m + G_i^m + E_i^m$ represents a decomposition of final demand for imports and $\sum_j a_{i,j}^m Y_j$ is total imports for intermediate inputs.

The capital market clearing condition, in the closed capital market case, implies

$$\bar{K}_j = \sum_i K_{i,j} \qquad j=1,..5 \tag{2.27}$$

The capital market clearing condition in the open capital market scenario implies

$$\bar{K}_j + FK_j = \sum_i K_{i,j} \tag{2.28}$$

and labour market clearing implies:

$$LS = \sum_i LS_i \tag{2.29}$$

where LD_i represents labour demand in the *i*th sector. We have not considered mobility of labour to and from UK economy explicitly in this model.

When there are *n* different markets in the economy, relative prices that clear *n*-1 markets clear the *n*th market as well. Because of the complexity of the model, analytical solutions are difficult to find, therefore it needs to be solved by a numerical technique.

Measuring welfare changes across alternative tax regimes

The essence of tax policy analysis lies in comparing welfare changes between a benchmark and counterfactual economy. How much a typical consumer has gained or lost because of changes in policy in money metric terms, or how much money is required to bring him/her back to the equivalent of original welfare, can be measured either in original or new prices. Hicksian equivalent variation (*EV*) is a measure of welfare change between benchmark and counterfactual scenarios using benchmark (old) prices. Hicksian compensating variation (*CV*), on the other hand, measures welfare changes in terms of new prices. A general rule of thumb is that a positive Hicksian EV is a measure of welfare gain, and corresponds to a negative Hicksian CV, which gives the amount of money to be taken away from the consumer in order to keep her at the old utility level. In general EV and CV are given by differences in money metric utility between old and new prices corresponding to benchmark and counterfactual solutions.

$$EV = E(U^N, P^0) - E(U^0, P^0) \tag{2.30}$$

$$CV = E(U^N, P^N) - E(U^0, P^N) \tag{2.31}$$

Superscripts *N* and *O* represent new and old values of the variable on which they appear, and *E* is money metric utility.

If utility functions are linear homogeneous, then original and new equilibria can be thought of in terms of a radial expansion in the utility surface. Therefore the change in welfare between benchmark and counterfactual solutions of the model is proportional to the change in income or the percentage change along the radial projection between two consumption points.

$$EV = \frac{U^N - U^0}{U^0} I^0 \tag{2.32}$$

$$CV = \frac{U^N - U^0}{U^N} I^N \tag{2.33}$$

Implementing the structure in GAMS

The early general equilibrium tax models typically used Scarf's algorithm for their solution (see Scarf (1967), Scarf and Hansen (1973), Shoven and Whalley (1984)) and were solved with codes written in FORTRAN. A large scale GE modelling has become much easier in recent years after the development of GAMS/MPSGE software.

The current model falls into the category of mixed complementarity non-linear programming problems. It is easily solved using GAMS/MPSGE software (Brook, Kendrick and Meeraus (1992), Rutherford (1997)) and PATH solver (Dirkse and Ferris (1995, 1997)). Technically there are five steps in the numerical implementation of the model: benchmarking, model declaration, benchmark replication, counterfactual solution and report writing. Model dimensions (sets) are declared and all base year data are read in tabular, parameter or scalar form in the base year model. Then modellers specify markets, production activities and budget constraints for each agent in the model declaration part. This part consist of blocks of equations for production technology, household preferences, revenues and income constraints. A model is calibrated when the base year data is reproduced by the model as its solution. This step is known as benchmark replication. In the fourth step various taxes or exogenous variables are changed in order to assess the efficiency and allocation effects of proposed changes in tax rates or transfers. Finally, model solutions are printed for review in the reporting stage. The MPSGE code is very concise for a standard Arrow-Debreu model. We give the GAMS/MPSGE codes for the UK model as an appendix to this report in order to present the details of these fives steps for a reader.

3

BENCHMARK DATA SOURCES FOR GE TAX MODEL OF THE UK ECONOMY

In this section we present the benchmark data set used to calibrate the GE tax model of the UK. The proper formulation of a micro-consistent data set is extremely important for tax policy analysis based on model solutions[1]. The Economics Unit of the Inland Revenue made a major contribution to the data work for this model. Frequent meetings between the Warwick modellers and the Economics Unit of the Inland Revenue were held to identify the data needs and to place joint requests to the Office of National Statistics. The data collection process dovetailed[2] with the construction of a micro-consistent data set fulfilling the calibration requirements for the benchmark year 1995.

This section discusses the structure of the data and its derivation closely follows the model structure outlined in the previous section. We report tax rates, elasticities and model parameter in the next section before presenting the model results in the final section.

DIMENSIONS AND CLASSIFICATION OF THE MODEL

The major source of data for the GE tax model of the UK for 1995 is the 123 sector input-output balances published by the Office of the National Statistics in London (ONS (1997)). The Inland Revenue worked out a 16 sector classification and consolidated the 123 sector input-output table to 16 sectors (see various tables in the appendix).

The sectoral details used in the current models are given in the first column in Table 1. It lists 16 sectors[3] included in the current model representing aggregations over the individual sectors given in column 2. The 1995 input-output balances have more disaggregation of service sectors than earlier input-output tables. This is particularly important as more than 62 percent of national income originates from service sectors, compared to about 30 percent in manufacturing sectors. The 1990 sectoral codes corresponding to these sectors are in column 3, with codes in accordance with the ONS classification for the 1995 tables given in the last column.

Table 1
Aggregation of 123 sectors into 16 sectors from 1990 Input-Output Sectoral Classification

Industry/Asset	*1990 I-O Sectors*	*1990 sectoral code*	*1995 sectoral code*
Agriculture	Agriculture, Forestry, Fishing	1,2,3	1-3
Extraction	Extraction – oil and gas	5	5
Other mining & quarrying	Coal extraction, stone, clay, sand, gravel, metal ores and minerals	4,14, 10	4,6,7
Chemicals	Coke ovens, oil proc, nuclear fuel, inorganic chemicals, organic chemicals, fertilisers, synthetic resins, paints, dyes, printing ink, special chemical for industry, pharmaceutical products, soap and toilet preparations, chemical products, man-made fibres	6, 20-29	35-46
Metals and mineral products	Iron and Steel, Aluminium, other non-ferrous metals, structural clay products, Cement, lime and plaster, concrete, asbestos, abrasive prods, glass, refractory and ceramic goods, metal casting, metal doors, windows, packaging products of metals, industrial plant and steel work, engineers small tools	11-13, 15-19, 30-34, 37	49-61
Engineering	Agricultural machinery and tractors, metal working machine tools, textile etc machinery, process machinery and contractors, mining equipment, mech power transmission equipment, other machinery, ordnance samll arms and ammunition, insulated wires and cables, basic electrical equipment, industrial electrical equipment, telecommunications etc. equipment, electronic components, electronic consumer goods, demestic electric appliances, electric lighting equipment, instrument engineering	35,36, 38-52, 57	62-76
Food, drinks and tobacco	Oils and fats, slaughtering and meat processing, milk and products, fruit vegetable and fish processing, grain milling and starch, bread, biscuits, sugar, confectionary, animal feeding stuffs, miscellaneous foods, alcoholic drink soft drinks, tobacco	58-70	8-20
Other manufacturing	Motor vehicles and parts, shipbuilding and repairing, aerospace etc, other vehicles, woollen and worsted, cotton spinning and weaving, hosiery and other knitted goods, textile finishing, carpets, jute, leather and leather goods, footwear, clothing furs, household and other textiles, timber and wood products, wooden furniture, pulp, paper and board,	53-56, 71-90	21-34, 47-48,77-84

Contd...

Industry/Asset	*1990 I-O Sectors*	*1990 sectoral code*	*1995 sectoral code*
	paper and board products, printing and publishing, rubber products, processing of plastics, jewellery and coins, sports goods and toys, other goods		
Electricity, gas and water	Electricity production, gas, water supply	7,8,9	85-87
Construction	Construction	91	88
Distribution, hotels, etc.	Wholesale distribution, retail distribution, distribution and vehicles repairs, hotels catering, pubs etc.	92,93,94,95	89-92
Transport, storage, and communication	Railways, road and other inland transport, sea transport, air transport, transport services, postal services, telecoomunication	96-102	93-99
Financial sector	Banking and finance, insurance, auxiliary financial services, estate agents, legal services, accountancy services, other professional services, advertising, computing services, other business services, renting of movables, owning and dealing in real estate, research and development	103-114, 118	100-103, 105-114
Public administration	Public administration	115	115
Education, health and social work	Sanitary services, education, health services, recreation and welfare services, personal services, domestic services	116, 117, 119-122	116-123
Housing services	Ownership of dwelling	123	104

The 16 sector input-output table consolidated from the 123-sector industry by industry input-output table for 1995 shows inter-sectoral linkages in production Table 2. Intermediate inputs used by a sector are given in the columns, along with labour and capital inputs and corresponding taxes in production. Rows of this table give the input that a particular sector provides to the other sectors. It is a well established convention in input-output analysis that the rows represents revenue for a sector and a column shows the cost of production to that sector. Some other information such as the revenue and transfer figures is taken from the National Account Blue Book for 1996.

REQUIREMENTS FOR A MICRO CONSISTENT DATA SET FOR THE MODEL

The benchmark data require three basic conditions of a general equilibrium model to be satisfied: a zero profit condition, market clearing and income balance. The zero profit conditions for producers in the benchmark data are met for various sectors of the economy when aggregate output equals gross of tax payments to labour and capital services and intermediate inputs. This essentially means that firms are just breaking even while producing goods and services and supplying them to markets. The market clearing condition for each sector implies that the total output or supply equals the aggregate demand - intermediate and final demands - for goods of that sector. The total supply of goods in the market comprises domestic output and imports. The income balance condition implies the expenditure of households and government is equal to their income or revenues gross of savings, the economy wide trade balance condition holds and the volume of savings equals the volume of investment in the economy. All of these three equilibrium conditions required for an empirical implementation of a GE tax model are satisfied in the data set contained in the input-output data in Table 3.2.

A column sum in that table represents supply of a product and a row sum represents total demand for that particular product. For market clearing, individual items in a row such as intermediate demand and final demand, add up to the column total for that sector. In the benchmark year, when the prices of inputs and outputs are equal to unity, the zero profit condition simply means that the total inputs used in production equal total supply of a product. The income balance condition is satisfied when the sum of value added, labour and capital income gross of taxes matches the total of final demands. In an open economy model, the value of exports needs to equal the value of imports, to meet the trade balance condition.

The 16 sector industry-by-industry input-output table presented in Table 3.2 meets all these four micro-consistency conditions for the UK economy for the benchmark year 1995. Gross output was equal to £1228 billion, split between intermediate demand (£487 billion) and final demand (£741 billion). Total demand equals total supply for each sector. The value of import equals the value of exports (£195 billion). The indirect taxes row is the sum of various taxes such as tariff, duties and levies, VAT and subsidies to intermediate and final demand. The original input-output balances do not dis-aggregate between labour and capital income. This break-down is done according to the method developed in the Inland Revenue.

Table 3.4 shows more detailed forward and backward linkages between the model sectors in the UK economy. For instance activities in the agriculture sector will have strong backward (12%) and forward linkages (21%) to the food and drink sector. On one hand the agriculture sector provides raw materials, such as grains, meat or milk, for the food and drink industry; on the other hand the agriculture sector itself uses inputs from the food and drink industry, eg. for feeding animals. Agriculture has some backward linkages to the financial (8%), chemicals (6%), and distribution (4.%) sectors.

The import use matrix corresponding to Table 3.2 is given in Table 3.3. For the purpose of data analysis we present coefficient forms of Table 3.2 in Tables 3.4-3.8.

The forward and backward inter-sectoral linkages emerging from the input-output table are important for the multi-sectoral analysis of production and consumption taxes in the UK GE tax model. The input-output table not only shows how much intermediate input a sector provides, either from domestic or imported sources, to other sectors, it also provides information on final demand, again decomposed by the domestic and foreign sectors, and the split of value added between inputs used in production.

Table 2

A 16 Sector Industry by Industry Input-Output Table of the United Kingdom 1995

I x I Domestic Use Matrix	*Agricul-ture*	*Extrac-tion*	*Other-Min ing*	*Chemi-cals*	*Metals*	*Engine-ering*	*Food, drink*	*Other Manuf.*	*Utili-ties*	*Constru-ction*	*Distri-bution*	*Trans-port*	*Finan-cial*	*Pub-lic Ad-min*	*Educ. Health,*	*Hous-ing*	*Total interme diate*	*Consu-mers' expen-diture*	*GG FC*	*GDF CF*	*Stocks*	*Exports*	*Total final demand*	*Total*
Agriculture	2,096	0	14	27	7	5	12,132	435	0	4	564	48	15	0	148	0	15,495	6,730	42	0	0	1,942	8,713	24,208
Extraction	0	2,439	0	4,697	3	0	0	0	3,622	0	0	0	0	0	0	0	10,762	0	0	0	0	6,942	6,942	17,704
Other Mining	20	0	353	218	846	26	45	130	1,897	401	105	17	8	0	57	0	4,124	339	47	0	0	983	1,369	5,493
Chemicals	1,433	10	37	3,899	433	546	571	1,484	466	737	1,299	1,254	913	0	3,204	19	16,304	3,764	3,116	0	261	28,663	35,804	52,108
Metals	110	162	192	1,225	7,249	6,320	1,831	5,197	50	7,074	503	389	5	0	84	0	30,392	346	588	7,158	779	10,230	19,101	49,493
Engineering	0	576	317	682	1,254	5,705	528	2,432	634	788	848	1,808	1,018	0	1,567	36	18,192	0	1,589	2,613	332	50,923	55,457	73,649
Food, drink	2,797	52	25	356	82	120	6,382	350	64	51	6,589	650	1,058	0	1,796	4	20,377	25,904	411	0	153	10,270	36,737	57,114
Other Manuf.	583	80	134	1,781	1,839	3,005	2,816	16,404	474	4,242	6,702	4,139	8,242	0	3,340	283	54,064	18,082	3,872	8,933	1,185	39,858	71,928	125,992
Utilities	279	0	160	1,330	1,596	1,189	931	1,980	12,273	272	1,201	857	1,184	0	705	23	23,981	16,353	1,323	0	0	62	17,738	41,719
Construction	172	0	122	109	32	56	0	31	0	21,085	603	151	1,985	0	146	3,929	28,420	3,521	4,414	47,764	285	0	55,983	84,404
Distribution	1,005	200	206	1,479	2,489	4,115	1,647	3,724	355	1,371	4,164	2,470	2,276	0	790	0	26,289	111,181	1,229	2,586	0	13,701	128,698	154,987
Transport	245	704	335	1,232	2,047	1,415	1,583	3,614	183	887	14,871	15,642	17,082	0	3,175	198	63,216	19,715	2,637	779	0	12,194	35,324	98,540
Financial	1,949	671	471	4,070	2,781	6,194	4,205	9,177	1,884	10,483	22,425	12,387	50,836	0	13,435	15,221	156,189	25,373	8,458	8,483	0	12,545	54,859	211,047
Public Admin	0	0	0	0	0	0	0	0	0	0	0	0	0	0	0	0	0	0	63,843	0	0	0	63,843	63,843
Educ. Health,	378	1	41	520	253	581	496	2,618	179	242	1,001	1,369	4,031	0	7,756	67	19,535	43,653	46,265	0	0	4,504	94,422	113,957
Housing	0	0	0	0	0	0	0	0	0	0	0	0	0	0	0	0	0	53,269	0	0	0	0	53,269	53,269
Total intermediate	11,067	4,895	2,410	21,626	20,912	29,276	33,168	47,576	22,081	47,638	60,876	41,182	88,652	0	36,201	19,781	487,339	328,229	137,832	78,316	2,995	192,816	740,188	1,227,527
Imports	1,630	989	425	10,639	7,613	15,965	8,827	30,336	3,612	5,151	3,532	4,895	3,949	0	2,960	19	100,541	52,021	9,995	28,174	1,563	2,494	94,248	194,789
Duty on imports	34	6	5	136	101	214	171	405	48	66	51	26	2	0	9	0	1,273	547	91	382	20	32	1,073	2,346
VAT	0	0	0	0	0	0	0	0	0	0	0	218	3,259	0	1,181	0	4,658	33,257	3,915	3,731	0	0	40,902	45,561
Duties and levies	211	2	103	1,175	344	176	460	331	1,378	130	1,275	2,026	896	0	344	36	8,887	22,713	434	0	0	0	23,147	32,034
Other taxes and sub sidies	-265	-25	-10	-50	-53	-46	-1,454	-212	-10	-34	-443	-404	-409	0	-186	-6	-3,607	4,559	-577	-45	4	-556	3,384	-223
Value added – Labour	7,143	1,409	1,822	10,151	15,790	18,529	9,691	36,483	5,492	29,947	61,877	35,191	70,149	60,316	69,067	0	433,059	0	0	0	0	0	0	433,059
Value added – Gross profits etc	4,388	10,428	738	8,432	4,786	9,536	6,250	11,074	9,118	1,505	27,820	15,406	44,549	3,527	4,381	33,440	195,376	0	0	0	0	0	0	195,376
Total inputs	24,208	17,704	5,493	52,108	49,493	73,649	57,114	125,992	41,719	84,404	154,987	98,540	211,047	63,843	113,957	53,269	1,227,526	441,325	151,691	110,558	4,582	194,786	902,942	2,130,468

Source: ONS, Input-Output Tables of the United Kingdom, 1995.

Table 3

Industry by Industry Import Use Matrix for the UK economy 1995

I x I Domestic Use Matrix	Agricul-ture	Extrac-tion	Other-Min ing	Chemi-cals	Metals	Engine-ering	Food. drink	Other Manuf.	Utili-ties	Constru-ction	Distri-bution	Trans-port	Finan-cial	Pub-lic Ad-min	Educ. Health.	Hous-ing	Total interme diate	Consu-mers' expen-diture	GG FC	GDF CF	Stocks	Exports	Total final demand	Total
Agriculture	462	0	0	2	0	0	2.342	394	0	0	546	9	0	0	0	0	3.755	1.471	0	0	0	46	1.517	5,272
Extraction	0	133	0	1.532	0	0	0	0	1.613	0	0	0	0	0	0	0	3.278	0	0	0	0	0	0	3.278
Other Mining	0	0	68	359	540	31	4	50	312	540	0	0	0	0	0	0	1.905	29	3	0	0	2.003	2.035	3.941
Chemicals	802	11	142	7.931	1.028	1.274	844	7.476	382	196	165	609	22	0	299	0	21.182	2.259	873	0	199	165	3.495	24,677
Metals	26	180	57	222	5.249	2.251	378	1.745	0	1.690	64	0	0	0	0	0	11.863	0	0	3	220	0	222	12.085
Engineering	45	161	61	13	286	11.980	22	2.177	855	770	46	791	78	0	119	0	17.403	6.220	3.123	22.859	148	164	32.513	49.916
Food, drink	291	0	0	275	0	0	4.641	36	0	0	936	53	0	0	0	0	6.232	8.812	348	0	18	19	9.198	15.430
Other Manuf.	0	0	79	300	478	369	565	18.399	12	1.900	1.206	641	60	0	357	0	24.365	24.075	2.893	5.312	979	98	33.357	57.722
Utilities	0	0	0	3	4	1	2	3	432	0	0	0	0	0	0	0	446	0	0	0	0	0	0	446
Construction	0	0	0	0	0	0	0	0	0	44	0	0	0	0	0	0	44	0	0	0	0	0	0	44
Distribution	0	0	0	0	0	0	0	0	0	0	0	0	0	0	0	0	0	3.518	0	0	0	0	3.518	3.518
Transport	0	504	11	0	5	0	4	0	0	2	530	2.720	375	0	60	0	4.211	4.036	342	0	0	0	4.378	8.590
Financial	4	1	8	0	20	50	22	0	4	10	35	33	3.369	0	886	19	4.463	0	1.328	0	0	0	1.328	5.791
Public Admin	0	0	0	0	0	0	0	0	0	0	0	0	0	0	0	0	0	0	416	0	0	0	416	416
Educ. Health.	0	0	0	1	3	8	2	55	2	0	3	38	45	0	1.238	0	1.395	1.035	669	0	0	0	1.704	3.099
Housing	0	0	0	0	0	0	0	0	0	0	0	0	0	0	0	0	0	566	0	0	0	0	566	566
Total Imports	1.630	989	425	10.639	7.613	15.965	8.827	30.336	3.612	5.151	3.532	4.895	3.949	0	2.960	19	100.541	52.021	9.995	28.174	1.563	2.494	94.248	194.789

Source: ONS, Input-Output Tables of the United Kingdom, 1995.

Table 4
A 16 Sector Industry by Industry Input-Output Coefficient Table of the United Kingdom 1995

	Agricul-ture	*Extrac-tion*	*Other Mining*	*Chemi-cals*	*Metals*	*Engine-ering*	*Food, drink*	*Other Manuf.*	*Utilities*	*Constru-ction*	*Distri-bution*	*Trans-port*	*Finan-cial*	*Public Admin*	*Educ. Health,*	*Housing*	*Total inter-mediate*
Agriculture	0.087	0.000	0.003	0.001	0.000	0.000	0.212	0.003	0.000	0.000	0.004	0.000	0.000	0.000	0.001	0.000	0.013
Extraction	0.000	0.138	0.000	0.090	0.000	0.000	0.000	0.000	0.087	0.000	0.000	0.000	0.000	0.000	0.000	0.000	0.009
Other Mining	0.001	0.000	0.064	0.004	0.017	0.000	0.001	0.001	0.045	0.005	0.001	0.000	0.000	0.000	0.000	0.000	0.003
Chemicals	0.059	0.001	0.007	0.075	0.009	0.007	0.010	0.012	0.011	0.009	0.008	0.013	0.004	0.000	0.028	0.000	0.013
Metals	0.005	0.009	0.035	0.024	0.146	0.086	0.032	0.041	0.001	0.084	0.003	0.004	0.000	0.000	0.001	0.000	0.025
Engineering	0.000	0.033	0.058	0.013	0.025	0.077	0.009	0.019	0.015	0.009	0.005	0.018	0.005	0.000	0.014	0.001	0.015
Food, drink	0.116	0.003	0.005	0.007	0.002	0.002	0.112	0.003	0.002	0.001	0.043	0.007	0.005	0.000	0.016	0.000	0.017
Other Manuf.	0.024	0.005	0.024	0.034	0.037	0.041	0.049	0.130	0.011	0.050	0.043	0.042	0.039	0.000	0.029	0.005	0.044
Utilities	0.012	0.000	0.029	0.026	0.032	0.016	0.016	0.016	0.294	0.003	0.008	0.009	0.006	0.000	0.006	0.000	0.020
Construction	0.007	0.000	0.022	0.002	0.001	0.001	0.000	0.000	0.000	0.250	0.004	0.002	0.009	0.000	0.001	0.074	0.023
Distribution	0.042	0.011	0.038	0.028	0.050	0.056	0.029	0.030	0.009	0.016	0.027	0.025	0.011	0.000	0.007	0.000	0.021
Transport	0.010	0.040	0.061	0.024	0.041	0.019	0.028	0.029	0.004	0.011	0.096	0.159	0.081	0.000	0.028	0.004	0.051
Financial	0.081	0.038	0.086	0.078	0.056	0.084	0.074	0.073	0.045	0.124	0.145	0.126	0.241	0.000	0.118	0.286	0.127
Public Admin	0.000	0.000	0.000	0.000	0.000	0.000	0.000	0.000	0.000	0.000	0.000	0.000	0.000	0.000	0.000	0.000	0.000
Educ. Health,	0.016	0.000	0.008	0.010	0.005	0.008	0.009	0.021	0.004	0.003	0.006	0.014	0.019	0.000	0.068	0.001	0.016
Housing	0.000	0.000	0.000	0.000	0.000	0.000	0.000	0.000	0.000	0.000	0.000	0.000	0.000	0.000	0.000	0.000	0.000
Total intermediate	0.457	0.276	0.439	0.415	0.423	0.398	0.581	0.378	0.529	0.564	0.393	0.418	0.420	0.000	0.318	0.371	0.397
Imports	0.067	0.056	0.077	0.204	0.154	0.217	0.155	0.241	0.087	0.061	0.023	0.050	0.019	0.000	0.026	0.000	0.082
Duty on imports	0.001	0.000	0.001	0.003	0.002	0.003	0.003	0.003	0.001	0.001	0.000	0.000	0.000	0.000	0.000	0.000	0.001
VAT	0.000	0.000	0.000	0.000	0.000	0.000	0.000	0.000	0.000	0.000	0.000	0.002	0.015	0.000	0.010	0.000	0.004
Duties and levies	0.009	0.000	0.019	0.023	0.007	0.002	0.008	0.003	0.033	0.002	0.008	0.021	0.004	0.000	0.003	0.001	0.007
Other taxes and subsidies	-0.011	-0.001	-0.002	-0.001	-0.001	-0.001	-0.025	-0.002	0.000	0.000	-0.003	-0.004	-0.002	0.000	-0.002	0.000	-0.003
Value added–Labour	0.295	0.080	0.332	0.195	0.319	0.252	0.170	0.290	0.132	0.355	0.399	0.357	0.332	0.945	0.606	0.000	0.353
Value added–Gross profits etc	0.181	0.589	0.134	0.162	0.097	0.129	0.109	0.088	0.219	0.018	0.179	0.156	0.211	0.055	0.038	0.628	0.159
Total inputs	1.000	1.000	1.000	1.000	1.000	1.000	1.000	1.000	1.000	1.000	1.000	1.000	1.000	1.000	1.000	1.000	1.000

DEMAND FOR DOMESTIC AND IMPORTED GOODS

The data from the input-output tables is presented in summary form in Tables 4-8.

As can be seen from Table 5, the financial sector is the largest of the 16 sectors included in the UK tax model, providing 17% of domestic gross output, followed by distribution (13%), other manufacturing (10%) and education and health (9%) . The other mining and metal sectors are the smallest in terms of gross output (0.4% each). Other smaller sectors are extraction (1.4%) and agriculture (2%).

Table 5

Demand composition of domestic output in intermediate and final demands for 1995

	Composition of total demand (A)		*Composition of final demands(B)*			
	Intermediate Demand	*Final Demand*	*Consu-mption*	*Government expenditure*	*Investment.*	*Exports*
Agriculture	0.640	0.360	0.772	0.005	0.000	0.223
Extraction	0.608	0.392	0.000	0.000	0.000	1.000
Other Mining	0.751	0.249	0.248	0.034	0.000	0.718
Chemicals	0.313	0.687	0.105	0.087	0.007	0.801
Metals	0.614	0.386	0.018	0.031	0.416	0.536
Engineering	0.247	0.753	0.000	0.029	0.053	0.918
Food, drink	0.357	0.643	0.705	0.011	0.004	0.280
Other Manuf.	0.429	0.571	0.251	0.054	0.141	0.554
Utilities	0.575	0.425	0.922	0.075	0.000	0.004
Construction	0.337	0.663	0.063	0.079	0.858	0.000
Distribution	0.170	0.830	0.864	0.010	0.020	0.106
Transport	0.642	0.358	0.558	0.075	0.022	0.345
Financial	0.740	0.260	0.463	0.154	0.155	0.229
Public Admin	0.000	1.000	0.000	1.000	0.000	0.000
Educ. Health,	0.171	0.829	0.462	0.490	0.000	0.048
Housing	0.000	1.000	1.000	0.000	0.000	0.000
Total	0.397	0.603	0.443	0.186	0.110	0.260

Data Source: Industry by industry table for 1995.

The data in Table 5 show the split between intermediate and final demands for 16 model sectors with a more detailed structure of final demand for domestic products. It can be noted that total intermediate demand accounts for 40 percent of gross output, while the remaining 60 percent is sold to final users. Consumption demand constitutes more than 44 percent of final sales, while nearly 26 percent of final sales is exported abroad. The government takes about 18.6 percent of final demand, leaving 11 percent to fulfil investment demand.

The final demand structure varies substantially across sectors. As seen from part A of Table 3.5, final demand is the most important component of total demand in housing (100%), public administration (100%), education and health (83%), distribution (83%), engineering (75%), food and drink (64%), chemicals (69%), construction (66%), and manufacturing (57%). Intermediate demand is larger in the other mining (76%), financial services (71%), agriculture (64%), transport (64%), extraction (61%), metals (61%) and utilities (58%) sectors.

In part (B) of Table 5, final demand is broken down further into private consumption, government consumption, investment and exports. Private consumption is the most important category of final demand in the housing (100%), utilities (92%), distribution (86%), agriculture (77%), and food and drink (71%) sectors. Government consumption is by far the most important category of final demand for the public administration (100%) and education and health (49%) sectors. Investment demand is prominent for construction (86%) and metals (42%) while export demand dominates final demand for extraction (100%), other mining (72%), engineering (92%), chemicals (80%), metals (54%) and other manufacturing (55%).

The external sector accounted for 15.6 percent of gross output in the UK economy during 1995. Major importing sectors are other manufacturing (30%), engineering (26%), chemicals(13%) and food and drink (8%). Imported products are more or less evenly split between intermediate and final use. Among final demand categories, imports are mainly used for consumption (55%) or investment (33%) purposes.

COMPOSITION OF INPUTS IN PRODUCTION

As can be seen from Table 6, domestic intermediate inputs constitute more than 50 percent of the production cost in construction (56%), utilities (53%) and food and drink (58%). The cost of labour is most significant in public administration (95%) and education and health (61%). Capital is most important in housing (62%), extraction (59%), financial services (21%) and utilities (21%).

Table 6
Input composition for domestic supplies in 1995

	Domestic intermediate inputs	*Imported intermediate inputs*	*Labour*	*Capital*	*taxes*	*Total*
Agriculture	0.457	0.067	0.295	0.181	-0.001	1.000
Extraction	0.276	0.056	0.080	0.589	-0.001	1.000
Other Mining	0.439	0.077	0.332	0.134	0.018	1.000
Chemicals	0.415	0.204	0.195	0.162	0.024	1.000
Metals	0.423	0.154	0.319	0.097	0.008	1.000
Engineering	0.398	0.217	0.252	0.129	0.005	1.000
Food, drink	0.581	0.155	0.170	0.109	-0.014	1.000
Other Manuf.	0.378	0.241	0.290	0.088	0.004	1.000
Utilities	0.529	0.087	0.132	0.219	0.034	1.000
Construction	0.564	0.061	0.355	0.018	0.002	1.000
Distribution	0.393	0.023	0.399	0.179	0.006	1.000
Transport	0.418	0.050	0.357	0.156	0.019	1.000
Financial	0.420	0.019	0.332	0.211	0.018	1.000
Public Admin	0.000	0.000	0.945	0.055	0.000	1.000
Educ. Health,	0.318	0.026	0.606	0.038	0.012	1.000
Housing	0.371.	0.000	0.000	0.628	0.001	1.000

Data Source: Industry by industry table for 1995.

Table 7
Composition of capital stocks for benchmark year 1995

Industry/Asset	*Buildings Life*	*P&M Long Life*	*P&M Short*	*Vehicles*	*Dwellings*	*Total Capital*	*Percent of Sectoral Cap.*
Agriculture	0.792	0.000	0.151	0.057	0.000	1.000	0.0123
Extraction	0.002	0.127	0.859	0.012	0.000	1.000	0.0145
Other mining & quarrying	0.367	0.000	0.609	0.023	0.000	1.000	0.0019
Chemicals	0.315	0.187	0.484	0.014	0.000	1.000	0.0223
Metals and mineral products	0.377	0.074	0.529	0.020	0.000	1.000	0.0221
Engineering	0.433	0.021	0.517	0.029	0.000	1.000	0.0225
Food, drinks and tobacco	0.469	0.032	0.476	0.023	0.000	1.000	0.0180
Other manufacturing	0.369	0.091	0.516	0.024	0.000	1.000	0.0415
Electricity, gas and water	0.547	0.424	0.024	0.005	0.000	1.000	0.0620
Construction	0.465	0.033	0.300	0.202	0.000	1.000	0.0053
Distribution, hotels, etc.	0.679	0.056	0.207	0.057	0.000	1.000	0.0705
Transport, storage, and communication	0.498	0.215	0.136	0.151	0.000	1.000	0.0637
Financial sector	0.680	0.006	0.197	0.117	0.000	1.000	0.0988
Public administration	0.828	0.029	0.125	0.017	0.000	1.000	0.0376
Education, health and social work	0.892	0.000	0.099	0.009	0.000	1.000	0.0643
Housing services	0	0	0	0	1.000	1.000	0.4426
Total assets (%)	0.331	0.058	0.137	0.032	0.443	1	1.0000

Source: Inland Revenue, 1998 (The ONS is in process of revising the capital stock data in early 1999).

Production taxes are highest in chemicals (2.4%) and utilities (3.4%). Imported intermediate inputs are important in the other manufacturing (24%), engineering (25%), chemicals (20%), and metals (15%) sectors. These sectors are also the most important export sectors in the UK economy.

In the model, production in each sector uses the services of homogenous labour. One unit of labour receives the same wage rate at the margin across sectors. Reallocation will occur until wages rates are equal.

The model includes five types of capital inputs. These assets are buildings, plant and machinery with short life (that with an expected life over 25 years), plant and machinery with long life, vehicles and dwellings. Information on the five different capital assets by sector, obtained from the Inland Revenue for the year 1995, in terms of the proportion of individual assets by sectors to total capital stock, are presented in Table 7.

As Table 7 shows, dwellings and buildings are two prominent capital assets in the UK. In the current data set housing services sector uses all dwelling assets which was about 44 percent of the total capital assets of the economy. All other 15 production and services sectors use only four type of capital assets as inputs: building, long and short lived plant and machinery and vehicles. Buildings assets refers to structures used for industrial and official uses. In aggregate buildings comprised 33 percent of the total assets. The asset share composition by sector in the Table 7 shows that asset composition varies by sector. The short lived plant and machinery are predominant capital asset in extraction, mining, chemicals, engineering, other manufacturing and food and drink sectors. Generally share of long lived plant and machinery and vehicle assets are lower than of building and short lived assets.

A more detailed description of the derivation of 1995 industry-by-industry symmetric input-output tables, from commodity-by-industry balances, is given in Graham Siddorn's notes in Appendix 1. Those notes include methods of converting balances valued at purchaser prices back to producer prices by stripping out product taxes and margins, and the process of getting industry-by-industry symmetric tables in basic prices by stripping out production taxes. In splitting value added between capital and labour, it takes the original split from the ONS, then subtracts an estimate of self-employment income from gross profits to correct the capital income reported in the original tables. For this computation, self-employment income was divided between labour and capital value added in the same proportion as non-self-employment value added appeared to be, within each industry, from the ONS data. These notes also show how to convert commodity-by-industry domestic use matrices and import use matrices into industry-by-industry symmetric matrices, using a make matrix for the 1995 data set.

NOTES

1. See St-Hilarie and Whalley (1983) on how to construct a micro-consistent data set for a GE model.
2. The Economics Unit of the Inland Revenue collected data for implementation of the UK GE tax model, particularly with a keen interest in assessing the efficiency effect of capital income tax applied to various assets and production sectors of the economy. While the co-operation between Warwick and the Inland Revenue team was close, various difficulties we encountered in obtaining a set of model admissible data at various stages of the project. Since a large scale general equilibrium analysis has not been regular practice in the UK after Piggott and Whalley (1985), we did not have any access to a readily available model consistent data set in the beginning. We started from scratch. It was quite challenging to obtain a model consistent data set. Initially we primarily focused on developing a prototype model that would show basic elements of the GE tax model by calibrating a prototype eight sector GE model to the 1988 data set. That basic platform was later extended to an eight sector 10 household model based on earning distributions published in the economic survey of 1994. However, it was realized then that benchmark year 1988 was too far in the past and would not be sufficient to capture the structural features of the economy in late 1990s. Until the 1995 data became available, we took the intermediate step of developing a 16 sector GE tax model calibrated to 1990 data. Thus another platform GE tax model was ready by early July of 1998. The basic tables had to be revised several times as various inconsistencies in value added, value added tax and tariffs re-appeared in the process of model implementation. It was only in the early weeks of November 1998 that we agreed on the data set and model structure which was calibrated to the 1995 data set. Then again this data set was revised in January 1999 for further elaboration in the tax

structure following the model result discussion meeting in early December. This section briefly contains a discussion of this data set which we have used for the final version of the model. While we had some preliminary data for 1988, we noticed that we needed some form of flexibility in generating P-tax rates so that the model had enough capacity to use the different P-tax rates necessary for the analysis of capital income tax policy. In the process, we re-coded P-tax from existing Turbo Pascal to GAMS.

3. See Graham Siddorn's notes on data in appendix 1.

4

TAX RATES, MODEL PARAMETERS AND ELASTICITIES

Implementation of the model specified in Section Two of this report requires tax rates, parameters and elasticities. Getting the right set of tax rates, parameters and elasticities is crucial as model results depend upon the configurations used. We have derived tax rates and parameters from the data contained in the previous section, and have taken elasticities from the literature. In this section, we briefly review the basis of our tax rate data, model parameters and elasticities used for our simulations in the results section.

AN OVERVIEW OF UK TAX POLICY IN 1995

The UK government collects revenue from taxes on capital and labour income, tariffs, duties and levies and value added taxes net of subsides on commodities. The multiplicity of tax instruments results from a set of multiple objectives of the tax system. Though the most important objective of any tax instrument is to raise revenue for the government while affecting the optimal choices of consumers and producers as little as possible, often each of these taxes is designed to meet a set of specific objectives. Capital income taxes aim to release investment resources in the most productive area and induce savings in the economy. Household income taxes aim to raise revenue while correcting the income distribution, as taxes from high income households finance transfers to low income households. Similarly, some of the value added taxes have the additional objective of reducing the consumption of injurious "sin goods" such as liquor, tobacco and cigarettes to promote public heath. These indirect taxes influence the prices of commodities, as well as the consumption spending of households. Other things remaining the same, households tend to avoid paying taxes by buying less of heavily taxed goods.

During our benchmark year, tax on household labour income was the most important source of revenue for the government. As shown in Table 1 it accounted for around 56 percent of total revenue. This is gross of national insurance contributions. Capital income tax contributed another 18.8 percent of the revenue. Indirect taxes- VAT on final consumption and investment, production taxes and tariffs-accounted for the remaining 25 percent of revenue.

Every tax system, however well designed it might be, distorts the choices of producers and consumers in the economy by changing the relative prices of goods and factors in the market place. None of the tax instruments is distortion free. Therefore the question of preferring one tax instrument against another on the basis of the excess burden of tax is really a relative issue. There is a long standing discussion in the public finance literature as to which one of these taxes is the most desirable tax, in terms of achieving objectives of efficiency and equity in the economy as a whole.

Table 1
Composition of government revenue 1995 (in %)

Household income tax	56.4
Capital income tax	18.8
VAT	15.6
Duties and levies	11.0
Subsidies and transfers	-2.6
Tariff	0.9
Total	100.0

Source: GE tax model of UK, 1998

How different taxes affect the choices of households and firms, how successful they are in raising revenue, and how harmful they are in reducing consumption and production in the economy are empirical issues. It is commonly believed that value added taxes are regressive, as they fall disproportionately on the consumption of poor households who spend a greater percentage of their income on consumption than rich households. On the other hand, income taxes are conventionally regarded as being progressive, since higher income people pay a larger amount in taxes. Usually it is thought that income taxes collected from high income households finance transfers to low income households. However, this redistribution issue is somewhat more complicated when the labour supply decisions of both low and high income households are taken into account. There often is a serious trade-off between the efficiency and equity of such a tax-transfer system in the economy. For instance, high taxes on income may improve equity in the economy, but usually discourage labour supply both by the rich (who pay the taxes) and the poor (who receive the benefit), thus reducing output and income in the economy. Differences in tax rates on capital income across sectors distort the allocation of capital resources between various sectors. It is likely that there may be over-investment in less taxed assets/sectors and under-investment in highly taxed assets/sectors.

In a competitive environment, taxes affect the economy through price based substitution and income effects, both in consumption and production. If the substitution effect is stronger than the income effect, consumption of a highly taxed commodity/factor will decrease, with some increase in the consumption or use of less taxed goods/factors. If the income effect is stronger, then higher taxes on one commodity may result in a general decline in spending on all other goods, as the consumer or producer has less purchasing power than in a no tax situation.

In general, resources tend to be diverted from heavily taxed sectors to less taxed sectors due to these income and relative price based substitution effects.

Although tax incidence analysis based on partial equilibrium models may be an appropriate tool for measuring the effect of small changes in the tax system, it is not an appropriate tool for capturing the widespread effects of the tax/subsidy system in the economy. Only a general equilibrium tax model can capture the wide ranging impacts of tax changes. The current model aims to evaluate the general equilibrium effect of a tax reform in the UK economy. It is a very useful framework for capturing the economy-wide income and substitution effects on consumption and production behaviour that affect households' decisions through market prices.

This section very briefly discusses the main characteristics of the tax system in the UK during 1995, which has undergone fundamental reforms since 1985. Rates of labour income taxes and capital income taxes have reduced substantially in most cases, while the value added tax rate and excise duties on cigarettes, tobacco and liquor have also changed during this period. The major argument advanced in the next section is that, despite these reforms, there still remains scope for substantial reform in the UK's tax system.

LABOUR INCOME TAX AND TRANSFERS

There has been a substantial change in the income tax system in the UK between 1985 and 1995. The figures in Table 2 show that all rates of income tax above 40 percent have been abolished, basic rates have been reduced from 30 to 25 percent, personal allowances have been increased in real terms, and the National Insurance Contribution has increased from 9 to 10% (Giles and Johnson (1994)).

Table 2
The UK Income Tax in 1985 and 1995

Types of taxes	*1985*	*1995*
Income tax	30%	25%
Basic rate	60%	40%
Highest rate	30%	20%
Lowest rate	£3,445	£3,445
Personal allowance	£1,950	£1,720
MCA rate	Marginal rate	15%
Basic rate limit	£25,300	£23,700
MIRAS ceiling	£46,800	£30,000
MIRAS rate	Marginal rate	15%
National insurance contributions		
Main rate	9%	10%

Source: Giles and Johnson (1994), p. 69.

The marginal income tax rates presented in Table 2 differ from the average effective income tax rates because of various kinds of allowances and rebates applied to different categories of household income, such as the personal allowance, married couple allowances and MIRAS allowances. For the GE tax model a single marginal effective tax rate on household (labour) income of 28 percent on employment earnings was estimated. Then an additional 10 percent was applied to take account of the national insurance contribution from the labour income. Thus, as in Table 3, the overall marginal labour income tax rate is equivalent to 38 percent in the current model.

Table 3
Household tax rates for year 1995 used in the UK tax model

Households	*Household,s marginal income tax rates*	*Net transfers as fraction of household income*
H1	38%	3.7%

This table also gives the effective rate for transfers, which was effectively 3.7 percent of gross household income. An additional exercise is necessary in order to accommodate inter household distribution issues in the model.

THE INLAND REVENUE P-TAX MODEL FOR CAPITAL INCOME TAX RATES

We use P-Tax formulae for generating capital income tax rates by assets and sectors in the GE tax model. The P-tax model has been in use in the Economics Unit of the Inland Revenue for a number of years. This version of the P-Tax model structure includes five different types of capital assets, three types of ownership, and three types of finances.

The five capital assets are plant and machinery of long life, plant and machinery of short life, vehicles, buildings and dwellings. The three types of ownership are households, tax exempt agents and insurance companies. The three types of financing methods are debt, equity and retained earnings. The variation in P-tax rates across assets and sectors is due to differentiated treatment of financial and economic depreciation rates, and tax rates also vary by financing methods for different owners and sectors.

The taxes on capital income by assets, generated using this tax calculator (P-Tax) of the Inland Revenue, are as given in Table 4[1]. It is obvious that tax rates differ substantially across sectors. From this table it becomes clear that buildings and dwellings are the heavily taxed capital service in the United Kingdom. The capital income tax rates for building services range from 40 to 51 percent. The tax rates on dwellings asset, which largely represents owner occupied houses, is crudely set to zero. This would not affect model results because the dwelling asset is input in production only in the housing services sector see Table 9. Tax rates on income from vehicle type assets is similar across sectors at around 21 percent, except for a lower rate in the agriculture sector and a slightly higher rate in the other manufacturing sector. Tax rates on income from plant and machinery are smaller compared to those on other assets. Plant and machinery with short life have generally higher capital income tax rates than plant and machinery with long life.

Table 4
Effective Tax Rates On Capital Income By Assets For Year 1995
Used In The Uk Tax Model

Industry/Asset	*Buildings*	*P&M Life Long*	*P&M Short Life*	*Vehicles*	*Dwellings*	*P&M Long Life (new Life '95)*
Agriculture	46.2	14.6	25.3	16.9	0.0	25.3
Extraction	51.1	15.9	27.8	21.3	0.0	27.8
Other mining & quarrying	44.3	14.6	23.3	21.3	0.0	23.3
Chemicals	39.9	13.0	17.9	21.3	0.0	17.9
Metals and mineral products	39.7	12.0	17.1	21.3	0.0	17.1
Engineering	39.7	12.0	18.3	21.3	0.0	18.3
Food, drinks and tobacco	39.7	12.4	17.8	21.3	0.0	17.8
Other manufacturing	39.7	12.9	19.1	22.7	0.0	19.1
Electricity, gas and water	40.8	13.6	30.0	21.3	0.0	30.0
Construction	39.7	14.6	23.5	21.3	0.0	23.5
Distribution, hotels, etc.	39.7	13.3	23.9	21.3	0.0	23.9
Transport, storage, and communication	39.7	16.4	26.5	18.5	0.0	26.5
Financial sector	50.7	13.3	24.7	21.3	0.0	24.7
Public administration	50.7	13.3	23.8	21.3	0.0	23.8
Education, health and social work	51.3	13.3	22.2	21.3	0.0	22.2
Housing services	0.0	0.0	0.0	0.0	0.0	0.0

Source: P-Tax calculator, Inland Revenue 1998.

One of the scenarios in our model computation concerns changing the life assumption of long lived plant and machinery assets. The last column of Table 4.4 includes the tax rates corresponding to the new life assumptions for long lived plant and machinery. The tax rates in the last column are higher than the original tax rates for long lived plant and machinery (third column).

A brief discussion on the methodology of calculating marginal capital income tax rates, P-tax rates, included in the current model follows. The P-Tax formula, which decomposes the total tax wedge on corporate income into personal and corporate wedges, was originally developed by Mervyn King in his books *Public Policy and the Corporation* and, with Don Fullerton, *The Taxation of Income from Capital*.

The basic starting point for a set of P-tax formulae is a definition of the nominal interest rate, which is equal to the real interest rate plus inflation

$$I = r + \pi \tag{4.1}$$

where r is real interest rate usually in line with the real yield on bond; π is the inflation rate and I is the nominal interest rate. This nominal rate of return may be different for different assets. If the real interest rate is 5 percent, and inflation is 2 percent, then the nominal interest rate is 7 percent.

A typical investor is interested in the post-tax return to investment. This is the real return net of tax on interest income.

$$S = I \times (1 - RM) - \pi \tag{4.2}$$

where S is post-tax return, and RM is the investor income tax rate on interest payments. As given by 2, it is obtained by removing inflation and taxes on interest income from the nominal interest rate.

The yield on government bonds is an anchor with which to compare the marginal effective tax rate (METR) on income generated from different types of investment. A *Marginal Tax Rate* is the tax rate on income from a marginal investment, that is capital income after all depreciation and other allowances are taken away from the investment income. Because of differing treatment under the tax regime, even with the assumption of a common rate of interest, the METR is generally different to the statutory tax rate (*e.g.* the 30% corporate tax rate) for each type of owner, type of finance, type of asset, and type of industry. The *effective capital income* tax rate is the tax amount expressed as a percentage of gross capital income, and thus is generally lower than the marginal tax rate.

There are several steps in determining the post tax rate of return from the initial assumption of the basic interest rate, *r,* applicable to an asset in a specific sector.

The effective capital gains tax rate, which differs across sectors and is applicable to equity finance but not to debt finance, is computed on realised capital gains (we suppress indices for asset types, sectors and owners just for clarity in exposition). This is computed as follows,

$$Z = \frac{ZS \times v\lambda}{v\lambda + S + \pi} \tag{4.3}$$

where ZS is the average marginal capital gains tax rate, $V\lambda$ is the percentage of accrued capital gains realised each year, and Z is the effective capital gains tax rate.

In order to arrive at an estimate of capital gains, capital income needs to be ascertained. In every capital income tax there is provision for depreciation allowances. The nominal corporate discount rate is computed differently for different methods of financing the capital asset. For retained earnings the discount rate is gross of the capital gains post-tax real rate of return, plus inflation

$$\rho = \frac{S}{1 - Z} + \pi \tag{4.4}$$

where r is the nominal corporate discount rate.

The corporate discount rate is adjusted for the imputation rate if the capital asset is financed by new equity. This is computed as:

$$\rho = \frac{S + \pi \times (1 - Z)}{\theta \times (1 - RM)} \tag{4.5}$$

where θ is the inverse of the dividend imputation rate.

The corporate discount rate for debt financed capital stock is the nominal return net of statutory corporate taxes.

$$\rho = I \times (1 - \tau) \tag{4.6}$$

where τ is the statutory corporate tax rate.

The present value of the available depreciation allowances against corporation taxable income is calculated for each type of physical asset (*e.g.* buildings, plant and machinery). Since the corporate discount rate is used to determine the present value of this stream of tax allowances, the value of tax allowances will be specific to the type of finance used, as well as the physical asset invested in. The formula has a different structure depending upon whether the tax allowances are calculated using a declining balance method or a straight-line method.

In the declining balance case, the present value of depreciation allowances is computed as

$$A = \frac{F_1 \times \tau \times ASS}{ASS + \rho} + F_2 \times \tau \tag{4.7}$$

where A is the present value of depreciation allowances; F_1 is the proportion of the asset qualifying for writing down allowance after the first year; F_2 is the first year capital allowance; and ASS is the rate of tax depreciation under declining balance.

The present value of depreciation allowances under the straight-line depreciation method uses a more complicated formula to compute allowances as

$$A = \frac{F_1 \times \tau \times AL \times \left(1 - e^{-(\rho F_1) \div AL}\right) + F_2 \times \tau}{F_1 \times \rho} \tag{4.8}$$

where AL is the rate of straight line depreciation and e is the exponential constant.

The corporate discount rate is reduced by the present value of tax allowances, and increased by the statutory corporate tax rate to give the required *pre-tax rate of return*. Additionally, where there is a corporate wealth tax on physical assets, this will increase the pre-tax rate of return. The pre-tax rate of return is net of depreciation allowances and gross of corporate wealth tax

$$P = (1 - A)\frac{\rho + DEP - \pi}{1 - \tau} + WC - DEP \tag{4.9}$$

where P is the real pre-tax rate of return; WC is the rate of corporate wealth tax; and DEP is the rate of economic depreciation of the asset. Thus P differs across assets and types of finance, depending on variations in allowances, depreciation and wealth tax rates.

The total tax wedge is the difference between the pre-tax and post-tax return. The total tax rate is this tax wedge divided by the pre-tax rate of return.

$$W = P - S \tag{4.10}$$

where W is total tax wedge.

In the 1995 tax regime an assumption is made that investing in government bonds would yield this post-tax rate of return (S), so it is then the required post-tax rate for each type of investor. Further, for each type of investor this post-tax return is common across all types of finance, that is arbitrage between types of finance by each investor is assumed (there is no risk/return trade off). The tax rate is increased by the personal tax rate (specific to both the type of investor *and* the type of finance), and reduced by any deductions from tax liability arising from the specific type of finance to give the *corporate discount rate*. The actual interest rate is reduced by the personal income tax rate on interest income (which is specific to the type of investor). These deductions are the tax credit available on dividend payments (which applies to new equity finance), and the allowance for debt interest payments from corporation tax (which applies to debt finance).

The UK model discussed in this report does not have the three different types of ownership or investment used in the P-tax computation. In order to arrive at a single rate for an asset in a particular sector, our P-Tax code assigns weights across finance types and ownership.

The weights across finance types for the base year were:

Debt	26.5%
New Equity	9.2%
Retained Earnings	64.3%

In addition, within each source of finance the following ownership shares are used for weighting to arrive at the effective tax rates by assets and sectors.

	Households	*Tax Exempt bodies*	*Insurance Co.s*
Debt New Equity &	76.6%	16.0%	7.4%
Retained Earnings	27.1%	62.1%	10.9%

Using these weights, we arrive at one average type of owner and financial source for each type of capital asset for each of the 16 industrial sectors considered in the model. The user cost of capital increases by the amount of tax rates on capital income. The varying rates of capital income tax across sectors and assets imply differences in user costs. The one effective tax rate per asset per sector reported in Table 4.4 are generated in this manner.

STRUCTURE OF VAT, PRODUCTION TAX AND TARIFF RATES

Indirect taxes on production and consumption contributed 25 percent of revenue in the benchmark year. The basic UK model captures four indirect tax instruments: import duties, duties and levies, value-added taxes, and subsidies on intermediate and final demand. These taxes are applied in the appropriate sequence. Subsidies on domestic sales and import duties on imported goods are applied on a net basis. Duties and levies are applied on gross of subsidy import prices of commodities.

Finally value added tax is imposed gross of all other types of indirect taxes. The total indirect tax rates on intermediate and final demand for the benchmark year are given in Tables 5 to 4.7. More details on the definition of these taxes are given in Appendix 1.

The effective value added tax rates differ across sectors for both public and private consumption. As shown in Table 5, the total indirect tax rates are higher on consumption than on investment and government demand. The total indirect tax rate on domestic and imported intermediate inputs are given in Tables 6 and 4.7 respectively. This variation, in spite of a standard VAT rate of 17.5 percent on commodities, is due to variations in specific indirect excise taxes such as excise duty on petrol (£1.69 per gallon), cigarettes (£1.13 per pack of 20), beer (£0.24 per pint), wine (£1.01 per bottle) or spirits (£5.50 per bottle). For instance, the very high total indirect tax rates in the chemical sector represents a high rate of duties and levies and high VAT for final consumption for fuel products.

Table 5
Composite Indirect Tax Rates on Final Demand Expressed as Per cent of Net Prices for year 1995

	Tax on household consumption		*Tax on investment*		*Tax in government consumption*	
	Domestic sales	*Imports*	*Domestic sales*	*Imports*	*Domestic sales*	*imports*
Agric	-10.9	4.9			-7.1	2.6
Minin	5.4	5.4			16.0	16.0
Chemi	163.1	167.2		1.5	14.7	16.3
Metal	17.3	17.3	3.3	4.7	17.5	17.5
Engin	15.4	16.9	5.0	6.6	16.6	18.2
Foodd	47.5	49.0			2.0	3.1
Othma	14.6	16.0	5.4	6.8	10.8	12.3
Power	9.0	9.0			16.9	16.9
Const	13.9	14.0	2.4	2.5	17.0	17.1
Distr	12.8	12.8			7.9	7.9
Trans	5.9	8.7	-2.2	0.3	6.7	9.3
Finan	1.1	1.1	0.3	0.3	6.1	6.1
Educa	6.3	7.5			-0.8	0.3
House	-2.0					

Source: GE data set, Inland Revenue 1998.

More details on indirect tax rates are given in Tables 8.a to 8.c based on the data received from the Inland Revenue.

The duties and levies on intermediate inputs, shown in Table 8.a, mainly represent taxes on energy inputs, *i.e.* petroleum products used in production process. These rates vary from 0.1 percent in one sector to more than 104 percent in other sectors. Some duties and levies are also imposed on the financial services sector. The value added tax on intermediate inputs, given in Table 8.b, are mainly concentrated in inputs used by transportation, financial services and education sectors.

Basic indirect tax rates on final demands on household and government consumption and investment goods are given in Table c. Among indirect taxes on

Table 6
Indirect tax rates on domestic intermediate inputs for year 1995

	Agric	*Extra*	*Minin*	*Chemi*	*Metal*	*Engin*	*Food*	*Othma*	*Power*	*Const*	*Distr*	*Trans*	*Finan*	*Educa*	*House*
Agric	-12.02		-7.14	-11.11	-14.29	-20.00	-11.63	-19.54			-19.68	-12.50	-6.67	-8.78	
Chemi	8.32		51.93	8.92	18.20	6.15	12.81	1.94	103.94	10.98	65.59	102.19	74.75	13.71	57.89
Metal					-0.04	-0.03	-0.05	-0.04		-0.03		0.77	20.00		
Engin						-0.05		-0.04				0.31	3.19	16.66	
Food	0.10	1.92		3.00	3.66	1.67	2.13	1.04		9.80	2.87	6.39	6.33	5.40	
Othma				-0.06	-0.05	-0.03	-0.04	-0.04		-0.02	-0.03	0.44	5.44	3.86	
Power	3.58		4.37	3.53	3.69	3.87	3.43	4.03	3.79	3.68	3.83	5.60	11.40	17.16	4.35
Constr										-0.03		1.99	11.18	2.74	-0.03
Distr												1.30	9.05	2.03	
Trans	-2.45	-3.55	-2.09	-2.27	-2.15	-2.19	-2.15	-2.19	-3.28	-2.25	-2.13	-1.93	3.38	2.15	-2.02
Finan	0.36		0.21	0.15	0.25	0.13	0.12	0.16	0.26	0.10	0.22	0.60	2.49	1.39	0.16
Educa	-1.06			-1.15	-1.19	-1.03	-1.01	-1.11	-1.12	-1.24	-1.10	-0.88	-0.45	-0.78	-1.49

Source: GE data set, Inland Revenue 1998. Sectors with zero taxes do not show up in this table.

Table 7
Indirect tax rates on imported intermediate goods for year 1995

	Agric	*Extra*	*Minin*	*Chemi*	*Metal*	*Engin*	*Food*	*Othma*	*Power*	*Const*	*Distr*	*Trans*	*Finan*	*Educa*	*House*
Agric	4.11						4.06	4.06			4.03			0.75	
Extra		1.5		1.31					1.3						
Minin			1.47	1.39	1.3			2	1.28	1.3					
Chemi	9.95		54.07	10.63	20.25	7.88	14.68	3.87	107.5	12.27	67.86	105.17	75.13	14.96	57.89
Metal		1.11	1.75	1.35	1.35	1.33	1.32	1.38		1.3	1.56	0.77	20		
Engin	2.22	1.24	1.64		1.4	1.35		1.38	1.4	1.3	2.17	1.57	4.51	17.64	
Foodd	1.13	1.92		4.12	3.66	1.67	3.28	1.04		9.8	3.97	8.4	6.33	5.4	
Othma			1.27	1.33	1.26	1.08	1.24	1.3		1.26	1.24	1.71	7.23	5.06	
Power	3.58		4.37	3.53	3.69	3.87	3.43	4.03	4.99	3.68	3.83	5.6	11.4	17.16	4.35
Const												1.99	11.24	2.74	
Distr												1.3	9.05	2.03	
Trans												0.49	5.6	4.36	
Finan	0.36		0.21	0.15	0.25	0.13	0.12	0.16	0.26	0.1	0.22	0.6	2.49	1.39	0.16
Educa												0.22	0.64	0.46	

Source: GE data set, Inland Revenue 1998. Sectors with zero taxes do not show up in this table.Total indirext tax rates on intermediate inputs vary across sectors. In aggregate agriculture, transport and education sector inputs are subsidised while the chemical and power sector inputs are taxed at higher rates. A comparison of tax rate figures in Table 4.6 and 4.7 reveals that in general tax rates are higher for domestic intermediate inputs than for imported intermediate inputs.

Table 8.a

Duties and levy rates on intermediate inputs in the base year 1995

	Agric	*Extra*	*Minin*	*Chemi*	*Metal*	*Engin*	*Food*	*Othma*	*Power*	*Const*	*Distr*	*Trans*	*Finan*	*Educa*	*House*
Chemi	8.5		51.9	9.3	18.8	6.5	13.2	2.6	104.8	11.1	65.8	102.3	68.6	6.8	57.9
Food	0.1	1.9		3.0	3.7	1.7	2.1	1.0		9.8	2.9	5.8	5.0	3.5	
Power	3.6		4.4	3.5	3.7	3.9	3.4	4.0	3.8	3.7	3.8	4.1	4.2	3.8	4.3
Finan	0.4		0.2	0.1	0.3	0.1	0.1	0.2	0.3	0.1	0.2	0.3	0.3	0.1	0.2

Source: GE data set, Inland Revenue 1998. Sectors with zero taxes do not show up in this table.

Table 8.c

Basic Indirect tax rates on final consumption in the base year 1995

	Tax rates in household consumption				*Tax rates in government consumption*				*Tax rates on investment goods*		
	Tariff rate	*VAT rate*	*Subsidy rate*	*Rate of duties and levies*	*Tariff rate*	*VAT rate*	*Subsidy rate*	*Rate of duties and levies*	*Tariff rate*	*VAT rate*	*Subsidy rate*
Agric	3.7	1.1	-11.9			2.6	-9.5				-11.9
Minin		5.4				16.0					
Chemi	1.2	15.8	-0.4	128.0	1.3	4.8	-0.1	9.7	1.5		-0.4
Metal		17.3				17.5			1.3	3.3	
Engin	1.3	15.4			1.3	16.7	-0.1		1.4	5.2	
Foodd	1.0	9.1		35.2	1.1	1.7		0.3			
Othma	1.2	14.6	-0.1		1.2	10.9	-0.1		1.3	5.4	-0.1
Power		5.8		3.1		12.9		3.5			
Const		14.0	0.0			17.1	0.0			2.5	0.0
Distr		12.8				7.9					
Trans		7.1	-2.5	1.5		9.3	-2.4			0.3	-2.5
Finan				1.1		6.1				0.3	
Educa		3.7	-1.1	3.6		0.3	-1.1				-1.1
House			-2.0								-2.0

Source: GE data set, Inland Revenue 1998. Sectors with zero taxes do not show up in this table.

final demand, import duties were highest for agricultural products, at roughly about 4 percent. For other sectors the tariff rates were 1 to 2 percent. VAT rates on final demand also differ by the category of final demand. VAT rates on consumption are higher than in investment or export demands.

Table 8.b
VAT rate in intermediate inputs in the base year 1995

	Trans	*Finan*	*Educa*
Agric			0.7
Chemi	0.3	3.9	6.6
Metal	0.8	20.0	
Engin	0.3	3.2	16.7
Food	0.5	1.3	1.8
Othma	0.5	5.5	3.9
Power	1.5	6.9	12.8
Const	2.0	11.2	2.7
Distr	1.3	9.1	2.0
Trans	0.5	5.6	4.4
Finan	0.3	2.2	1.3
Educa	0.2	0.6	0.5

Sectors with zero taxes do not show up in this table.

CALIBRATED SHARE PARAMETERS IN PRODUCTION AND CONSUMPTION

Data on input-output transactions, value-added, taxes and final demand presented in Tables 1 and 2 are used to calibrate shift and share parameters for the consumption and production sides in the UK model, as shown in Table 9.

The share of labour is highest in the public administration, construction, mining and quarrying, engineering and other manufacturing, health and education and financial sectors. On average labour's share stands around 70 per cent across sectors though these shares vary from 97.5 per cent for the public administration and education sectors to 15 per cent in the extraction sector. The share of capital is highest in the housing services (note that no labour input used in this sector), extraction, power and chemical sectors.

Among various assets within industry, the share of buildings type assets is the highest followed by short and long lived plant and machinery. The share of vehicle assets in sectoral output is the lowest among all assets. Dwellings are the only input in the housing services sector.

From the data set we establish that the representative household spends 63.4 per cent of their broadly defined income (full income) on consumption, and the remaining 36.6 per cent on leisure. This partly reflects our assumption that the leisure to labour supply ratio is three to four in the benchmark year. The allocation of spending on the composite commodity to various goods by consumers, government and investors is given in Table 10. This table shows that the sectors accounting for the highest shares of consumer spending are distribution and hotels (30%), housing services (12%), education, health and social work(11%), food and drinks (12%) and other manufacturing products (11%). The major part of public consumption is composed of education (31%).

Table 9
Calibrated share parameters in production and consumption in UK tax model, 1995

Industry/Asset	*Buildings*	*P&M long life*	*P&M short life*	*Vehicles*	*Dwellings*	*Share of capital total*	*Share of labour total*	*Value added net of tax*
	Share of individual capital assets in production					*Share in factors in value added*		
Agriculture	0.193	0.051	0.021		0.0	0.265	0.735	9716
Extraction	0.001	0.123	0.710	0.011	0.0	0.845	0.155	9101
Other mining & quarrying	0.065	0.148	0.006		0.0	0.219	0.781	2332
Chemicals	0.096	0.083	0.202	0.005	0.0	0.387	0.613	16563
Metals and mineral products	0.056	0.016	0.108	0.004	0.0	0.185	0.815	19363
Engineering	0.098	0.007	0.158	0.009	0.0	0.272	0.728	25437
Food, drinks and tobacco	0.125	0.012	0.172	0.008	0.0	0.317	0.683	14192
Other manufacturing	0.055	0.020	0.104	0.005	0.0	0.183	0.817	44654
Electricity, gas and water	0.247	0.279	0.013	0.003	0.0	0.541	0.459	11972
Construction	0.014	0.001	0.011	0.008	0.0	0.034	0.966	30996
Distribution, hotels, etc.	0.142	0.017	0.055	0.016	0.0	0.229	0.771	80261
Transport, storage, and communication	0.100	0.060	0.033	0.041	0.0	0.235	0.765	46020
Financial sector	0.155	0.002	0.069	0.043	0.0	0.269	0.731	96018
Public administration	0.023	0.001	0.005	0.001	0.0	0.031	0.969	62229
Education, health and social work	0.027	0.005	0.000		0.0	0.032	0.968	71341
Housing services	0.0	0.0	0.0	0.0	1.0	1.000	0.000	33440

Source: The Inland Revenue, for the GE tax model of the UK 1998.

Table 10
Share of Spending of Households, Government and Investors

Industry	*Share of household spending on goods*	*Share of government spending on goods*	*Share of investor's spending on goods*
Agric	0.0174	0.0003	
Minin	0.0009	0.0004	
Chemi	0.0367	0.0303	0.0040
Metal	0.0009	0.0046	0.0733
Engin	0.0168	0.0366	0.2399
Foodd	0.1183	0.0051	0.0015
Othma	0.1121	0.0497	0.1510
Power	0.0411	0.0102	
Const	0.0093	0.0341	0.4274
Distr	0.2981	0.0087	0.0225
Trans	0.0582	0.0210	0.0066
Finan	0.0591	0.0685	0.0739
Pubad	0.4236		
Educa	0.1095	0.3071	
House	0.1216		

Source: UK tax model 1998.

The input-output table contains investment by origin for different sectors. The construction sector provides 43 per cent of investment goods and another 24 per cent originates from the engineering sector. The other manufacturing (15%), metal and mineral products (7.6%) and financial (7%) sectors are other important providers of investment goods.

ELASTICITIES OF SUBSTITUTION IN PRODUCTION AND CONSUMPTION

The elasticities of substitution in production and consumption are very important in determining the model results in a general equilibrium model. The sizes of welfare changes and measures of the marginal excess burden of taxes across model scenarios depend crucially upon the values of these elasticities. The classic intuition on the role of elasticities in welfare analysis of taxes is provided by the Harberger

Table 11
Elasticity Parameters used in the UK tax model (central case)

Industry	*(a)* *Elasticity of substitution between labour and capital*	*(b)* *Elasticity of substitution among capital assetsl*	*(c)* *Elasticity of substitution among domestic supplies and imports*	*(d)* *Elasticity of transformation between domestic supplies and exports*	*(e)* *Central tendency values of own price elasticities of household demand functions*
Agriculture	0.90	0.90	2.12	1.46	-0.475
Extraction	1.19	1.19	2.82	1.93	-0.305
Other mining & quarrying	1.11	1.11	2.63	1.80	-0.362
Chemicals	1.18	1.18	2.80	1.92	-0.542
Metals and mineral products	1.22	1.22	2.89	1.98	-0.503
Engineering	1.11	1.11	2.63	1.80	-0.275
Food, drinks and tobacco	0.74	0.74	1.75	1.20	-0.795
Other manufacturing	1.18	1.18	2.80	1.92	-0.530
Electricity, gas and water	1.11	1.11	2.63	1.80	-0.000
Construction	0.74	0.74	1.75	1.20	-0.000
Distribution, hotels, etc.	1.18	1.18	2.80	1.92	-0.489
Transport, storage, and communication	1.18	1.18	2.80	1.92	-0.321
Financial sector	1.22	1.22	2.89	1.98	-0.000
Public administration	0.67	0.67	1.58	1.08	-0.481
Education, health and social work	1.18	1.18	2.80	1.92	-0.253
Housing services	0.74	0.74	1.75	1.20	-0.000

Source: Piggott and Whalley (1985)..

(1962) triangle, which relates welfare cost to the square of tax rates times the price elasticity of the taxable factor. When direct econometric studies are not available, numerical methods are used to derive substitution elasticities from price elasticities. Given the size of the current model, it is hard to find direct evidence on all the different types of elasticities used in the model. Some estimates are available in the literature, while for some others a modeller needs to rely on sensitivity analyses and connection between own price elasticities and the elasticity of substitution.

We take elasticity figures from Piggott and Whalley (1985) for our basic calculation. Then we set up medium and high elasticity tables scaling up these basic elasticities. These elasticities explain the degree of substitution among capital assets and between labour and capital in the production functions, between domestic supplies and imports in the Armington function, among consumption goods in the composite consumption function and between composite consumption and leisure in the utility function. Besides the elasticities specified in Table 11 the elasticity of substitution between goods and leisure, σ_h, is set equal to 0.5, and the elasticity of substitution among composite goods, σ_y, is also set to 0.5.

In the unit elasticity specification, the figures in columns (a) and (b) of Table 4.11 are replaced by unit elasticities to check the sensitivity of model results to these elasticities.

5

ANALYSIS OF MODEL RESULTS: EFFICIENCY, ALLOCATION IMPACTS AND MARGINAL EXCESS BURDENS OF PUBLIC FUNDS IN THE BASIC UK GENERAL EQUILIBRIUM TAX MODEL[1]

Internal consistency of a general equilibrium model is assured when a model reproduces the benchmark data set, with calibrated model parameters, as its solution. Though equilibria could be computed for a wide range of parameter sets and elasticities, only those parameter sets and elasticities which can generate base year quantities and prices as model solutions are relevant. In this section we use the multisectoral general equilibrium tax model calibrated to 1995 data in order to analyse the efficiency and allocation effects of various taxes in the UK economy.

For each tax policy scenario, we compute changes in total money metric aggregate welfare by summing up money metric equivalent variations for households, investors and government. The money metric equivalent variation measures the amount of money required to compensate agents to move to the new equilibrium, from an old equilibrium with goods evaluated in terms of new prices. A positive equivalent variation represents a gain compared to the old equilibrium and a negative equivalent variation represents a loss. To be comprehensive, we take changes in total money metric equivalent variation in response to tax changes as a percentage of UK GDP for various alternative tax policies. Then we check the robustness of the model results by computing the sensitivity of the EV/GDP ratio to moving to a set of relevant substitution elasticities.

We use the model mainly to assess the impacts of taxes on five types of capital assets, labour income taxes and four types of indirect taxes. The five types of capital assets are buildings, short and long lived plant and machinery, vehicles and dwellings; the four types of indirect taxes are import duties, subsidies, duties and levies and value added taxes on intermediate and final demands.

1. An earlier version of this chapter has been published in the European Research Studies Journal 6:3-4, 177-205, 2003.

Figure 1
Flow Chart of Model Use

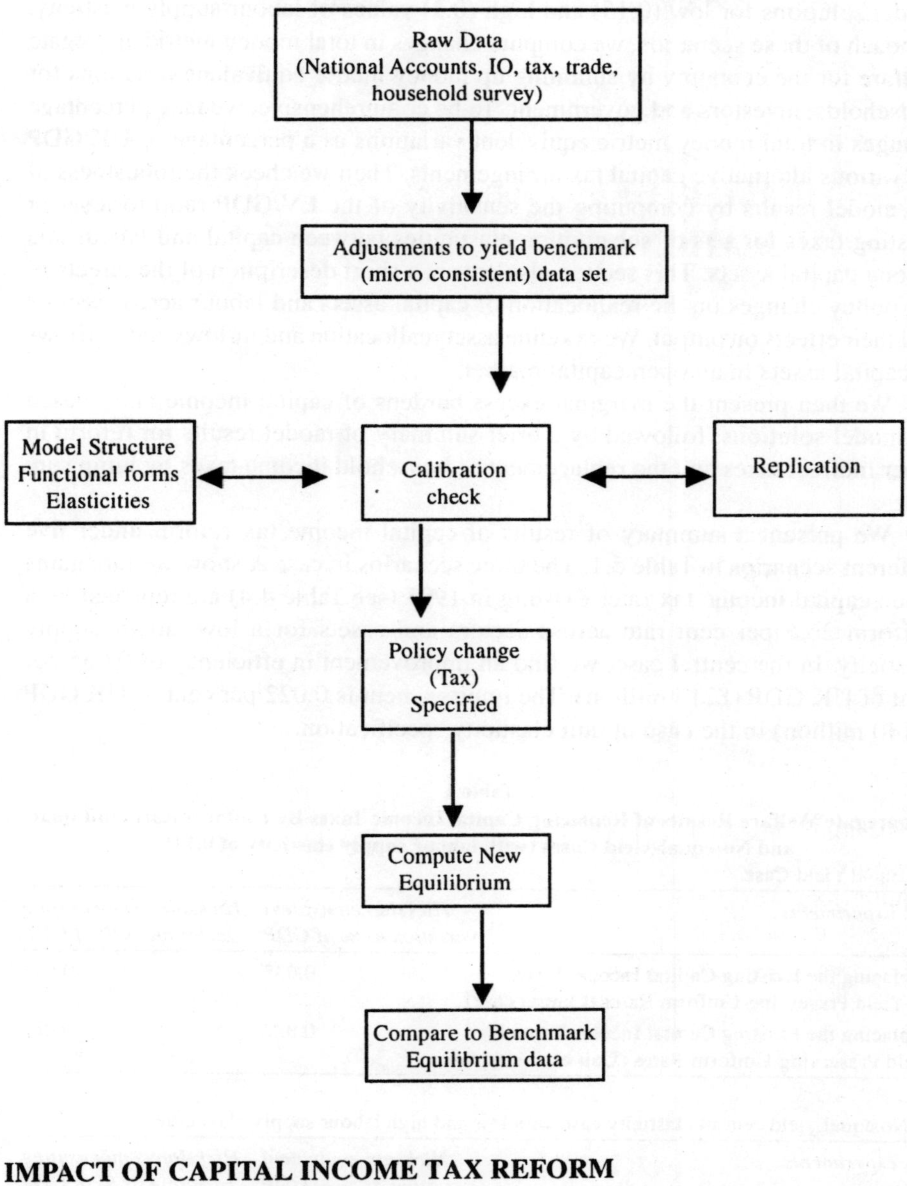

IMPACT OF CAPITAL INCOME TAX REFORM

The major focus of this section of the report is on evaluating the impacts of capital income taxes. First, we consider four different scenarios to assess the impact of capital income taxes on the economy. These scenarios consist of moving to a uniform yield preserving 26.5 per cent tax rate from the existing taxes for central and unit elasticity cases, and moving to a uniform 30 per cent tax rate from the existing taxes without any equal yield requirements for low and high labour elasticity cases. The robustness of each of these experiments is checked by using model solutions for low (0.15) and high (0.3) values of labour supply elasticity. For each of these scenarios, we compute changes in total money metric aggregate welfare for the economy by summing up money metric equivalent variations for households, investors and government. To be comprehensive, we take percentage changes in total money metric equivalent variations as a percentage of UK GDP for various alternative capital tax arrangements. Then we check the robustness of the model results by computing the sensitivity of the EV/GDP ratio to a set of existing taxes for sets of substitution elasticities between capital and labour and among capital assets. This section also covers a short description of the effects of tax policy changes on the reallocation of capital assets and labour across sectors and their effects on output. We examine asset reallocation and inflows and outflows of capital assets in an open capital market.

We then present the marginal excess burdens of capital income taxes based on model solutions, followed by a brief summary of model results for reform in other indirect taxes and the replacement of household income taxes by lump sum taxes.

We present a summary of results of capital income tax reform under five different scenarios in Table 5.1. The three scenarios in case A show welfare gains when capital income tax rates existing in 1995 (see Table 4.4) are replaced by a uniform 26.5 per cent rate across sectors and assets for a low labour supply elasticity. In the central case, we find an improvement in efficiency of 0.035 per cent of UK GDP (£217 million). The improvement is 0.022 per cent of UK GDP (£140 million) in the case of unit elasticity specification.

Table 1
Aggregate Welfare Results of Replacing Capital Income Taxes By Uniform Rates in Equal and No-equal-yield Cases (with labour supply elasticity of 0.15)

A. Equal Yield Case

Tax Experiments	*Hicksian equivalent variation as % of GDP*	*Hicksian compensating variation as % of GDP*
Replacing the Existing Capital Income Taxes By Yield Preserving Uniform Rates (Central case)	0.035	-0.036
Replacing the Existing Capital Income Taxes By Yield Preserving Uniform Rates (Unit elasticity case)	0.022	-0.022

B. No equal yield central elasticity case with low and high labour supply elasticities

Tax experiments	*Hicksian equivalent variation as % of GDP*	*Hicksian compensating variation as % of GDP*
Replacing the Existing Capital Income Taxes By Uniform Rates (Low case)	0. 281	-0.279
Replacing the Existing Capital Income Taxes By Uniform Rates (High case)	0.283	-0.281

Note: See section 4 for numerical values of substitution elasticities in central and unit cases.

We relax the equal yield requirement in the no equal yield scenarios, in Cases B of Table 1. The size of government can, and usually does, change after the tax reform without any adjustment to other taxes. The efficiency gain from replacing existing taxes by uniform capital income tax rates in the no equal yield capital tax reform was about 0.281 per cent of UK GDP for the low labour supply elasticity case and 0.283 per cent for the high labour supply elasticity.

In an earlier version of the model, the computed efficiency gain from replacing capital income tax by yield preserving lump-sum taxes was 0.3 per cent of the UK GDP.

The improvement in aggregate efficiency reported here reflects removal of distortions existing in the economy by introducing uniform tax rates on capital. We have checked robustness of these results with respect to high and low labour supply elasticities.

ROBUSTNESS OF MODEL RESULTS

We check the robustness of the welfare impact results outlined above by means of sensitivity analysis of the results to four different sets of substitution elasticities among assets (σ_κ), keeping elasticities of substitution between labour and capital (σ_v) fixed; and four different sets of elasticities of substitution between labour and capital, keeping substitution elasticities among assets fixed. Table 2 includes the results of sensitivity analysis for replacing the existing level of capital income taxes by yield preserving uniform capital income tax rates, for both low and high labour supply elasticities.

For all pairs of elasticities, the welfare impacts of moving to a yield preserving capital income tax from a set of existing taxes is positive and almost linear in the value of substitution elasticities among assets, for a particular set of elasticities of substitution between labour and capital assets. Similarly, it is also almost linear in the values of substitution elasticities between capital and labour for any particular value of substitution elasticities among capital assets.

Table 2

Sensitivity of aggregate welfare as a percentage of UK GDP to substitution elasticities between capital and labour, and to substitution elasticities across capital assets

A. Labour supply elasticity 0.15

σ_κ σ_v	*0.75*	*1.0*	*3.0*	*5.0*
0.75	0.01513	0.01705	0.0316	0.04594
1.0	0.01951	0.0223	0.03607	0.05046
3.0	0.04999	0.05252	0.06898	0.08426
5.0	0.07694	0.08039	0.09992	0.11647

When both σ_v and σ_κ are very high, each assuming a value of 5.0, the welfare impact of switching to a uniform tax rate was about 0.11 per cent of UK GDP, which amounts to nearly £691 million.

B. Labour supply elasticity 0.3

σ_{κ} σ_{v}	0.75	1.0	3.0	5.0
0.75	0.01496	0.01688	0.03143	0.04576
1.0	0.0193	0.02124	0.03587	0.05026
3.0	0.04947	0.05206	0.06866	0.08399
5.0	0.07616	0.07971	0.09953	0.11618

Note: σ_{v} is the elasticity of substitution between capital and labour
σ_{κ} is the elasticity of substitution among capital assets.

REALLOCATION OF CAPITAL ASSETS AND LABOUR IN PRODUCTION

Firms use capital services and labour services in production. Following convention in general equilibrium analysis, before tax prices of these factors are set to unity in the benchmark. Producers, or users of these inputs, however, pay the gross of tax prices but the owners of these factors receive net of tax payments. Government collects the tax revenue. In this model capital income taxes are collected at the sectoral level. The labour tax does not differ by sector. In our model construction labour income taxes are collected from households[1].

In 15 out of 16 sectors, capital services are split between four different assets: buildings, short lived plant and machinery, long lived plant and machinery, and vehicles. Labour is homogeneous across all these sectors. The housing services sector is peculiar in terms of input use, as it uses dwellings as its only input. It uses none of the other assets nor any labour. Housing sector is isolated from other sectors.

The relative prices of capital assets differ across sectors in the benchmark, mainly for the reason that capital income tax rates differ by assets and sectors. The equal yield uniform tax reform reduces these inter-sectoral and inter-asset differences in the relative user cost of capital in the counterfactual scenarios. Consequently we see a significant reallocation of capital and labour resources across sectors occurring in comparison to the base year. The capital reallocation results in Table 3 show intra-asset reallocation of capital assets with the central case elasticity specification for both low and high labour supply elasticity cases. The model results confirm our assertion about the reallocation effects of changes in the relative prices. Based on changes in relative prices of capital between sectors, we expect more use of building type assets in the agriculture, extraction, financial services, public administration and education sectors. The relative prices of building type assets decrease in these sectors when capital income taxes become uniform across sectors and assets, compared to the benchmark relative prices. The sector-by-sector results in the first row in Table 5.3 show that in the case of a low labour supply elasticity, reallocation is actually happening in our model solutions. The use of building type assets increases by 21 per cent in education, 19 per cent in public administration, 21 per cent in extraction, 14 per cent in financial services, and around 2 per cent in the agriculture sector. The use of buildings decreases in

Central Case Specification of Elasticities

Table 3

Capital Asset Reallocation from Equal Yield Replacement of Capital Income Taxes by Uniform Tax Rates By Industry

A. % Change in Capital Use (By Asset By Sector)

Asset Class	*Agric*	*Extr*	*Min*	*Chem*	*Metal*	*Eng*	*Food*	*OTHMA*	*Power*	*Constr*	*Distr*	*Trans*	*Fin*	*PubAD*	*EducA*
Buildings	2.05	21.17	-1.47	-8.98	-11.62	-12.06	-5.87	-6.74	-6.26	-8.31	-10.82	-11.56	14.18	18.89	20.89
PM Long		-0.45		-0.52	-4.93	-5.88	-1.08	-1.97	0.38	-1.15	-1.66	3.34	-8.78	-5.02	
PM Short	2.76	10.26	0.30	-5.79	-9.55	-8.12	-3.72	-3.45	20.12	0.85	4.68	9.65	-1.34	0.91	-2.55
Vehicles	-5.30	2.11	2.49	7.88	4.81	3.06	4.64	4.24	6.89	1.92	5.63	-1.03	-2.01	2.03	1.96

C. Capital income tax rates in the base case

Asset Class	*Agric*	*Extr*	*Min*	*Chem*	*Metal*	*Eng*	*Food*	*OTHMA*	*Power*	*Constr*	*Distr*	*Trans*	*Fin*	*PubAD*	*EducA*
Buildings	46.2	51.1	44.3	39.9	39.7	39.7	39.7	39.7	4 0.8	39.7	39.7	39.7	5 7	5 0.7	51.3
PM Long		15.9		13.0	12.0	12.0	12.4	12.9	13.6	14.6	13.3	16.4	13.3	13.3	
PM Short	25.3	27.8	23.3	17.9	17.1	18.3	17.8	19.1	30 0	23.5	23.9	26.5	24.7	23.8	22.2
Vehicles	16.9	21.3	21.3	21.3	21.3	21.3	21.3	22.7	21.3	21.3	21.3	18.5	21.3	21.3	21.3

Note: The capital income tax rates used here may be different from the capital income tax rates in use in the Inland Revenue.

Equal yield uniform capital tax rate: 26.5%

Aggregate Welfare Effect: +£218.1 mill (95)

= 0.0347% of UK 1995 GDP

Unit Elasticities

Table 4

Capital Asset Reallocation from Equal Yield Replacement of Capital Income Taxes by Uniform Tax Rates By Industry

A. % Change in Capital Use (By Asset By Sector)

Asset Class	*Agric*	*Extr*	*Min*	*Chem*	*Metal*	*Eng*	*Food*	*OTHMA*	*Power*	*Constr*	*Distr*	*Trans*	*Fin*	*PubAD*	*EducA*
Buildings	2.10	16.21	-0.60	-5.15	-7.29	-8.76	-5.51	-7.04	-3.96	-7.91	-6.60	-7.00	9.42	12.12	13.39
PM Long		2.46		-0.46	-3.53	-5.05	-1.24	-2.28	-0.02	-1.23	-1.24	1.99	-5.60	-3.27	
PM Short	2.17	9.15	0.09	-3.63	-6.41	-6.51	-3.82	-3.85	12.92	0.86	2.82	5.97	-0.73	0.58	-1.54
Vehicles	-4.63	4.06	1.46	4.58	2.54	0.92	4.52	4.69	4.29	1.86	3.31	-0.76	-1.25	1.19	1.22

Equal yield uniform capital tax rate : 26.5%

Aggregate Welfare Effect : +£140 mill (95) = 0.0223% of UK 1995 GDP the other sectors because of a rise in the relative price of building assets in those sectors compared to the base year.

The reallocation results for other assets, long and short lived plant and machinery and vehicles could also be interpreted in this manner. We see positive changes in the use of a particular asset in which the user cost of the asset has reduced relative to the base year.

Besides inter-sectoral reallocation, we also see inter-asset substitution and capital labour reallocation after the uniform tax reform. Given that we have a fixed endowment of each type of capital asset in both the benchmark and the counterfactual scenarios, total reallocation is subject to this capital stock constraint.

Reallocation between asset types also occurs when the relative prices of these assets change in counterfactual scenarios. Inter-asset reallocation in response to capital tax reform is reflected in terms of positive changes for some assets, followed by negative changes in the use of other assets within a sector. For every sector, some assets change positively and some other assets change negatively in response to the uniform tax reform. For instance, in the agriculture sector, use of the buildings type asset increases by 2 per cent, use of plant and machinery with short life also increases by 2.8 per cent, while there is a reduction of 5.3 per cent in the use of vehicle type assets.

The capital reallocation effect explained in this section is sensitive to elasticity configurations. We consider a unit elasticity case in Table 4. Generally the direction of changes in the allocation of assets is the same as in the central elasticity specification outlined in Table 5.3, while the magnitude of such changes is smaller for the unit elasticity specification than in the central elasticity specification.

Besides inter-sectoral and inter-asset redistribution, changes in the relative user cost of capital have a significant effect on the use of labour across sectors. When capital inputs become relatively cheaper than the labour input, producers tend to substitute capital for labour. As outlined above, capital becomes relatively cheaper in certain sectors such as agriculture, finance, public administration, and education, and relatively expensive in some other sectors, particularly manufacturing, after a uniform tax reform. For this reason we see substitution between capital and labour in the model solutions.

The figures in Table 5 show that replacing low capital income tax rates in the base year by a 26.5 per cent uniform tax rate increases the user cost of capital in manufacturing sectors and some service sectors (chemicals, metals, engineering, food, other manufacturing, power, construction, distribution and transport). We see substitution of capital by labour in these sectors. Thus the effect of the reduction in capital assets is not completely compensated for by increased use of labour. Therefore output decreases in most of the manufacturing sectors, though not by as much as would have been warranted by the reduction in the use of capital in these sectors. Figures in Table 5 also show that labour is substituted by capital assets, because capital becomes less expensive, in the financial services and education sectors. Benefiting from cheaper capital services, these sectors substitute capital for labour and experience positive changes in output. For instance, two

Central Case
Specification
of Elasticities

Table 5
% Changes in Employment and Output
Equal Yield Replacement of Capital Income Taxes By Uniform Tax Rates

	Labour supply elasticity 0.15	
Industry	*% change in employment(labour use)*	*% change in output*
Agric	-0.989	-0.065
Extra	-0.843	1.606
Minin	-0.207	-0.367
Chemi	4.758	-0.251
Metal	1.850	-0.731
Engin	0.352	-0.970
Food	2.797	-0.044
Othma	0.951	-0.241
Power	4.084	-0.262
Constr	0.130	-0.040
Distr	2.673	-0.121
Trans	1.818	-0.015
Finan	-4.757	0.124
PubAD	-0.827	0.035
EducA	-0.897	0.107
House		0.01

extreme cases of factor substitution are seen in the financial and chemical sectors: capital substitutes for labour substantially in the financial sector while labour substitutes for capital in the chemical sector.

OPENING UP THE CAPITAL MARKET IN THE GE TAX MODEL OF THE UK ECONOMY

We have extended the small open economy assumption of the commodity market to the capital market to assess equilibrium stocks of capital resources where inflow and outflow can occur in response to tax changes in the UK economy. We fix the net user cost of the capital asset at unity to open up the capital market. This allows inflows and outflows of the capital asset in the model. We notice a higher supply of heavily taxed building assets, with some lower supply of less heavily taxed assets.

The results from opening up the capital market with the uniform capital tax experiment are presented in Table 8. The net overseas ownership of UK assets and UK ownership of overseas assets are presented in a small table.

We see inflows of capital assets for which the user cost of capital has decreased because of the taxes, such as buildings, and outflows of assets for which the user cost has increased after the tax changes, such as long and short lived plant and machinery and vehicles. However, it should be noted that the capital inflows and outflows mentioned in this table may take a long time to adjust before they settle down to the levels seen from the comparative static studies. The inflows and outflows of assets are not very sensitive to labour supply elasticities.

Open capital market scenario
Central case of elasticities

Table 8

Equal Yield Replacement of Capital Income Taxes by Uniform Tax Rates: Open Capital Market Case

A. % Change in Capital Use (By Asset By Sector)

Asset Class	*Agric*	*Extr*	*Min*	*Chem*	*Metal*	*Eng*	*Food*	*OTHMA*	*Power*	*Constr*	*Distr*	*Trans*	*Fin*	*PubAD*	*EducA*
Buildings	12.36	33.04	17.19	12.34	13.04	14.44	8.18	7.31	13.04	6.65	9.97	11.79	24.34	27.18	29.24
PM Long		-15.09		-17.31	-16.71	-13.87	-10.30	-9.11	-14.90	-10.43	-17.76	-13.94	-20.85	-19.04	
PM Short	-7.89	-3.65	-7.91	-13.23	-12.57	-8.89	-7.38	-6.02	-0.33	-5.31	-8.73	-4.65	-11.47	-10.25	-11.12
Vehicles	-13.67	-10.26	-9.63	-10.14	-8.84	-6.32	-5.33	-4.07	-8.72	-6.67	-11.17	-12.23	-14.51	-12.56	-11.91

Inflows(+) and Outflows (-) of Capital Assets

Buildings	*PM Long*	*PM Short*	*Vehicles*	*Dwellings*
7959	-1776	-3130	-1078	192

Equal yield uniform capital tax rate : 25.6%

Aggregate Welfare Effect : = 0.366% of UK 1995 GDP

OPENING UP OF THE CAPITAL MARKET AND TRADE IMBALANCE

Balance in international trade is a property of a pure general equilibrium model. The values of imports and exports offset each other. However, when the pure general equilibrium structure is distorted by fixing the domestic rate of return to capital assets to the international capital market rate, the model loses one degree of freedom for adjustment in quantities and prices. Therefore, trade balance is not automatically guaranteed. Inflows and outflows of capital services occur until the marginal product of capital equals this exogenously fixed rate of return. The values of exports and imports do not offset each other.

Table 5.9
Exports, imports and trade balance with open capital markets

	Low elasticity of labour supply (0.15)		
	export volume (£ illions)	*Import volume (£millions)*	*Trade imbalance (£ millions)*
Agric	1860	5304	-3443
Extra	6952	3330	3623
Minin	1032	1973	-941
Chemi	29262	25020	4242
Metal	10671	12487	-1817
Engin	55941	51096	4845
Foodd	10618	15596	-4978
Othma	40958	58410	-17452
Power	64	452	-388
Const		44	-44
Distr	14447	3549	10897
Trans	12506	8713	3793
Finan	13855	5839	8016
Pubad		397	-397
Educa	4641	3131	1511
House		571	-571
Total	202807	195912	6895

In aggregate, the total imbalance in the capital account created by opening up the capital market is matched by balances in the trade account. Two basic points are noteworthy. First, the imbalance in trade varies across sectors. For instance, the other manufacturing sector had the greatest imbalance in absolute terms, nearly £17.5 billion, irrespective of low or high values of labour supply elasticity. The financial sector realises a surplus of £8.1 billion. Secondly, these trade flows and imbalances are not influenced by the set of elasticity configurations used in the model. In separate computations we noticed a greater impact of capital market opening when elasticities of substitution in production and trade were high than when they were low.

MARGINAL EXCESS BURDEN OF TAXES IN THE UK MODEL

The marginal excess burden (MEB) of taxes measures the extra cost to society, in terms of money metric welfare, of each pound of revenue raised by means of a certain tax instrument. We have computed the MEB for each tax instrument included in the UK model by dividing the change in welfare (ΔW_t) by the net change in the government revenue (ΔR_t). The net change in government revenue reflects the share (g) of revenue retained by the public sector.

$$MEB_t = \frac{\Delta W_t}{g.\Delta R_t} \tag{5.1}$$

The popular measure of the marginal excess burden of taxes, given by the area of the Harberger triangle, is related with the elasticity of demand for goods.

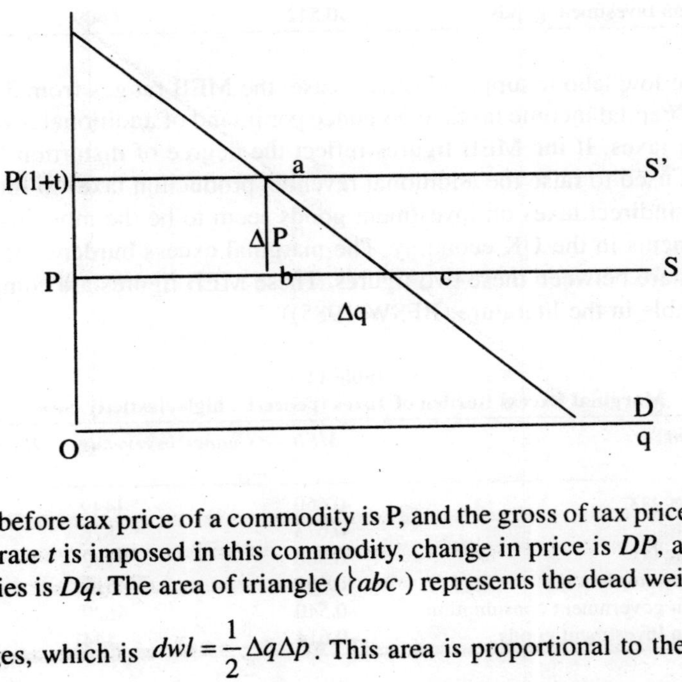

Here before tax price of a commodity is P, and the gross of tax price is P(1+t). After tax rate *t* is imposed in this commodity, change in price is *DP*, and change in quantities is *Dq*. The area of triangle (}*abc*) represents the dead weight loss of tax changes, which is $dwl = \frac{1}{2}\Delta q \Delta p$. This area is proportional to the square of the tax rate and the elasticity of demand. The price elasticity of demand is $e = \frac{\Delta q}{\Delta p}\frac{p}{q}$. Then the relation between the change in quantity and the elasticity is $\Delta q = \frac{\Delta pq}{p} e$. Inserting this value of Δq in the equation for the dead weight loss formula we get $dwl = \frac{1}{2}\left(\frac{\Delta pq}{p}\right) e\Delta p$. The tax rate and change in prices are equal, implying $\Delta p = t$ and normalising $p = 1$, $dwl = \frac{1}{2} t^2 eq$.

The results show that MEB figures differ according to the type of tax instrument used to raise additional revenue. Results of the UK model in terms of changes in revenue, Hicksian EVs and MEB are given in Table 10.

Table 10
Marginal Excess Burden of Taxes (pence/£: low elasticity case)

Tax instrument	*MEB*	*Change in revenue*	*Hicksian money metric EV*
Capital income tax	-0.350	11305	-3962
Production tax	-0.544	6585	-3582
Labour income tax	-0.435	7984	-3473
Household consumption tax	-0.517	6911	-3574
Indirect tax on government consumption	-0.540	6629	-3578
Indirect tax on Investment goods	-0.542	6609	-3581

For the low labour supply elasticity case, the MEB ranges from 35 pence in the case of capital income taxes to 54 pence per pound of additional revenue from production taxes. If the MEB figures reflect the degree of distortion for the tax instrument used to raise the additional revenue, production taxes in intermediate goods and indirect taxes on investment goods seem to be the most distortionary tax instruments in the UK economy. The marginal excess burdens (MEB) of all other taxes are between these two figures. These MEB figures are comparable to rates available in the literature (BFSW(1985)).

Table 11
Marginal Excess Burden of Taxes (pence/£ : high elasticity case)

Tax instrument	*MEB*	*Change in revenue*	*Hicksian money metric EV*
Capital income tax	-0.660	4449	-2936
Production tax	-0.673	876	-590
Labour income tax	-0.580	8182	-4750
Household consumption tax	-0.669	4519	-3025
Indirect tax on government consumption	-0.540	6629	-3578
Indirect tax on Investment goods	-0.614	344	-211

We find MEB measures to be sensitive to the elasticities of substitution in both the consumption and production sides of the economy. As figures in Tables 10 and 11 show, MEB figures are higher for higher values of elasticities compared to corresponding numbers with lower elasticities.

AGGREGATE WELFARE FOR INDIRECT TAX REFORM

The basic UK model included here has four types of indirect taxes on intermediate inputs and final demand: tariffs, subsidies, duties and levies, and value added tax. Rates of indirect taxes vary across sectors and final demand categories as reported in the previous section.

The aggregate welfare impacts of replacing a non-uniform indirect tax by a uniform tax rate and lump sum taxes are reported in Table 12.

For the central case specification, the welfare gain from replacing equal yield non-uniform VAT by uniform VAT was about 0.019 per cent of UK GDP. Such a welfare gain occurs because of the removal of distortions caused by differentiated VAT rates in the base year.

Equal yield replacement of all differentiated indirect tax rates by uniform tax rates across sectors leads to a gain of 0.017 per cent of UK GDP. This figure is also very close to the gains from the uniform VAT case.

Finally, when we replace indirect tax rates by an equal yield lump sum tax, the welfare gain rises to 1.72 per cent of UK GDP, which is bigger than in all the other tax experiments reported earlier.

Table 12
Aggregate Welfare for other cases
(as % of GDP)

Equal Yield Replacement of non-uniform VAT By Uniform Rates - Central Case Specification of Elasticities -	0.0186% of UKGDP
Equal Yield Replacement of all Indirect Taxes By Uniform Indirect Tax Rates	0.01704% of UKGDP
Equal Yield Replacement of all Indirect Taxes By equal yield lump-sum Tax	1.723% of UKGDP
Equal Yield Replacement of household income taxes By equal yield lump-sum tax	3.67% of UKGDP

NOTES

1. Though social security, national insurance contributions could be thought of as taxes on labour use.

PART - II

DYNAMIC GENERAL EQUILIBRIUM TAX MODEL OF THE UK ECONOMY

6

DYNAMIC MULTISECTORAL GENERAL-EQUILIBRIUM TAX MODEL OF THE UK ECONOMY[2]

INTRODUCTION

This paper describes specification, calibration, and replication of a sixteen-sector dynamic open-economy general equilibrium tax policy model of the UK economy and its application to study sectoral growth paths and dynamic efficiency effects for various tax reform scenarios using 1995 as the reference year. Dynamic model discussed here builds on a static model discussed in detail in an earlier paper (Bhattarai (1999)). The sectoral classification as well as the tax structure built into the model reflect the modelling requirements of the Economics Unit of the Inland Revenue.

This model consists of a dynamic multisectoral representation of the UK economy. On the demand side, an infinitely lived dynastic household allocates lifetime income between consumption and savings to maximise intertemporal utility. On the supply side, investors allocate investment among various production sectors based on their profitability. On the policy side, the government collects revenue from direct and indirect taxes and allocates them to purchase goods and services for public consumption and to make transfers to the households. Prices in each period adjust until the markets for goods, capital, and labour clear.

The major advantage of the dynamic model presented here, in comparison to the static version of the model, lies in its ability to track both short- and long-run impacts of tax and trade policy measures on the growth path of the economy via their effects on capital formation. The process of capital accumulation, both in the short and in the long run, is determined endogenously through consumption-saving decisions of households and investment allocation decisions of producers who may or may not have any anticipation of tax policy shocks to be introduced by the government. Sectoral investment flows, which depend on sector specific marginal productivity of capital, add to the capital stock in a sector. Capital assets are modelled as sector-specific, which enables us to examine the differential impacts of tax reform on investment by sector and capture the possibility of transitory shutdown in sectoral investment.

2. An earlier version of this chapter has been published in the Applied Economics 39: 1545-1563, 2007.

This model differs from the earlier dynamic model of the UK by Hutton and Kenc (1994) in terms of structure, solution technique, model dimensionality and flexibility of model application to various policy issues.

Dynamic applied general equilibrium models have been used to analyse growth and intergenerational equity issues over the past two decades. Most of the early dynamic general equilibrium models were one sector models (Auerbach and Kotlikoff (1987), Perroni (1995), Kotlikoff (1998)) emphasizing the impacts of tax changes on long-run growth, investment, savings, and capital formation. More disaggregated dynamic general equilibrium models have started appearing only recently (Rutherford (1995), Bhattarai (1997), DREAM (1997)). These dynamic models are suitable tools for analysing long-run dynamics in decentralised economies with many consumption and production sectors and many economic agents interacting with each other through the market. Developments in computational technology in the 1990s have made it possible to construct fully-fledged multisectoral dynamic models for highly disaggregated specifications rather than relying on recursive dynamics used in earlier applied general equilibrium literature as found in Ballard, Fullerton, Shoven, and Whalley (1984). Here we use GAMS/MPSGE software in order to write the code of the model (Meeraus et al. (1992), and Rutherford (1995)) and the PATH solver to solve it (Dirkse and Ferris (1996)).

Transitional effects of tax reform may differ significantly across sectors even when long-run impacts are similar. With the present model it is possible to look at sector-specific impacts of tax changes both in the short and in the long run. The explicit dynamic specification of demand and supply of commodities and factors of production allows the transition paths of output, employment and capital formation in various sectors to be assessed in response to a certain policy change that causes reallocation of resources through changes in factor and commodity prices. It is an advantage of a dynamic model over static general equilibrium models which rely mainly on a comparative static framework for policy analysis in line with Leontief (1949), Harberger (1959), and Robinson (1989).

The model is used to perform a number of equal-yield tax replacement experiments, whereby a certain tax is reduced and the remaining taxes increased in order to guarantee a constant period-by-period level of government spending. This implies no change in the public sector borrowing in the current model, which is close to public finance practice in the UK in recent years. For each experiment, we report transitory and long run effects on sectoral output, employment, and capital formation, as well as overall dynamic efficiency impacts. These experiments are carried out in different scenarios concerning the openness of capital markets and the private sector's ability to anticipate tax changes.

We use this model to evaluate dynamic efficiency effects and growth path impacts of reforms in each of seven different taxes included in the model. The dynamic efficiency effects associated with each experiment are measured in terms of the welfare gain or loss to the representative household over the entire model horizon, and in each scenario the sectoral growth of output, employment, investment, and capital in the transition to a new balanced-growth path is compared to the reference status-quo growth path. We perform these experiments both under the assumption that reform is unanticipated by private agents, and under the assumption that private agents are able to anticipate tax reform before it is implemented. We also explore the implications of international openness for capital markets.

When distortionary capital income tax rates ranging from 24 to 48 per cent in the base year are replaced by a uniform capital income tax rate of 25 per cent, the dynamic efficiency gains are about 0.77 per cent of the base year GDP. Some sectors, such as agriculture, where the capital input cost has reduced relatively in the counterfactual scenario due to lower capital income tax rates, experience an expansion. Other sectors, where the capital income tax has not reduced that much in the counterfactual scenario relative to the benchmark, such as engineering, experience slower growth. Reducing labour income tax from 24 per cent in the benchmark year to 15 per cent results in a welfare loss of up to 2.05 per cent of the base year GDP, mainly because more distortionary taxes have to be increased to make up for lost revenues. Replacing differential tax rates on production by a uniform 5 per cent rate across sectors results in a welfare gain of 1.4 per cent of the base year GDP. Similarly, replacing differentiated household consumption tax rates by a uniform 5 per cent rate generates a welfare gain of 0.6 per cent of GDP. We find similar welfare gains for a reform in government consumption taxes and tariffs. The private sector's ability to anticipate reform affects transitional effects as well as the dynamic efficiency effects of reform, raising them in some cases and lowering them in others. Simulation results appear to be robust with respect to changes in the degree of international openness of capital markets.

This paper is organised as follows. In Section II, we describe the structure of the multisectoral dynamic general equilibrium tax model, discussing intertemporal utility and saving consumption choices of households, investment criteria for the producers, production technologies, trade, public consumption and the competitive equilibrium conditions for the model. In Section III we discuss how an infinite horizon problem can be approximated by means of a finite period problem, and how the model is calibrated to a balanced-growth path. Section IV describes parameters, elasticities and tax rates used for calibration to a balanced-growth path. Section V presents simulation results obtained from the model, for seven different equal-yield tax reform experiments, and includes a brief discussion of the associated dynamic efficiency effects. In Section VI we briefly discuss some possible extensions to the current model. A conclusion of the current study is presented in Section VII. Section VIII gives an extensive list of references on dynamic general equilibrium modelling. Notes on the data set, figures for all scenarios, and a GAMS/MPSGE code for the current model are presented in appendices.

MODEL STRUCTURE

The dynamic general equilibrium tax model described in this paper is a large-scale, small open-economy model. It captures the circular flow of output, income and expenditure in the goods and factor markets accounting for price-based backward and forward linkages across various production sectors in the UK economy over the entire model horizon. In each period, households, endowed with labour and capital, supply factors of production to firms, which use these inputs in producing goods and services. As suppliers of factor inputs, households are remunerated according to the marginal contribution of factor services in production. Income earned from work and/or from supplying capital services is then either spent on consumption of domestic or foreign products, or saved for future consumption. Firms use those savings to purchase investment goods, which replenish and add to their capital stocks. Ex post total investment equals the ex-ante amount of savings in the economy.

Both households and firms make optimal choices given their intertemporal budget constraint. Net investment amounts are determined by the profit maximizing prospects across sectors, more investment occurring in sectors with higher marginal productivity of capital. The government and investors also make choices consistent with dynamic optimisation. The government collects revenue, and spends it either for public consumption or to make transfers to households. In every period, solutions to the model are given by prices that guarantee equality between the demand for and supply of goods.

Labour is mobile across sectors in this model. Labour services will flow to a sector with a higher marginal revenue product from one with a lower marginal revenue product until the net of tax remuneration is equal across sectors. In contrast, we assume that capital goods (such as buildings, machinery etc.) once installed in a sector cannot be redirected to other sectors.

Demand for and supply of goods and factors readjust until all excess demands and excess supplies are eliminated through changes in prices. The forces of perfectly competitive markets operate to determine these equilibrium prices. Furthermore, in equilibrium, no sector earns above-normal profits, market clearing prevails for all factors and products, and the value of imports for intermediate use and final demand equals the value of export earnings.

This model includes an explicit representation of current UK taxes, as they affect the economic incentives of producers and consumers. Changes in taxes thus affect economic behaviour and ultimately market prices via the model's equilibrium conditions. To quantify the economic effects of tax policy changes as well as their impact upon the growth path of the economy, we simulate the effects of equal-yield tax replacements, whereby a specific tax is exogenously reduced and other taxes are endogenously adjusted to maintain constant revenues in real terms. This approach enables us to isolate the effects of tax changes from the effects of changes in government spending.

There are several limitations to the current model. Simulation results are based on a deterministic calibration procedure. Also, although applied dynamic general equilibrium models contain a more detailed representation of a competitive economy in comparison to real business cycle models, they ignore the stochastic elements that may affect both the production and consumption sides of the economy. As a consequence, they assume that both consumers and producers have perfect knowledge of both current and future market conditions (*perfect foresight*). Solution methods for stochastic shocks in production and consumption in multisectoral models, however, have not yet been fully developed in the literature.

In addition, the model assumes that the UK economy is perfectly competitive: both consumers and producers take market prices as given. Including imperfect competition in the current model is possible but requires further work.

Finally, the model assumes that all resources are fully employed, and is a "real" model, where only relative prices matter and money is neutral. Inflation and unemployment issues are therefore outside the scope of our analysis. The model is appropriate for studying real impacts of tax policies but is not suitable for examining impacts on short-run economic fluctuations occurring through monetary channels or disequilibrium phenomena.

Intertemporal preferences and household demand

We assume forward-looking behaviour by consumers and producers, in the sense that they have perfect foresight with regard to their income, resources and prices of commodities in the economy. In the model, infinitely-lived households allocate lifetime income to maximise lifetime utility, which is defined as

$$\sum_{t=0}^{\infty} \beta^{t} \frac{U_t^{1-\sigma} - 1}{1-\sigma} \tag{1}$$

where β is the discount factor, which depends on the rate of time preference; U_t is composite commodity in the instantaneous utility function. This composite commodity is made of consumption and leisure. We choose a constant relative risk aversion (CRRA) CES functional form for this utility function in (1)[1] in which *1/s* measures the elasticity of substitution between the present and future composite commodity. The smaller is *s*, the more slowly marginal utility falls as the quantity of the composite commodity rises, so households are more willing to allow changes in the composite commodity over time. Thus a smaller *s* implies a higher elasticity of substitution between current and future consumption or a higher degree of consumption smoothing and substitution over time.

Instantaneous utility U is a function of composite consumption and leisure:

$$U(C_t, L_t) = \left(\alpha_c C_t^{\frac{\gamma-1}{\gamma}} + (1-\alpha_c) L_t^{\frac{\gamma-1}{\gamma}} \right)^{\frac{\gamma}{\gamma-1}} \tag{2}$$

where C_t is composite consumption in period t, and L_t is leisure in period t. Here g represents the elasticity of substitution between consumption and leisure; the larger the value of g, the more responsive are consumption and labour supply to changes in commodity prices and wage rates.

The representative household faces an intertemporal budget constraint whereby the present value of its consumption and leisure stream in all periods cannot exceed the present value of infinite lifetime full income (wealth constraint). Life-time income in this model includes the value the household's labour endowment and other income:

$$\sum_{t=0}^{\infty} R_t^{-1}(P_t(1+t^{vc})C_t + w_t(1-t_l)L_t) = W \tag{3}$$

where, $\mu(t) = \prod_{s=0}^{t-1} \frac{1}{1+r_s}$ is a discount factor; r_s represents the real interest rate on assets at time s; P_t is the price of composite consumption (which is based on goods' prices), t^{vc} is value added tax on consumption, t^l is labour income taxes, and C_t is composite consumption, which is composed of sectoral consumption goods, i.e. $P_t = \vartheta \prod_{i=1}^{n} p_{i,t}^{\alpha_i}$, and $C_t = \prod_{i=1}^{n} C_{i,t}^{\alpha_i}$ where α_i gives the share of spending on good i by the representative household, $C_{i,t}$ is a composite of domestic and foreign sector j products and $p_{i,t}$ its gross-of-tax price, and ϑ is a constant price index in the base year. W is the life time wealth of the household, defined as

$$W_{0,h} = \frac{J_{0,h}}{1+r_0^c} + \frac{J_{1,h}}{(1+r_0^c)(1+r_1^c)} + \ldots + \frac{J_{t,h}}{\Pi_s^t(1+r_s^c)} + \ldots = \sum_{t=0}^{\infty} \mu(t) J_{t,h} \tag{4}$$

where J_t is disposable household full income in period t, which includes the value of labour endowments and capital income plus transfers:

$$J_t = (1-t_l)w_t\overline{L}_t + (1-t_k)r_t K_t + TR_t \tag{4'}$$

where w_t is the wage rate, $\overline{L}_t$ is labour supplied, r_t is the rental rate of capital, K_t is the capital stock, TR_t is the transfer from the government to the household, t_l is the tax rate in labour and t_k is the tax rate in capital.

We combine equations (1) to (4) to form the Lagrangian for the consumer's inter-temporal allocation problem in (5).

$$\Im = \sum_{t=0}^{\infty} \left(\frac{1}{1+\rho}\right)^t \frac{\left(\left(\alpha_c C_t^{\frac{\gamma-1}{\gamma}} + (1-\alpha_c)L_t^{\frac{\gamma-1}{\gamma}}\right)^{\frac{\gamma}{\gamma-1}}\right)^{1-\sigma} - 1}{1-\sigma} + \tag{5}$$

$$\lambda[\sum_{t=0}^{\infty} R_t^{-1}(P_t(1+t^{vd})C_t + w_t(1-t_l)L_t) - W_t]$$

Here, γ is the intratemporal elasticity of substitution between consumption and leisure, λ is the shadow price of income in terms of the present value of utility, and β in (1) is replaced by $\frac{1}{1+\rho}$, where $\rho > 0$ is the rate of time preference, which indicates the degree to which the household prefers leisure and consumption in earlier rather than in later years. The larger the value of ρ, the more the household is willing to spend resources under its disposal earlier in life. This parameter is thus crucial in determining the amount of saving that the household wants to carry out in each period. Non-satiation in preferences implies that the intertemporal budget constraint will hold with equality at an optimum.

The instantaneous utility function used to model intratemporal substitution possibilities by consumers contains three nesting levels as represented in Figure 1, in Appendix A. At the top level, utility is a function of leisure and composite consumption, as in (1). How a single composite consumption good is made from sixteen sub-composite goods is shown in the second level of the nest. Finally each sub-composite good again represents a combination of domestic and imported goods.

Like consumption, investment and government consumption demand also comprise domestic and imported sources, but their composition is depends on relative price of commodities .

Saving, investment, and labour supply

Economy wide savings, S_t, is the total of household savings (we assume that the government pursues a balanced budget policy over the model horizon). Household savings are the part of income that is not consumed:

$$S_t = J_t - P_t(1+t^{vc})C_t \tag{6}$$

For a given rate of time preference and intertemporal rate of substitution (and if some other conditions are satisfied), individuals will save more when the rate of interest is higher than when it is lower. The lower the intertemporal elasticity of substitution and the smaller the time preference parameter, the larger are the savings in the economy. A higher rate of interest on savings raises the cost of current consumption in terms of future consumption. At the same time, it raises lifetime wealth. The first effect tends to induce more savings, while the second tends to raise consumption. If the former effect dominates the latter, which is the case given our model parameterisation, savings will rise.

Note that, in reality, it is possible that the rate of return on saving received by households may be less than the cost of capital to the investors if financial intermediaries charge interest on the mobilisation of resources, the transaction cost of intermediation thus taking the form of a wedge between the prices faced by savers and investors. Here, we simply assume that the gross-of-intermediation cost of capital is equal to the return on savings.

Economy wide balance requires that income be equal to total expenditure. Government revenue is constrained to be equal to its expenditure. In the closed-capital market version of the model, we also assume trade balance (equality between the value of imports and the value of exports) in each period; whereas when we allow for international capital flows, trade balance must be satisfied in present value terms over the model horizon (see the next section).

Investors employ savings to purchase investment goods. The market rental rate of capital is determined by the equality of the demand for and the supply of capital. Total investment demand equals the use of investment goods from domestic and imported sources:

$$I_t = \sum_i PD_{i,t} ID_{i,t} + \sum_i PM_{i,t} IM_{i,t} \tag{7}$$

where $ID_{i,t}$ is domestic supply of investment goods, and $IM_{i,t}$ is imported investment goods. Ideally one would need to include a capital composition matrix to specify how a unit of investment good in a particular sector is made from the capital inputs from various sectors. In the absence of information on the sectoral composition of investment by sector of origin, we simply specify a composite investment good using information on total investment demand from the input-output table. This composite good is then allocated to sector-specific investment so as to equalize the marginal productivity of capital across sectors.Investment opportunities are arbitraged when the net rate of return from each investment activity does not exceed the rate of interest, and is equal to it when investment is undertaken at a positive level in that sector, i.e.

$$R_{i,t} - \delta_i \le r_t$$

$$I_{i,t} \ge 0$$

$$I_{i,t}(R_{i,t} - \delta_i - r_t) = 0 \tag{8}$$

where $R_{i,t}$ is the gross-of-depreciation rate of return in sector *i* at time *t*, δ_i is the sector-specific depreciation rate, and r_t is the rate of interest at *t*. This arbitraging condition implies that sectors with higher gross return $R_{i,t}$ and lower depreciation rate generate more gross investment demand. On a balanced-growth path, investment will grow at the same rate in all sectors, and the return to capital will be equalized everywhere. However, during the transition to a balanced-growth path, it is possible for the net return in a sector to fall below the return elsewhere in the economy, and, as a result, for investment to "shut down" in that sector.

Sectoral assets are subject to economic depreciation. Thus, in every period, gross sectoral investment replenishes depleted capital, and increases the capital stock (*net* investment). Capital accumulation in sector *i* in period *t+1* then is given by the capital stock of period *t* net of depreciation and investment:

$$K_{i,t+1} = K_{i,t}(1-\delta_i) + I_{i,t} \tag{9}$$

Growth in sectoral output depends both upon the growth of employment and the growth of the capital stock in that sector. On a balanced-growth path, where all prices are constant and all real economic variables grow at a constant rate, capital stocks must grow at a fast enough rate to sustain growth. This condition can be expressed as

$$I_{i,T} = K_{i,T}(g+\delta_i) \tag{10}$$

where the subscript *T* denotes the terminal period of the model.

Note that assuming a closed capital market may not be realistic for the UK economy. The representation of capital mobility in small open-economy models is not yet quite satisfactorily developed in the applied general equilibrium literature. Goulder, Shoven and Whalley (1983) model capital markets for the US by assuming that the capital endowment of the rest of the world is five times the US endowment, the implicit assumption being that the US economy constitutes about a fifth of the world economy. If we follow the same route for the UK, we may roughly assume that the rest of the world is endowed with twenty-five times more capital than UK households (considering UK GDP to be equal to 4 percent of world GDP). For simplicity, in the open capital markets version of the dynamic model we simply assume the UK to be a price taker in capital markets, and allow capital inflows and outflows to take place so as to ensure that the UK rate of interest remains constant and equal to the world rate of return. A more realistic analysis of capital asset flows would require a model structure where the UK economy is explicitly modelled as part of the global economy.[1]

Labour supply, LS_t, for each household is given by the difference between the household labour endowment, and the demand for leisure, L_t.

$$LS_t = \overline{L}_t - L_t \tag{14}$$

In equilibrium, the wage rate must be such that the labour supplied by the household equals the total demand for labour derived from the profit maximising behaviour of firms (as set out in the following section).

Technology and trade

The structure of production in the model is shown in Figure A2 in appendix A. At the bottom of the figure one type of composite capital stock[2] combines with labour to form value added for the sixteen sectors in the model. Then this value added aggregate combines with domestic and imported intermediate inputs from sixteen sectors to produce gross output for each sector. Gross output is either sold in domestic markets or exported to the rest of the world.

Following a well-established convention in open-economy applied general equilibrium models, we adopt an "Armington" specification whereby products are differentiated according to the location of production. Thus domestic and imported goods, even in the same sector, are qualitatively different and are not perfect substitutes, and intra-industry trade can occur. The Armington aggregation function, with given shares and substitution elasticity, describes how the domestic and imported goods are combined:

$$A_{i,t} = \Phi\left(\delta_i^d D_{i,t}^{\frac{\sigma_m - 1}{\sigma_m}} + \delta_i^m M_{i,t}^{\frac{\sigma_m - 1}{\sigma_m}}\right)^{\frac{\sigma_m}{\sigma_m - 1}} \quad (15)$$

where $A_{i,t}$ is the Armington CES aggregate of domestic supplies $D_{i,t}$ and import supplies $M_{i,t}$ for each sector, δ_i^d is the share of domestically produced goods, δ_i^m is the share of good *i* imports, σ_m is the elasticity of substitution in the aggregate supply function, and Φ is the shift parameter of the aggregate supply function.

The aggregate value of supply in the economy must be equal to the sum of the values of domestic supplies and imports:

$$PA_{i,t} A_{i,t} = PD_{i,t} D_{i,t} + PM_{i,t} M_{i,t} \quad (16)$$

where $D_{i,t}$ and $M_{i,t}$ are domestic and import supplies respectively, $PD_{i,t}$ is gross price of domestic supplies, $PM_{i,t}$ is price of imported goods gross of tariffs, and $PA_{i,t}$ is the gross price of composite commodity *i*.

Overall market clearing in the product market implies

$$A_{i,t} = CC_{i,t} + G_{i,t} + I_{i,t} + \sum_j DI_{i,j,t} + \sum_j MI_{i,j,t} \quad (17)$$

where $CC_{i,t}$ is composite consumption, $G_{i,t}$ and $I_{i,t}$ represent composite consumption by the government and investment respectively (discussed below), $DI_{i,j}$ is the demand for domestic intermediate input and $MI_{i,j}$ is demand for imported intermediate inputs,.

Domestic supply, $D_{i,t}$, in equations (15,16), is the part of gross output sold in the domestic market. The rest of domestic output is exported. The split between domestic sales and exports is given by a constant elasticity transformation function:

$$GY_{i,t} = \Theta\left((1-\delta_i^e)D_{i,t}^{\frac{\sigma_y-1}{\sigma_y}} + \delta_i^e E_{i,t}^{\frac{\sigma_y-1}{\sigma_y}}\right)^{\frac{\sigma_y}{\sigma_y-1}} \tag{18}$$

where $GY_{i,t}$ is output (gross of intermediate inputs), $E_{i,t}$ is exports, $D_{i,t}$ is domestic supplies, σ_y is the elasticity of transformation in total supply, δ_i^e is the share of exports, and Q is the shift or scale parameter in the transformation function. The value of gross supplies in the economy must be equal to the sum of the gross values of domestic supplies and exports:

$$P_{i,t}GY_{i,t} = PD_{i,t}D_{i,t} + PE_{i,t}E_{i,t} \tag{19}$$

where $D_{i,t}$ and $E_{i,t}$ are domestic and export supplies respectively, $PD_{i,t}$ is gross prices of domestic supplies, $PE_{i,t}$ is price of exported goods gross of export taxes, and $P_{i,t}$ is the price of domestic supplies of commodity i.

The import and export prices in equations (16) and (19) will generally differ from domestic prices because of tariffs and export taxes applied considering product differentiation between domestic and foreign products. The gross-of-export-tax prices of exportable goods and the gross-of-tariff prices of importable commodities tend to get closer to world prices as the elasticity of transformation between domestic sales and exports in production and the elasticity of substitution between domestically produced goods and imports in consumption approach infinity.

On the production front, producers use labour and capital in each of N sectors to produce value added. The amount of each type of these inputs employed by a producer in a particular sector is based upon the sector specific production technology and input prices. We use a CES function to express this relationship:

$$Y_{i,t} = \Omega_i\left((1-\delta_i)(K_{i,t})^{\gamma_i} + \delta_i(LS_{i,t})^{\gamma_i}\right)^{\frac{1}{\gamma_i}} \tag{20}$$

where $Y_{i,t}$ is the gross value added of sector i, Ω_i is a shift or scale parameter in the production function, $K_{i,t}$ and $LS_{i,t}$ are the amounts of capital and labour used in sector i, δ_i is the share parameter of labour in production, and γ_i is the CES substitution elasticity parameter. This is a constant returns to scale production function. Euler's product exhaustion theorem implies that total output (value added) equals payments to labour and capital and each factor receives remuneration at the rate of its marginal productivity:

$$PY_{i,t}Y_{i,t} = w_t LS_{i,t} + r_t K_{i,t} \tag{21}$$

where w_t is the gross-of-tax wage rate and r_t is the gross rental rate of capital.

The relationship between the intermediate inputs and gross output is expressed by input-output coefficients, which form a fixed physical non-price based constraint in the production system. The general form of production function is

$$GY_{i,t} = \min\left(Y_{i,t}, \left(\frac{DI_{i,j,t}}{a^d_{i,j}}\right)_{i=j}, \left(\frac{MI_{i,j,t}}{a^m_{i,j}}\right)_{i=j} \right) \tag{22}$$

where $a^d_{i,j}$ are input-output coefficients for domestic supply of intermediate goods; $a^m_{i,j}$ are input-output coefficients for imported supply of intermediate goods, $DI_{i,j}$ is the supply of domestic intermediate input and $MI_{i,j}$ is the supply of imported intermediate inputs. The presence of input-output linkages in the model enables us to assess various kinds of backward and forward impacts of policy changes. For instance a tax on agricultural output has a direct effect on demands for agricultural goods, and a backward impact that spreads to many other sectors which provide inputs to that sector. Similarly, through forward linkages, the tax affects the cost of agricultural inputs to other sectors.

The objective of a firm in the *j*th sector of the economy is to maximise the present value of profits subject to production technology constraints. Sectoral profits are given by the differences between the revenue from sales and the cost of supply. The unit revenue function is a constant elasticity transformation (CET) composite of the unit price of domestic sales and the unit price of exports. The unit costs are divided between value added, i.e. payments to labour and capital, and domestic and imported intermediate inputs:

$$\Pi^y_{j,t} = [((1-\delta^e_i)PD_{i,t}^{\frac{\sigma_y-1}{\sigma_y}} + \delta^e_i PE_{i,t}^{\frac{\sigma_y-1}{\sigma_y}})]^{\frac{1}{\sigma_y-1}} \tag{23}$$

$$-\theta^v_j PY^v_{j,t} - \theta^d_j \sum_i a^d_{i,j} P_{i,t} - \theta^m_j \sum_i a^m_{i,j} PM_{j,t}$$

where:

$\Pi^y_{j,t}$ is the unit profit of activity in sector *j*

$PE_{j,t}$ is the export price of good *j*

$PD_{j,t}$ is the domestic price of good *j*

$PY^v_{j,t}$ is the price of value added per unit of output in activity *j*

s_y is a transformation elasticity parameter

$P_{i,t}$ is the price of final goods used as intermediate goods

δ_j^e is the share parameter for exports in total production

θ_j^v is the share of costs paid to labour and capital

θ_j^d is the cost share of domestic intermediate inputs

θ_j^m is the cost share of imported intermediate inputs

$a_{i,j}^d$ are input-output coefficients for domestic supply of intermediate goods

$a_{i,j}^m$ are input-output coefficients for imported supply of intermediate goods

In equilibrium, with free entry and perfect competition, profits will be zero in each period. The zero-profit condition for sector j in period t can be written in dual form in terms of composite prices of commodities and inputs (see appendix for details):

$$\Pi_{j,t}^y \leq 0 \tag{24}$$

With respect to international trade, zero trade balance is a property of any general equilibrium model. In the version with no international capital flows, we have, therefore, assumed that the value of exports (gross of UK taxes and subsidies) equals the value of imports (net of UK taxes and subsidies) in equilibrium in each period:

$$\sum_i PE_{i,t} E_{i,t} = \sum_i PM_{i,t} M_{i,t} \tag{25}$$

No inter-temporal borrowing occurs in this case. In the version with international capital flows, we have that this condition must be satisfied in present value terms, *i.e.*

$$\sum_t (1+r^W)^{-t} \sum_i PE_{i,t} E_{i,t} = \sum_t (1+r^W)^{-t} \sum_i PM_{i,t} M_{i,t} \tag{26}$$

where r^W is the world rate of interest.

Public consumption

The government collects revenue from various taxes and spends that revenue to purchase goods and services for public consumption and to make transfers to households.

The value of government consumption is given by

$$G = \sum_i PA_i GD_i + \sum_i PA_i GM_i \tag{27}$$

where GD_i is government consumption of domestic goods, and GM_i is government consumption of imported goods. Like households, the government chooses between domestic and imported goods for its consumption on the basis of their relative prices.

Tax revenue is collected through taxes on capital and labour income and value added taxes on final demand, production taxes on intermediate inputs, and tariffs on imports:

$$REV_t = \sum_i t_i^k r_t K_{i,t} + \sum_i t_i^{vc} P_{i,t} CC_{i,t} + \sum_i t_i^{vg} P_{i,t} G_{i,t} \tag{28}$$

$$+ \sum_i t_i^{vk} P_{i,t} I_{i,t} + \sum_i t_l w LS_t + \sum_i t_i^m PM_{i,t} M_{i,t} + \sum_i t_i^p P_{i,t} GY_{i,t}$$

where REV_t is total government revenue and t_i^k is a composite tax rate on capital income from sector *i*. These rates are derived from the P-Tax model of capital income tax rates, originally written by King and Robson (1988) using methodology devised by King and Fullerton (1984); and used in the Inland Revenue for a number of years. t_l^{vc} is the *ad valorem* tax rate on final consumption by households, t_i^{vk} is that on public consumption and t_i^{vk} is the ad valorem tax rate on investment. t_l is the tax rate on labour income of the household, t_i^p is the tax on production, and t_i^m is the tariff on imports. All of these taxes, particularly when they are levied at different rates on different sectors and households, have distortionary impacts on the allocation of resources in the economy.

Tax revenues are either used to finance public consumption, or to make transfers to households in lump sum form:

$$REV_t = G_t + TR_t \tag{29}$$

DEFINITION OF A DYNAMIC COMPETITIVE EQUILIBRIUM

A dynamic competitive equilibrium is a combination of sequences of prices of gross output $P_{i,t}$, price of domestic supplies, $PD_{i,t}$; import prices, $PM_{i,t}$; export prices, $PE_{i,t}$; prices of value added, $PY_{i,t}$; prices of capital goods, $P_{j,t}^k$; prices of terminal capital, $PTK_{j,t}$; wage rates of labour, w_t; prices of government services, PG_t; values of transfers to households, PR_t; prices of composite of consumption and leisure, PU_t; rental rate of capital for each sector, r_1^k : R+ →R, and sequences of gross output, $GY_{i,t}$; total supply of domestic intermediate inputs, $DI_{i,j,t}$ and imported intermediate inputs, $MI_{i,j,t}$; sectoral capital stock, $K_{i,t}$; labour demands, $LS_{i,t}$; value added, $Y_{i,t}$; sectoral investment, $I_{i,t}$; exports, $E_{i,t}$; imports, $M_{i,t}$

government revenue, REV_t ; services, G_t ; consumption of households, CC_t ; labour supply, $LS_{i,t}$ and leisure demand, L_t ; and level of household utility from consumption, U_t , such that given these prices and quantities, the following conditions are satisfied:

1. households maximise intertemporal utility subject to their wealth constraint;
2. investors maximise intertemporal profits subject to arbitrage conditions in capital markets;
3. producers minimise costs subject to technology constraints;
4. unit profits are zero in all production sectors;
5. markets for goods and services clear;
6. the government account constraint is satisfied;
7. the balance of payments condition is fulfilled
8. the economy grows at a constant rate beyond a certain terminal period T.

In such an equilibrium, consumers have perfect foresight, capital accumulation is consistent with household's and producers' optimisation and income and expenditures balance over the life period. An agent is doing the best he or she can in light of actions taken by others, and actions taken together are feasible given technologies and resources.

NOTES

1. In a separate project document, we report on a static global economy model (from a UK perspective), based on the GTAP4 data set, in which perfectly competitive international capital markets are modelled explicitly.
2. Disaggregation of assets into five different capital assets ¾ long-lived plant and machinery, short lived plant and machinery, vehicles, buildings and dwellings, as in our static model, is left for a future version of the model.

7

CALIBRATION AND APPLICATION OF DYNAMIC MULTISECTORAL GENERAL-EQUILIBRIUM TAX MODEL OF THE UK ECONOMY

CALIBRATION TO A BALANCED-GROWTH PATH AND MODEL SOLUTION

Implementation of a dynamic general equilibrium model requires three steps: calibration of model parameters, replication of the benchmark economy, and computation of transitional dynamics corresponding to policy shocks in the model economy.

A numerical model can only be solved for a finite number of periods. Some adjustment is therefore necessary to approximate an infinite horizon by a finite horizon. The most common way of approximating an infinite horizon equilibrium is to use a terminal balanced-growth condition (see Rutherford et al. (1997) for a discussion of other approximation methods). The idea is to write utility as

$$U = \sum_{t=1}^{T} \beta^t U(C_t) + \sum_{t=T+1}^{\infty} \beta^t U(C_t) \tag{30}$$

The second term in this utility function degenerates into a constant term. The terminal condition in investment $I_T = K_T(g + \delta)$ (dropping sectoral subscripts) is used to leave the economy on its balanced path after the terminal condition.

To calibrate the model, we take 1995 UK data and assume that in 1995 the UK economy was on a balanced growth-path, with all sectors growing at the same rate, g. The benchmark rate of return, r, is taken to be exogenously given and equal to five per cent. We then select model parameters such that, starting from current levels of capital stock and current prices, the model yields a dynamic solution path which is consistent with balanced growth. For this purpose, we exploit the relationship between the current and future prices of capital and investment goods.

Specifically (abstracting from the presence of distortionary taxes), one unit of investment in period t must produce one unit of capital stock in period $t+1$ from one unit of output of the investment goods in period t. One unit of capital at the beginning of period t earns a rate of return today, r_t^k and delivers $1\text{-}d$ units of capital for the start of the $t+1$ period. We therefore must have:

$$P_1^k = r_1^k + (1-\delta)(1-r)P_1^k \tag{32}$$

where P_t^K is the price of capital good at the end of period t. The gross return covers depreciation and interest earning of each unit of investment

$$r_t^k = (r+\delta)P_t^k \tag{33}$$

where r is the real rate of interest. Equations (32) and (33) together imply

$$\frac{P_{t+1}^k}{P_t^k} = \frac{1}{1+r} \tag{34}$$

which means the price of the capital good next period relative to its current price is equal to the market discount factor in the model.

We compute values for sectoral capital stocks from sectoral capital earnings in the base year. If capital income in sector i in the base year is $\overline{V}_i$, we can write $\overline{V}_i = r_t^k K_i$. Since the return to capital must be sufficient to cover interest and depreciation, we can also write $\overline{V}_i = (r+\delta_i)K_i$, or

$$K_i = \frac{\overline{V}_i}{(r+\delta_i)} \tag{35}$$

On a balanced growth path, where all sectors grow at a rate g, we have $I_i = (g+\delta_i)K_i$, and thus

$$I_i = \frac{(g+\delta_i)}{(r+\delta_i)}\overline{V}_i \tag{36}$$

In the benchmark equilibrium, all reference quantities grow at the rate of labour force growth, g, and reference prices are discounted on the basis of the benchmark rate of return.

To solve the model, we allow for a time horizon sufficient for a balanced-growth path to be attained. In our simulations we use a sixty-five year horizon. In practice, the model's variables typically converge to an approximate balanced-growth path after about twenty to thirty years. We formulate and solve the model using the GAMS/MPSGE software.

PARAMETERS, ELASTICITIES AND TAX RATES

Internal consistency of a general equilibrium model is assured when a model is able to reproduce the benchmark data set, with calibrated model parameters, as its solution. Though equilibria could be computed for a wide range of parameter sets and elasticities, only those parameter sets and elasticities which can generate base year quantities and prices as model solutions are relevant. The basic steps for implementation of a general equilibrium model are as shown in Figure 1.

Figure 1
Steps for Implementing a General Equilibrium Model

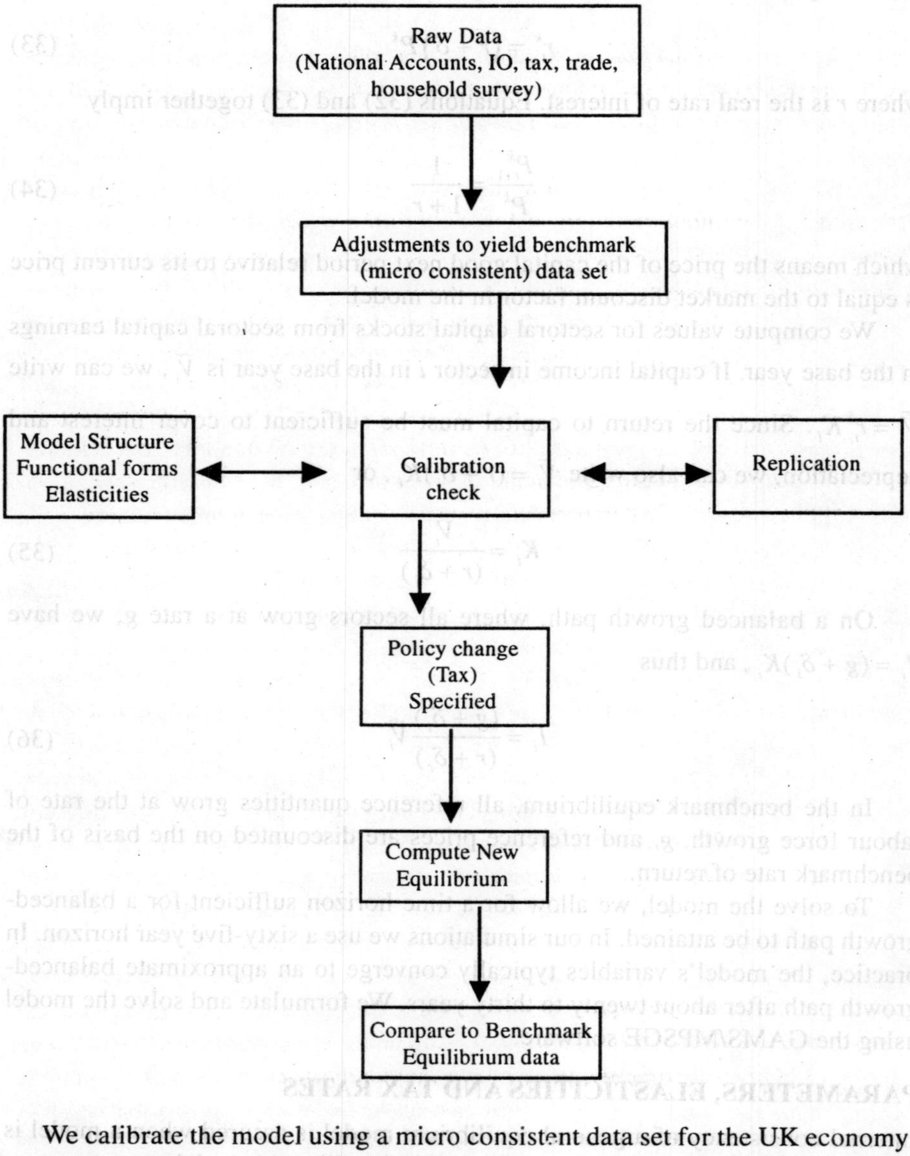

We calibrate the model using a micro consistent data set for the UK economy for the year 1995, assuming that the UK economy was on a balanced-growth path in that year. Once the model is calibrated in this way, the baseline growth path shows how the economy would move forward, *ceteris paribus*, if the current economic policies were to continue.

A careful selection of model parameters is crucial to the performance of general equilibrium models, and any model solutions must be interpreted within the context of the parameters used. Crucial parameters which determine the behaviour of the current model are the intertemporal rate of substitution in households' utility functions, elasticity of substitution between composite consumption and leisure, the elasticity of substitution between domestic and imported commodities, the elasticity of substitution between the capital and labour inputs in production, the elasticity of transformation between domestic and foreign trade, popularly known as the Armington elasticity, growth rates of the labour force, the benchmark rate of interest, and rates of depreciation by sector.

Table 1 and Table 2 below list the values assumed for these parameters in the current model. We briefly discuss the rationale for selecting these values below.

Intertemporal elasticity of substitution: The intertemporal elasticity of substitution, *1/s*, measures the responsiveness of the composition of a household's current and future demand for the composite consumption good (composite of consumption and leisure) to relative changes in the rate of interest. This parameter is a crucial determinant of households' savings. No consensus exists in the literature regarding a reasonable value of such an elasticity. Ogaki and Reinhart (1998a,1998b) estimate such elasticity to be between zero and 0.1 in case of durable goods. Hall (1988) finds them very small, even negative. Hansen and Singleton (1996) note considerably less precision in the measure of the elasticity of intertemporal substitution. Hutton and Kenc (1994) used 0.4 for a consumption tax exercise for the UK economy; Auerbach and Kotlikoff (1987) assume it to be about 0.25; Kydland and Prescott (1992) assume it to be 1. We use a value of 0.5 in the current model.

Intratemporal elasticity of substitution between consumption and leisure: This determines how consumers' labour supply responds to changes in real wages. Indirect evidence on this elasticity is derived from various estimates of labour supply elasticities that are available in the literature (Killingsworth (1983)). Here we adopt a value of 0.5 for this substitution elasticity. Further discussion on how to derive numerical values of substitution elasticities from labour supply elasticities is provided in one of our earlier studies on tax incidence analysis (Bhattarai and Whalley (1999)).

Intratemporal elasticity of substitution between consumption goods: This captures the degree of substitutability among goods and services in private final consumption. A higher value implies more variation in consumption choices when the relative prices of goods and services change. Consistently with Piggott and Whalley (1985), we specify a value of 0.5 for this parameter.

Armington elasticities: The Armington transformation elasticity determines how the composition of production between goods produced for the domestic markets and goods produced for export responds to relative price changes in domestic and export prices, while the Armington substitution elasticity determines how relative price changes in domestic and import prices affect the composition of domestic demand between domestically produced goods and imports. Higher values of substitution and transformation elasticities mean a greater impact of foreign prices in domestic markets. Various estimates exist in the literature about the value of these elasticities, Reinert and Roland-Holst (1992) report estimates of substitution elasticities for 163 US manufacturing industries and find these elasticities to remain between 0.14 and 3.49. Piggott and Whalley (1985) suggest using import and export price elasticities to calibrate substitution and transformation elasticities used in these trade functions. They take central tendency values of these elasticities to be around 1.25. We use 2.0 for both substitution and transformation elasticities to account for increased integration of the UK in the global economy.

Elasticity of substitution between capital and labour in production: Early estimates of the elasticity of substitution between capital and labour are found in Arrow, Chenery, Minhas, and Solow (1961). They estimated constant elasticities of substitution for US manufacturing industries using a pooled cross country data set of observations on output per man and wage rates for a number of countries. Again, we rely on Piggott and Whalley (1985) central tendency values of elasticities between capital and labour for our current model which are given in the first column of Table 2.

Growth rate and benchmark interest rate: We take two per cent to be the initial balanced growth rate and five per cent to be the benchmark rate of interest in the model. These rates seem to be realistic based on the experience of the UK economy. (The economic growth rate in the UK has remained around two per cent on average in the last decade and the real interest rate has remained around five per cent.)

Depreciation rates: We derive sector specific aggregate depreciation rates using asset specific rates (five types) and weighting them by value of asset types. This asset type breakdown was sector specific and based on ONS figures adjusted by the Inland Revenue.The Inland Revenue figures did not provide a depreciation figure for the housing sector, entirely dwelling in this sectoral breakdown; for this reason we set the depreciation rate in the housing sector equal to 2 per cent. Thus depreciation rates for this model vary from two per cent in the housing sector to seventeen per cent in the extraction sector as shown in Table 2.

Tax rates: For the current version of the model we use tax rate data obtained from the Inland Revenue in December 1998 as presented in Table 2. All direct and indirect taxes vary across sectors (see Bhattarai (1999) for details). Though these data need updating in line with more recent data, which presents a more satisfactory diaggregation of the indirect taxes (see also Siddorn (1999)), most tax rates presented in Table 2 still reflect the structure of the tax system existing in the UK in 1995. The capital income tax rates by sectors are derived using asset specific weights in the P-Tax rates by assets and sectors.

Flow data: A brief discussion of the sectoral data used for the calibration of the multisectoral dynamic UK model is presented in the input-output table of the

UK for 1995 is given in Table A2 in Appendix A. This table contains information on input-output transactions, value added, final demand and taxes for the year 1995.

Table 1
Basic Parameters of the UK Model

Steady state growth rate for sectors (g)	0.02
Net interest rate in non-distorted economy (r)	0.05
Reference quantity index of output, capital and labour for each sector,	
Reference price index output, capital and labour *(of what, capital?)* for each sector,	
Elasticity of transformation between UK's domestic supplies and exports to the Rest of the World (ROW),	1.5
Elasticity of substitution between UK's domestic products and imports from Rest of the World (ROW), σ_y	1.5
Intertemporal elasticity of substitution,	0.5
Intra temporal elasticity of substitution between leisure and composite goods,	0.5
Elasticity of substitution in consumption goods across sectors, s_c	0.5

Table 2
Depreciation, Capital Income and Indirect Tax Rates (%)

Industry	*Electicity of subsititu-tion between capital (γ_i)*	*Deprecia-tion rate (annual %)*	*Capital income tax rate*	*Indirect tax on private consump-tion*	*Indirect tax on public consump-tion*	*Indirect tax on invest-ment*	*Produc-tion tax rates*	*Tariff rates*
Agric	1.2	8.3	41.4	1.6	7.7		-10.9	2.5
Extra	1.7	16.6	26.2					2.5
Minin	1.5	10.4	31.0	12.5			-0.6	2.5
Chemi	1.7	5.6	24.0	15.4	8.3		14.3	2.5
Metal	1.6	5.4	25.3			3.8	0.0	2.5
Engin	1.5	6.0	27.6		31.1	4.9	0.0	2.5
Food	1.0	5.4	28.0	17.0	3.5		12.2	2.5
Othma	0.9	6.4	26.2	26.3	19.	6.1	0.0	2.5
Power	1.5	4.1	28.9	5.7	22.1		3.4	2.5
Constr	1.0	9.4	30.3	13.3	27.8	2.5	-0.1	
Distr	1.6	5.9	33.9	4.4			5.4	
Trans	1.6	7.5	29.7	8.3	15.3	0.1	-2.2	2.5
Finan	1.6	6.9	41.9	1.0	11.0	0.3	2.0	2.5
PubAD	1.6	4.	45.8					2.5
EducA	1.6	3.8	48.1	7.5	0.6		1.9	2.5
House	1.0	2.0					-0.3	2.5

Source and notes: We use Piggott and Whalley (1985) for the elasticity of substitution between labour and capital,; aggregate depreciation rate per sector is derived from the P-tax sector-asset specific discount rates; tax and tariff rates rely on Bhattarai (1999) and Siddorn (1998).

TAX POLICY EXPERIMENTS: EQUAL-YIELD TAX REPLACEMENTS

Tax reforms aim for an efficient, fair and simple tax system. A key factor for achieving these goals is the choice of an appropriate tax base, a central issue in the tax reform literature. In what follows, we use the dynamic tax model described in the previous sections to assess the dynamic efficiency effects and the long- and short-run sectoral impacts of replacing various existing UK taxes (in place in 1995). We simulate the effects of equal-yield tax changes, mainly to explore four different questions:

1. What are the dynamic efficiency effects of tax reform over the model horizon?
2. How do unanticipated tax changes affect sectoral output, employment and capital formation in the economy?
3. How do anticipated tax changes affect sectoral output, employment and capital formation?
4. Does the international openness of capital markets alter the dynamic effects of tax changes?

Although the specification of economic relationships in each period is very similar to that of the static version of the model, simulation results can be expected to differ between the two models, mainly for the following three reasons: (i) long-run capital stocks are endogenous in the dynamic model, resulting in an elastic long-run capital supply response; as a result, any tax-induced changes in the net-of-tax return to capital, which would be fully borne by capital in the static model, are dampened in the dynamic model by supply responses; (ii) sectoral effects during the transition to a new balanced-growth path are affected by the sector-specificity of capital assets; although in the long run the return to investment must be equalised across sectors, which is equivalent to a static specification with sectorally mobile capital, in the short run the return to assets may differ across sectors, leading to the shutdown of investment in some sectors; (iii) in the open capital market case, there is a further possibility of inflows and outflows of capital stocks into and from the economy which result in the rate of return being pegged to the world rate of return.

Table 3
Counterfactual tax rates in the dynamic UK model

Tax experiment	*Capital income tax rate*	*Indirect tax on private consumption*	*Indirect tax on public consumption*	*Indirect tax on investment*	*Production tax rates*	*Tariff rates*	*Household income tax rate*
Counterfactual tax rates	25.0	10.0	5.0	5.0	5.0	1.0	15.0

We solve the model separately for seven different types of tax reform experiments, and for three different scenarios. In each experiment, a given tax rate is lowered relative to its benchmarked level as described in Table 3 below. In addition to the counterfactual taxes being lower, in most cases, the uniform counterfactual replaces a non-uniform tax across the 16 sectors (see Table 2).

Removing this distortion can also be expected to improve welfare, regardless of welfare effects from a change in the overall level of one of these taxes.

As discussed previously, in each case, the remaining taxes are proportionally adjusted so as to guarantee a constant level of government spending in each period, under a period-by-period government budget constraint (*i.e.*, no new government debt is allowed).

For each of these seven experiments we explore three scenarios:

1. Unanticipated tax change with no international capital flows;
2. A five-year anticipated tax change with no international capital flows;
3. Unanticipated tax change with international capital flows.

In the "anticipated" scenario, we assume that private agents can foresee the tax change occurring five years before it is implemented, and can therefore immediately adjust their choices in anticipation of the change. All reforms are assumed to take place in the year 2000; in the "anticipated" scenario, reforms take place in 2000 but are announced in 1995.

A selection of results from the model-based numerical simulations for the various experiments and scenarios is presented in Figures 1A-21B in Appendix B. These show impacts on sectoral investment, capital stocks, output and employment relative to the baseline "business as usual" reference path case. Note that in the baseline all real variables are growing at a rate of two per cent per year; hence all figures must be interpreted as being relative to a growing reference growth path (*i.e.*, they are "de-trended" figures). In each figure, left panels and right panels depict effects for different subsets of sectors in the economy.

Results for the closed-economy no-announcement case are presented in Figures 1A to 7B in Appendix B. Results for the closed-economy five-year announcement case are presented in Figures 8A to 14B. Results from a closed economy case with no announcement effects are given in Figures 15A to 21B.

Following standard practice in applied general equilibrium modelling exercises, in order to assess the overall efficiency effects of tax reform, we measure how much a typical consumer has gained or lost because of changes in policy in terms of the implied change in his or her real purchasing power, i.e., by computing the monetary compensation that is required to bring him/her back to the original level of welfare experienced before the reform took place. The equivalent variation (*EV*) is a measure of welfare change between benchmark and counterfactual scenarios which uses benchmark (old) prices to define real purchasing power. The compensating variation (*CV*), on the other hand, measures welfare changes in terms of new prices.

Following this tradition we use model solutions to compute equivalent variations in consumer welfare from given changes in policy regimes. The *EV* for this model can be computed as the change in the present value of lifetime utility expressed as a per centage of base year UK GDP:

$$UW = 100\ \ (LU - 1)\frac{C_0}{GDP_0} \tag{41}$$

Here UW is a measure of the present value of welfare to the representative household for the period of the model horizon, LU is the composite lifetime utility, C_0 is the composite of consumption and leisure in the base year, and GDP_0 is the base year GDP (the adjustment factor $\frac{C_0}{GDP_0}$ corrects for the fact that the value of household consumption in the model includes the value of leisure).

Table 4
Efficiency effects of tax reform in the dynamic UK model
Change in life time utility as a per centage of base GDP (%)

	Closed capital market with no announcement	*Closed capital market with announcement*	*Open capital market with no announcement*
Capital income tax	0.699	0.633	0.768
Labour income tax	-2.054	-2.054	-2.195
Production tax	1.421	1.284	1.442
Investment tax	-0.085	-0.048	-0.106
Household consumption tax	0.112	0.557	0.693
Government consumption tax	0.297	0.256	0.317
Tariffs	0.070	0.053	0.081

The dynamic welfare effects associated with the various experiments are shown in Table 4. Equal-yield tax reform has a positive impact in most tax reform experiments except in labour income tax and investment tax reform. Note that, in the current model, the reduction in revenue due to a reduction in one tax is compensated for by an equi-proportional increase in other taxes. Hence, a positive figure indicates that the tax to be replaced is relatively more distortionary than the rest of the tax system as a whole. Although the picture is not that clear since some of the counterfactual taxes replace a non-uniform tax regime over the sixteen sectors, and this reduction in distortions can be expected to increase welfare regardless.

The model solutions show that dynamic welfare effects are generally larger when there are international capital flows. The presence of announcement effects, however, has an ambiguous effect on the welfare impacts of tax reform. On the one hand, announcing tax changes in advance enables the private sector to better adjust to the change, immediately undoing some of the distortions associated with the taxes to be reduced. On the other hand, when new distortionary policies are introduced, announcing policy changes in advance actually raises the efficiency costs of the policy, as individuals' choices are immediately affected by the change.

We comment more extensively on the results in the following subsections.

Capital income tax reform

Capital income taxation creates an intertemporal distortion by affecting the savings decisions of households. As discussed earlier, the effect of capital income taxes on savings and capital accumulation is ambiguous (Boskin (1978), Fullerton, Shoven, and Whalley (1983), Bradford (1986), Auerbach and Kotlikoff (1987). A standard argument is that higher taxes on capital income increase the cost of future consumption and thus reduce savings. Whether income effects offset this substitution effect, and how much such taxes affect savings, is essentially an empirical question.

The relative prices of capital assets differ across sectors in the benchmark, mainly for the reason that capital income tax and depreciation rates differ by sectors. Such distortion affects both the supply and demand sides of the capital market. On the supply side, higher tax rates affect the saving decision of the households and thus affect the aggregate volume of capital stock available in the economy. On the demand side, inter-sectoral differences in taxes affect the relative user cost of capital and hence the sectoral allocation of capital.

Capital income taxes range from twenty-four per cent in the chemical sector to forty-eight per cent in the education sector in the base year. We set a uniform twenty-five per cent capital income tax rate across all sectors to evaluate the degree of distortions due to differentiated rates in the base year.

The growth paths of investment, capital stock, employment and output relative to the reference economy following such a reform are given in Figures 1A-B, 8A-B, and 15A-B in Appendix B. These figures show that the primary impact of capital tax reform is felt as an increase in the level of investment across sectors, after an initial sharp reduction due to the initial impacts of changes in other taxes. An unanticipated capital income tax reform increases investment to more than fifteen per cent in production sectors and other sectors. Then its level settles down to more than five to fifteen per cent of the reference path of the economy depending on the sector. The agriculture, finance, distribution, mining and construction sectors experience more expansion than other sectors. In contrast, housing investment shuts down for more than five years and remains depressed afterwards.

Capital stocks follow the growth in investment. In the long run, the capital stock in agriculture remains above fifteen per cent higher than in the baseline; other sectors experience a ten per cent increase compared to the reference path. We can see that the relative size of this effect by sector is related to the baseline capital income tax and depreciation rate for that sector. For instance, the growth path of the capital stock in the chemical sector does not deviate much from the reference path, due to the capital tax rate in that sector remaining relatively unaffected by the reform.

The general pattern of investment and capital stock effects described above is preserved when the capital market is open (Figure 15A), the only difference being that convergence is faster and "smoother" in the open capital market case.

Besides inter-sectoral asset reallocation, changes in the relative user cost of capital have a significant effect on employment across sectors. When capital inputs become relatively cheaper than the labour input, producers tend to substitute capital for labour. As outlined above, capital becomes relatively cheaper in certain sectors such as agriculture, finance, public administration, and education, and relatively expensive in some other sectors, particularly manufacturing, after a uniform tax reform.

The levels of employment and output under a uniform capital income tax reform remain between –5 and 5 per cent of the reference path in this model. Growth of the agriculture sector is above the reference path across all market scenarios, while that of the engineering sector remains below the reference path in all scenarios. This reflects the fact that the capital income tax in the agriculture sector has reduced from 41 per cent to 25 per cent and it has a relatively lower depreciation rate compared to other sectors. The construction sector experiences a big shock after the tax change, but bounces back to above the benchmark reference path over time.

The presence of announcement effects causes investment to begin adjusting earlier, in anticipation of the new taxes. When tax changes are known in advance, there are incentives, immediately after the announcement, to postpone investment to periods where it enjoys relatively better tax treatment. As the time of the reform approaches, however, investment changes go in the same directions as the post-reform changes (with the exception of the initial spike immediately following the reform).

We may conclude that the impact of capital income tax reform varies across sectors and the size of this impact depends upon the benchmark rates of capital income tax and depreciation. Sectors subject to higher tax rates and lower depreciation rates in the benchmark realise growth paths significantly above the reference path of the economy and sectors with lower tax and depreciation rates stay on or below the reference path.

The general equilibrium impacts of capital income tax changes affect the reference paths of employment and output but the size of the employment and output effects are smaller than those in investment and capital stock by sector. Changes in the capital stock have some knock on effects on employment and then on the output. Output effects are more extreme in the extraction and distribution sectors, which are more capital-intensive than service sectors such as public administration and education.

The overall efficiency effects of such reforms range from 0.63 per cent to 0.77 per cent of the base year UK GDP, suggesting that, in comparison to the rest of the tax system, capital taxation is significantly more distortionary.

Labour income tax reform

Taxes on labour income contribute more than 55 per cent of total UK tax revenue. Like all other taxes on market activities, labour income taxation distorts the labour-leisure choices of households, but in this model it does so more "neutrally" than other taxes do.

Income taxes are conventionally regarded as being progressive, since higher income people pay a larger amount in taxes. Usually it is thought that income taxes collected from high income households finance transfers to low income households. However, this redistribution issue is somewhat more complicated when the labour supply decisions of both low and high income households are taken into account. There is a crucial trade-off between the efficiency and equity effects of such a tax-transfer. High taxes on income may improve equity in the economy, but usually discourage labour supply both by the rich (who pay the taxes) and the poor (who receive the benefit), thus reducing output and income.

We simulate the effects of a simple labour income tax reform consisting of a reduction in the tax rate from 24 per cent in the benchmark economy to 15 per cent. Results from the model for this tax reform experiment are presented in Figures 2A-B, 9A-B, and 16A-B. An equal-yield replacement of labour income taxes with other taxes increases other tax-induced distortions in the economy. In particular, we see the levels of investment, capital stock, employment and output fall below the reference path. Only the housing sector expands due to a reduction in labour income tax.

In the closed-capital markets, no-announcement case, this replacement generates a substantial dynamic efficiency loss of 2.05%, indicating that labour taxes are by far the least distortionary form of taxation in the model. The efficiency loss with open capital markets is even more substantial.

Production tax reform

Unified business rates, subsidies and excise taxes are applied into the use of inputs in production. These rates distort input choices by producers ultimately resulting in a less efficient combination of inputs in production. Production taxes vary across sectors from -11 per cent to 14 per cent in the base year. As these taxes reduce the profit margin of the producers, when these tax rates are reduced profit margins increase and producers expand their output.

In our counterfactual experiment, we replace all sector-specific rates by a uniform rate of 5 per cent. This production tax reform has a strong impact on the growth paths of investment, capital stock, employment and output as shown in Figures 3A-B, 10A-B, and 17A-B. The magnitude of shocks in the various sectors closely corresponds to the size of production tax or subsidy rates in the benchmark economy.

There is little variation between the open and closed capital markets cases. In both scenarios, the overall efficiency effect of the replacement is a sizeable 1.4 per cent of the base year GDP, indicating that these taxes are very distortionary. With announcement effects, this welfare gain falls to 1.2%.

Investment goods tax reforms

In the model a single composite investment good is produced and demanded by the different sectors. Taxes on investment goods are levied at this stage. Just as capital income taxes do, taxes on investment goods negatively affect savings and investment.

Reform of indirect tax rates on investment goods exhibits a very different pattern of impacts on the model economy in comparison with other experiments, and we see a significant difference between the open and closed capital market scenarios, with and without announcement effects (Figures 4A-B, 11A-B, 18A-B). Since investment taxes are small, however, all associated impacts are relatively modest.

In the long run, the growth paths of most sectors are 2 per cent above or below the reference path. The efficiency loss from moving to a uniform 5 per cent investment tax from the existing differentiated but lower tax rates ranges from 0.08 per cent of base year GDP -0.1 per cent, suggesting that this tax is relatively more distortionary than other taxes.

Household consumption tax reform

Indirect taxes on consumption goods increase the cost of consumption to households, who tend to substitute cheaper (less taxed) goods for expensive (heavily taxed) goods. While some of the indirect taxes on goods are imposed to reduce the consumption of injurious "sin goods" such as liquor, tobacco and cigarettes with a broader interest of promoting public heath, consumption taxes mainly aim at raising revenue[2]. Differential taxation of different consumption categories distorts the composition of consumption demand. Also, taxation of consumption distorts labour supply decisions (the choice between consumption and leisure) just as taxation of labour income does.

Indirect taxes on commodities are typically viewed as being regressive in the public finance literature, the standard argument being that they fall disproportionately on the consumption of poor households who spend a greater per centage of their income on consumption than rich households.

In the current model tax rates on household consumption vary from 1.6 per cent in the agriculture sector to 26 per cent in 'other manufactures' in the base year. In our experiment, these differentiated rates are replaced by a flat ten per cent rate.

The pattern of growth effects relative to the reference path varies significantly across sectors (Figures 5A-B, 12A-B and 19A-B). Production sectors generally experience higher growth rates relative to the reference path while other sectors experience a negative impact. This pattern is very different from what we observe for other tax experiments.

The overall efficiency effect of this tax reform is a gain of 0.1 per cent of UK GDP, again denoting that this source of revenue is relatively more distortionary than the combination of other taxes in the economy. This welfare gain increases significantly with announcements (0.6 per cent) and when capital markets are open (0.7 per cent).

Government consumption tax reform

Public spending accounts for around 40 per cent of GDP, a significant amount of which is in the form of public consumption. The share of public final consumption demand in total sectoral demand in relation to the total final demand by households, investors, the government and the rest of the world is shown in Table 5. The proportion of public consumption in total final demand varies significantly across sectors, ranging from 0.5 per cent in agriculture to 49 per cent in the education sector and up to 100 per cent in the public administration sector. Tax rates by sectors on public consumption are different from those on private consumption or on investment Table 2. Taxes on public consumption vary from 0.6 per cent to 32 per cent in the data. Such differentiated tax rates on public consumption create distortions in public demand choices. In our counterfactual experiment, we reduce these rates to a uniform rate of 5 per cent.

Simulation results (Figures 6A-B, 13A-B, 20A-B) show that most of the sectors experience increased growth. Again, sectors with higher tax rates in the base year are above the reference path, and sectors with taxes on public consumption do not show much variation.

Table 5
Composition of final demand

	Consumption	*Government expenditure*	*Investment.*	*Exports*
Agriculture	0.772	0.005	0.000	0.223
Extraction	0.000	0.000	0.000	1.000
Other Mining	0.248	0.034	0.000	0.718
Chemicals	0.105	0.087	0.007	0.801
Metals	0.018	0.031	0.416	0.536
Engineering	0.000	0.029	0.053	0.918
Food, drink	0.705	0.011	0.004	0.280
Other Manuf.	0.251	0.054	0.141	0.554
Utilities	0.922	0.075	0.000	0.004
Construction	0.063	0.079	0.858	0.000
Distribution	0.864	0.010	0.020	0.106
Transport	0.558	0.075	0.022	0.345
Financial	0.463	0.154	0.155	0.229
Public Admin	0.000	1.000	0.000	0.000
Educ. Health,	0.462	0.490	0.000	0.048
Housing	1.000	0.000	0.000	0.000
Total	0.443	0.186	0.110	0.260

The dynamic efficiency gain from reducing taxes on the government sector in the no-announcement, closed-capital markets case is less than 0.3 per cent of the base year GDP, which is higher than that from reducing taxes on private consumption. This is in spite of lower tax rates applied to public consumption. Announcement effects and the opening of capital markets do not change the results significantly.

Tariff reform

Tariffs, like taxes, increase the price of a commodity to a consumer or a producer in the economy. Specifically, they increase the cost of imported commodities relative to comparable domestically produced commodities. Thus, tariffs distort trade with the rest of the world.

The small economy assumption as used here essentially means that a representative consumer and producers in the UK can purchase and sell unlimited amounts of goods and services without affecting international market prices. The main reason for such an assumption is that the UK's trade volume is small compared to trade volumes at the global level. By this assumption we rule out the existence of commodities in which the UK might be a dominant supplier or consumer in the global market.

Following a long process of intra-regional and international trade liberalisation over more than five decades, very little room is left for further gains only through liberalisation of commodity trade. Still we find some mild efficiency effects and more or less uniformly positive distributed effects of tariff reform across sectors.

Tariff rates are about 2.5 per cent in the benchmark year. We investigate the effects of a reduction in tariffs to 1 per cent (Figures 7A-B, 14A-B, 21A-B), compensated by a revenue-preserving equi-proportional increase in all other taxes. The overall efficiency effect of such tariff reform ranges from 0.07 to 0.08 per cent of the base year GDP. These results show that as the UK economy is quite liberalised already, gains from such moves may be very small, even when dynamic linkages are taken into account.

POSSIBLE EXTENSIONS

We can think of a number of possible extensions to the current model. Such extensions could consist of improvements in the modelling methodology, adding more dimensionality, and widening policy application.

On the methodological side, the single agent structure could be meaningfully augmented by including overlapping generations (Kotlikoff (1988), Ballard and Kim (1995), Rutherford *et al.* (1998). Such a model structure would allow for the study of retirement and social security issues and intergenerational distribution. A multiple household structure could also be used to study the effects of tax reform on income distribution patterns. Another natural extension could be augmenting the model with a regional multihousehold structure to study income distribution. Also, the current small open economy formulation could be extended to a global trade model formulation incorporating several regions, especially accounting for UK-EEC and the Rest of the World linkages separately in the global economy.

As we have discussed, the current general equilibrium structure is based on perfect competition and deterministic calibration. It would be more realistic to incorporate imperfect market structure and a stochastic process of asset returns, with multiple capital assets and portfolio choices, although the latter extension may prove computationally forbidding, even with the high speed of currently available computers and solution algorithms.

With respect to policy issues, this model could easily be augmented to study the effects of various labour and capital market policies adopted by the government besides tax policies such as the New Deals for Work welfare programme. With very small alterations one could use this model to explore the long-term impacts of education and health policies through human capital formation and to assess the impacts of environmental policies on economic growth and distribution.

CONCLUSION

The major advantage of the dynamic model presented here, in comparison to the static version of the model described in an earlier report, lies in its ability to track both short- and long-run impacts of tax and trade policy measures on the growth path of the economy via their effects on capital formation. In the dynamic model, the process of capital accumulation, both in the short and in the long run, is determined endogenously through consumption-saving decisions of households and investment allocation decisions of producers. The structure of the model allows us to look at the differential impacts of tax reform on investment by sector and capture the possibility of transitory shutdown in sectoral investment.

The model is calibrated using 1995 micro consistent data for the UK economy. It is then used to perform a number of equal-yield tax replacement experiments, whereby a certain tax is reduced and the remaining taxes increased in order to guarantee a constant period-by-period level of government spending without any change in public borrowing. For each experiment, we report transitional and long run effects on sectoral output, employment, and capital formation, as well as overall dynamic efficiency impacts. In each case, we investigate whether impacts differ when people can anticipate tax changes occurring in the future or when they encounter tax changes all of sudden without any anticipation. We also investigate how results in a closed capital market specification differ from those in an open capital market setting.

The dynamic efficiency effects and the growth path impacts of tax reform vary significantly across experiments. When distortionary capital income tax rates ranging from 24 to 48 per cent in the base year are replaced by a uniform capital income tax rate of 25 per cent, the dynamic efficiency gains are about 0.77 per cent of the base year GDP. Some sectors, such as agriculture, where the capital input cost has been reduced relatively in the counterfactual scenario by lower capital income tax rates, experience an expansion. Other sectors,such as engineering, where the capital income tax has not reduced that much in the counterfactual scenario relative to the benchmark, experience slower growth.

Reducing labour income tax from 24 per cent in the benchmark year to 15 per cent results in a welfare loss of up to 2.05 per cent of the base year GDP, mainly because more distortionary taxes have to be increased to make up for lost revenues. Replacing differential tax rates on production by a uniform 5 per cent rate across sectors results in welfare gain of 1.4 per cent of the base year GDP. Similarly replacing differentiated household consumption tax by a uniform 5 per cent rate causes a gain of 0.6 per cent of GDP. We find similar gains in welfare from a reform in the taxes on government consumption and tariffs.

The private sector's ability to anticipate reform affects transitional effects as well as the dynamic efficiency effects of reform, raising them in some cases and lowering them in others. Simulation results appear to be robust with respect to changes in the degree of international openness of capital markets. In all cases, convergence to a new balanced-growth path occurs more quickly when private agents anticipate future tax changes and when capital markets are internationally open.

NOTES

1. This paper reports on activity undertaken as part of an ESRC project on General Equilibrium and Dynamic Modelling for the Analysis of UK Policy Issues. We are grateful to the ESRC for financial support and to Graham Siddorn at the Economics Unit of the Inland Revenue for data support and to Bill McNie, Tobi Kendall, Carlo Perroni and John Whalley at the Warwick University and a seminar group in the Hull University for discussions and suggestions. Correspondence address: K.R.Bhattarai@econ.hull.ac.uk, phone: 44-1482-466483; fax: 44-1482-466216.
2. The main excise duties on tobacco, alcohol and fuel were included in 'Production Taxes' here in line with ONS Input-Output definitions; although in a later tax aggregations provided by the Inland Revenue and used in our Static Model (Bhattarai (1999)) such excise taxes were incorporated within consumption taxes (see also Siddorn (1999)).
3. See Graham Siddorn's notes on data in Appendix 1 of Bhattari (1999).

REFERENCES

Abel, A., and O. J. Blanchard (1983), "An Intertemporal Model of Saving and Investment." *Econometrica* 51 3 pp. 675-692.

Arrow, K.J., H.B. Chenery, B.C. Minhas and R.M. Solow (1961), "Capital-Labour Substitution and Economic Efficiency," *Review of Economics and Statistics* 43, 225- 250.

Auerbach, A.J. and L.J. Kotlikoff (1987), *Dynamic Fiscal Policy*. Cambridge University Press.

Ballard, C.J. and J.J. Kim (1995), "Using a Computational General Equilibrium Model with Overlapping Generations," in conference volume for 6th CGE Modelling Conference, University of Waterloo.

Ballard, C.L., D. Fullerton , J.B. Shoven and J. Whalley (1985), *A General Equilibrium Model for Tax Policy Evaluation*. University of Chicago Press, Chicago.

Barro, R.J. and X. Sala-I-Martin (1995), *Economic Growth*, McGraw Hill, London.

Bhattarai, K. (1999), *General Equilibrium Tax Policy Model of the UK Economy: A Report to the ESRC and the Inland Revenue*, University of Warwick, Coventry.

Bhattarai, K. (1997), *Financial Deepening and Economic Development in Nepal: A Forward Looking CGE Model with Financial Liberalization*. Ph.D. Dissertation, Northeastern University, Boston, USA.

Bhattarai, K. and J. Whalley (1999), "The Role of Labour Demand Elasticities in Tax Incidence Analysis with Heterogeneous Labour," forthcoming in *Empirical Economics* 24(4) November.

Bhattarai, K. and J. Whalley (1999), "A World Trade Model and a Small Open Economy Model from a UK Perspective" *mimeo*, University of Warwick, July.

Blanchard, O.J. and S. Fischer (1990), *Lectures on Macroeconomics*. MIT Press.

Boehringer, C., A. Pahlke, T. F. Rutherford (1997), "Environmental Tax Reforms and the Prospects for a Double Dividend. An Applied General Equilibrium Analysis for Germany," *Mimeo*: University of Stuttgart and University of Colorado.

Boskin, M.J. (1978), "Taxation Saving and the Rate of Interest," *Journal of Political Economy* 86:s3-s28.

Bradford, D. (1986), *Untangling the Income Tax*, Harvard University Press.

Broer, D.P. and J. Lassila, eds. (1996), *Pension Policies and Public Debt in Dynamic CGE Models*, Heidelberg: Physica.

Brook, A K., D. Kendtrick, A. Meeraus (1992), *GAMS: User's Guide,* Release 2.25, The Scientific Press, San Francisco, CA.

Cass, D. (1965), "Optimal Growth in an Aggregative Model of Capital Accumulation," *Review of Economic Studies* 32:233-240.

Debreu, G. (1954), *The Theory of Value*. Yale University Press, New Haven.

Diamond, P. (1965), "National Debt in Neo-Classical Growth Model," *American Economic Review* 55, 126-1150.

Dirkse, S. P. and M.C. Ferris (1996), "A Pathsearch Damped Newton Method for Computing General Equilibria," *Annals of Operations Research,* 211-232.

Fair, R.C. (1984), *Specification, Estimation, and Analysis of Macroeconometric Models.* Harvard University Press, Cambridge, MA.

Fullerton, D. and D.L. Rogers (1993), *Who Bears the Lifetime Tax Burden?* Brookings Institution, Washington D.C.

Fullerton, D., J. Shoven and J. Whalley (1983), "Dynamic General Equilibrium Impacts of Replacing the US Income tax with a Progressive Consumption Tax," *Journal of Public Economics* 38, 265-96.

Goodman A. and Webb S. (1994), "For Richer, For Poorer: The Changing Distribution of Income in the UK, 1961-91," *Fiscal Studies* 15, 29-62.

Goulder, L.H., and L.H. Summers (1989), "Tax Policy, Asset Prices, and Growth: A General Equilibrium Analysis," *Journal of Public Economics*, 38, 265-296.

Hall, R.E. (1988), "Intertemporal Substitution in Consumption," *Journal of Political Economy* 96 339-57.

Hansen, L.P. and K.J. Singleton (1996), Efficient Estimation of Linear Asset-pricing Models with Moving Average Errors," *Journal of Business and Economics Statistics* 14, 53-68.

Hamermesh, D. S. (1993), *Labour Demand*, Princeton University Press, New Jersey.

Harberger A.C. (1962), "The Incidence of the Corporation Income Tax," *Journal of Political Economy* 70, 215-40.

Harrison, W.J. and K.R. Pearson (1996), "Computing Solutions for Large General Equilibrium Models Using GEMPACK," *Computational Economics* 9, 83-127.

Hutton, J. and T. Kenc (1994), "Representative UK Income Tax with a Progressive Consumption Tax," University of Cambridge Department of Applied Economics *Working Paper* 9413, June.

Jenkins, S.P. (1996), "Recent Trends in the UK Income Distribution: What Happened and Why?," *Oxford Review of Economic Policy* 12.

Jonson, P. and S. Webb (1993), "Explaining the Growth in UK Income Inequality: 1979-1988," *The Economic Journal* 103, 429-435.

Killingsworth, M. (1983), *Labor Supply*, Cambridge University Press.

King and Fullerton (1984), "The taxation of Income form Capital", *The University of Chicago Press Ltd.*

King and Robson (1988), "Manual for TURBO PTAX", *London School of Economics Financial Markets Group.*

Kotlikoff, L.J. (1988), "Intergenerational Transfers and Savings," *Journal of Economic Perspectives* 2, 41-58.

Kotlikoff, L.J., Shoven J. and Spivak A. (1986), "The Effect of Annuity Insurance on Savings and Inequality," *Journal of Labor Economics* 43, S183-S215.

King, R.G. and R. Levine (1993), "Finance and Growth: Shumpeter Might Be Right,"

Quarterly Journal of Economics, Aug., pp.717-737.

Koopmans, T.C. (1965), "On the Concept of Optimal Growth," in *The Econometric Approach to Development Planning*. Chicago: Rand McNally.

Kydland, F.E. and E.C. Prescott (1977), "Rules Rather than Discretion: The Inconsistency of Optimal Plans," *Journal of Political Economy* 85, 473-491.

Lucas, R. Jr. (1988), "On the Mechanics of Economic Development," *Journal of Monetary Economics,* 223-42.

Lumsdaine, R.L., J.H. Stock and D.A. Wise (1992) "Pension Plans Provisions and Retirement: Men and women, Medicare, and Models," *NBER Working Paper* No. 4201.Cambridge MA.

Machina, M.J. (1989) "Dynamic Consistency and Non-Expected Utility Models of Choice Under Uncertainty," *Journal of Economic Literature* 27, 1622-1668.

Mercenier, J. and T.N. Srinivasan ed. (1994)_*Applied General Equilibrium and Economic Development: Present Achievement and Future Trends*. University of Michigan Press, Ann Arbor.

Miles, D.K (1990) "Financial Liberalization of the Housing Market and Current Account," *Birkbeck College Discussion Paper in Financial Economics* FE 6/90, July.

Pemberton, J. (1997) "The Empirical Failure of the Life Cycle Model with Perfect Capital Markets," *Oxford Economic Papers*. 49, 129-151.

Ogaki, M. and C.M. Reinhart (1998a) "Intertemporal substitution and durable goods:long-run data," *Economics Letters* 61 85-90.

Ogaki, M. and C.M. Reinhart (1998b) "Measuring Intertemporal Substitution: The Role of Durable Goods," *Journal of Political Economy*, 106, 5, 1078-1098.

Perroni, C. (1995), "Assessing the Dynamic Efficiency Gains of Tax Reform When Human Capital is Endogenous," *International Economic Review* 36, 907-925.

Piggott, J. and J. Whalley (1985) *UK Tax Policy and Applied General Equilibrium Analysis.* Cambridge University Press.

Rankin, N. (1987), "Disequilibrium and the Welfare Maximising Levels of Government Spending, Taxation and Debt," *Economic Journal* 97, 65-85.

Ramsey, F.P. (1928), "A Mathematical Theory of Saving," *Economic Journal* 38, 543-559.

Reinert, K.A and D.W. Roland-Holst (1992), "Armington Elasticities for United States Manufacturing Sectors," *Journal of Policy Modelling* 14, 631-639.

Rebelo, S. (1991), "Long-run Policy Analysis and Long-run Growth," *Journal of Political Economy* 99, 500-521.

Robinson, S. (1991), "Macroeconomics, Financial Variables, and Computable General Equilibrium Models," *World Development* 19, 1509-1523.

Romer, D. (1996), *Advanced Macroeconomics*. McGraw Hill.

Romer, P.M. (1986), "Capital Accumulation in the Theory of Long-Run Growth," in Barro, R. (ed.) *Business Cycle Theory*. Harvard University Press.

Rutherford, T.F. (1995), "Extension of GAMS for Complementary Problems Arising in Applied Economic Analysis," *Journal of Economic Dynamics and Control* 19, 1299-1324.

Rutherford, T.F, C. Bohringer and A. Pahlke (1998), "Carbon Abatement, Revenue Recycling and Intergenerational Burden Sharing," Presented at the Dynamic CGE Conference, Denmark, 1998.

Rutherford, T.F., Lau, M. I., and A. Pahlke (1997), "Modelling Economic Adjustment: A Primer in Dynamic General Equilibrium Analysis," *Discussion Paper*, Department of Economics, University of Colorado, Boulder.

Rust, J. P. (1989), "A Dynamic Programming Model of Retirement Behaviour," in David A.W. (ed.) *The Economics of Aging*. Chicago: U. of Chicago Press.

Rust, J. (1997), "Using Randomization to Break the Curse of Dimensionality," *Econometrica*. 65, 487-516.

Rust, J. (1997), "How Social Security and Medicare Affect Retirement Behaviour in the World of Incomplete Markets," *Econometrica* 65, 781-831.

Samuelson, P.A. (1958), "An Exact Consumption-loan Model of Interest with or without the Social Contrivance of Money," *Journal of Political Economy* 66.

Sargent, T.J. (1987), *Dynamic Macroeconomic Theory*. Harvard University Press.

Siddorn, G. (1999), Derivation of 1995 Industry-by-Industry Use Matrices, *mimeo*, *Economics Unit*, Inland Revenue, F4 West Wing, Somerset House, Strand, London WC2R 1LB.

Solow, R.M. (1956), "A Contribution to the Theory of Economic Growth." *Quarterly Journal of Economics* 70, 65-94.

St-Hilaire, F. and J. Whalley (1983), "A Micro Consistent Equilibrium Data Set for Canada for Use in Tax Policy Analysis," *Review of Income and Wealth*, 29, 175-204.

Shoven, J.B. and J. Whalley (1984), "Applied General-Equilibrium Models of Taxation and International Trade: An Introduction and Survey," *Journal of Economic Literature* 22, 1007-1051.

Shoven, J.B. and J.Whalley (1992), *Applying General Equilibrium*. Cambridge University Press, 1992.

Slemrod, J. (1992), "Taxation and Inequality: A Time-exposure Perspective," *NBER Working paper* no. 3999.

Stock, J.H. and D.A. Wise (1997), "Pensions, the Option Value of Work and Retirement," *Econometrica* 58, 1151-1180.

Stokey, N. L. and R. E. Lucas (1989), *Recursive Methods in Economic Dynamics*. Harvard University Press.

Summers, L.H. (1980), "Capital Taxation and Accumulation in a Life Cycle Growth Model," *American Economic Review* 71, 533-44.

Taylor, J.B. and H. Uhling (1990), "Solving Nonlinear Stochastic Growth Models: A Comparison of Alternative Solution Methods," *Journal of Business and Economic Statistics* 8.

Uzawa, H. (1962), "On a Two-Sector Model of Economic Growth," *Review of Economic Studies* 29, 40-47.

Uzawa, H. (1964), "Optimal Growth in a Two-Sector Model of Capital Accumulation," *Review of Economic Studies* 31,1-25.

Walras, L. (1954), *Elements of Pure Economics*. Allen and Unwin, London.

Weizsacker, R.K.V. (1996), "Distributive Implications of an Aging Society" *Journal of European Economic Review* 40, 729-746.

Wendner, R. (1999), "A Calibration Procedure of Dynamic CGE Models for Non-Steady-State Situations using GEMPACK," *Computational Economics* (forthcoming).

Wise, D. A. (1989), Ed. *The Economics of Aging* Chicago: University of Chicago Press.

Whalley, J. (1985), *Trade Liberalization Among Major World Trading Areas*, MIT Press, Cambridge.

Whalley, J. and B. Yeung (1983), "External Sector `Closing' Rules in Applied General Equilibrium Models" *Journal of International Economics*,15, pp.1-16.

APPENDIX A

A brief note on the data set

Table A1

Aggregation of 123 sectors into 16 sectors from 1990 Input-Output Sectoral Classification

Industry/Asset	*1990 I-O Sectors*	*1990 sectoral code*	*1995 sectoral code*
Agriculture	Agriculture, Forestry, Fishing	1,2,3	1-3
Extraction	Extraction – oil and gas	5	5
Other mining & quarrying	Coal extraction, stone, clay, sand, gravel, metal ores and minerals	4,14, 10	4,6,7
Chemicals	Coke ovens, oil proc, nuclear fuel, inorganic chemicals, organic chemicals, fertilisers, synthetic resins, paints, dyes, printing ink, special chemical for industry, pharmaceutical products, soap and toilet preparations, chemical products, man-made fibres	6, 20-29	35-46
Metals and mineral products	Iron and Steel, Aluminium, other non-ferrous metals, structural clay products, Cement, lime and plaster, concrete, asbestos, abrasive prods, glass, refractory and ceramic goods, metal casting, metal doors, windows, packaging products of metals, industrial plant and steel work, engineers small tools	11-13, 15-19, 30-34, 37	49-61

Contd....

Industry/Asset	*1990 I-O Sectors*	*1990 sectoral code*	*1995 sectoral code*
Engineering	Agricultural machinery and tractors, metal working machine tools, textile etc machinery, process machinery and contractors, mining equipment, mech power transmission equipment, other machinery, ordnance samll arms and ammunition, insulated wires and cables, basic electrical equipment, industrial electrical equipment, telecommunications etc. equipment, electronic components, electronic consumer goods, demestic electric appliances, electric lighting equipment, instrument engineering	35,36, 38-52, 57	62-76
Food, drinks and tobacco	Oils and fats, slaughtering and meat processing, milk and products, fruit vegetable and fish processing, grain milling and starch, bread, biscuits, sugar, confectionary, animal feeding stuffs, miscellaneous foods, alcoholic drink soft drinks, tobacco	58-70	8-20
Other manufacturing	Motor vehicles and parts, shipbuilding and repairing, aerospace etc, other vehicles, woollen and worsted, cotton spinning and weaving, hosiery and other knitted goods, textile finishing, carpets, jute, leather and leather goods, footwear, clothing furs, household and other textiles, timber and wood products, wooden furniture, pulp, paper and board, paper and board products, printing and publishing, rubber products, processing of plastics, jewellery and coins, sports goods and toys, other goods	53-56, 71-90	21-34, 47-48,77-84
Electricity, gas and water	Electricity production, gas, water supply	7,8,9	85-87
Construction	Construction	91	88
Distribution, hotels, etc.	Wholesale distribution, retail distribution, distribution and vehicles repairs, hotels catering, pubs etc.	92,93,94,95	89-92
Transport, storage, and communication	Railways, road and other inland transport, sea transport, air transport, transport services, postal services, telecoomunication	96-102	93-99
Financial sector	Banking and finance, insurance, auxiliary financial services, estate agents, legal services, accountancy services, other professional services, advertising, computing services, other business services, renting of movables, owning and dealing in real estate, research and development	103-114, 118	100-103, 105-114
Public administration	Public administration	115	115
Education, health and social work	Sanitary services, education, health services, recreation and welfare services, personal services, domestic services	116, 117, 119-122	116-123
Housing services	Ownership of dwelling	123	104

The dynamic general equilibrium model of the UK contains 16 sectors representing the production system of the UK economy sectors and their 1990 and 1995 sectoral codes are given in Table A1. These 16 sectors[3] together represent 123 input-output sectors (as determined by the ONS), as shown in column 2. The 1990 sectoral codes corresponding to these sectors are in column 3, with codes in concordance with the 1995 ONS Input-Output tables given in the last column. The 1995 input-output table has more disaggregation of service sectors compared to earlier input-output tables. This is particularly important as more than sixty-two per cent of national income originates from service sectors, compared to about thirty per cent in manufacturing sectors. Intermediate inputs used by a sector are given in the columns, along with the primary factors of production such as labour and capital inputs and corresponding taxes on primary inputs. Rows of an input-output table give the input that a particular sector supplies to other sectors. It is a well established convention in input-output analysis that rows represent revenue of a sector and columns show the cost of production to that sector. Some other information such as the revenue and transfer figures, given in the right bottom corner of the input-output table, are taken from the National Account Blue Book for 1996.

Every general equilibrium model requires a micro consistent data set in order to calibrate the model parameters and validate the model by replicating the base year data as a solution to the model (see St-Hilaire and Whalley (1983)). Mainly the benchmark data for a general equilibrium model require three basic conditions to be satisfied: a zero profit condition, a market clearing condition and income balance. The zero profit conditions for producers in the benchmark data are met for various sectors of the economy when aggregate output equals gross of tax payments to labour and capital services and intermediate inputs. This essentially means that firms are just breaking even while producing goods and services and supplying them to markets. The market clearing condition for each sector implies that total output or supply equals aggregate demand, which is composed of intermediate and final demands. The total supply of goods in the market comprises domestic output and imports. The income balance condition implies that the expenditure of households and government must be equal to their income or revenues gross of savings, the economy wide trade balance condition holds and the volume of savings equals the volume of investment in the economy.

The 16 sector industry-by-industry input-output table presented in Table A2 meets all these micro-consistency conditions for the UK economy for the benchmark year 1995. All of these three equilibrium conditions required for an empirical implementation of a GE tax model are satisfied in the data set contained in the input-output data in Table A2.

Gross output was equal to £1228 billion, split between intermediate demand (£487 billion) and final demand (£741 billion). Total demand equals total supply for each sector. The value of imports equals the value of exports (£195 billion). The indirect taxes row is the sum of various taxes such as tariffs, duties and levies, VAT and subsidies to intermediate and final demand. The original input-output balances do not disaggregate between labour and capital income. This breakdown is done according to a method developed in the Inland Revenue.

More detailed explanation of the various data elements for the current model are contained in our earlier report (Bhattarai (1999)).

Table A2

A 16 Sector Industry by Industry Input-Output Table of the United Kingdom 1995 *(in millions of £s)*

I x I Domestic Use Matrix	Agriculture	Extraction	Other Mining	Chemicals	Metals	Engineering	Food, drink	Other Manuf.	Utilities	Construction	Distribution	Transport	Financial	Public Admin	Educ. Health,	Housing	Total intermediate	Consumers' expenditure	GG FC	GDF CF	Stocks	Exports	Total final demand	Total
Agriculture	2,096	0	14	27	7	5	12,132	435	0	4	564	48	15	0	148	0	15,495	6,730	42	0	0	1,942	8,713	24,208
Extraction	0	2,439	0	4,697	3	0	0	0	3,622	0	0	0	0	0	0	0	10,762	0	0	0	0	6,942	6,942	17,704
Other Mining	20	0	353	218	846	26	45	130	1,897	401	105	17	8	0	57	0	4,124	339	47	0	0	983	1,369	5,493
Chemicals	1,433	10	37	3,899	433	546	571	1,484	466	737	1,299	1,254	913	0	3,204	19	16,304	3,764	3,116	0	261	28,663	35,804	52,108
Metals	110	162	192	1,225	7,249	6,320	1,831	5,197	50	7,074	503	389	5	0	84	0	30,392	346	588	7,158	779	10,230	19,101	49,493
Engineering	0	576	317	682	1,254	5,705	528	2,432	634	788	848	1,808	1,018	0	1,567	36	18,192	0	1,589	2,613	332	50,923	55,457	73,649
Food, drink	2,797	52	25	356	82	120	6,382	350	64	51	6,589	650	1,058	0	1,796	4	20,377	25,904	411	0	153	10,270	36,737	57,114
Other Manuf.	583	80	134	1,781	1,839	3,005	2,816	16,404	474	4,242	6,702	4,139	8,242	0	3,340	283	54,064	18,082	3,872	8,933	1,185	39,858	71,928	125,992
Utilities	279	0	160	1,330	1,596	1,189	931	1,980	12,273	272	1,201	857	1,184	0	705	23	23,981	16,353	1,323	0	0	62	17,738	41,719
Construction	172	0	122	109	32	56	0	31	0	21,085	603	151	1,985	0	146	3,929	28,420	3,521	4,414	47,764	285	0	55,983	84,404
Distribution	1,005	200	206	1,479	2,489	4,115	1,647	3,724	355	1,371	4,164	2,470	2,276	0	790	0	26,289	111,181	1,229	2,586	0	13,701	128,698	154,987
Transport	245	704	335	1,232	2,047	1,415	1,583	3,614	183	887	14,871	15,642	17,082	0	3,175	198	63,216	19,715	2,637	779	0	12,194	35,324	98,540
Financial	1,949	671	471	4,070	2,781	6,194	4,205	9,177	1,884	10,483	22,425	12,387	50,836	0	13,435	15,221	156,189	25,373	8,458	8,483	0	12,545	54,859	211,047
Public Admin	0	0	0	0	0	0	0	0	0	0	0	0	0	0	0	0	0	0	63,843	0	0	0	63,843	63,843
Educ. Health,	378	1	41	520	253	581	496	2,618	179	242	1,001	1,369	4,031	0	7,756	67	19,535	43,653	46,265	0	0	4,504	94,422	113,957
Housing	0	0	0	0	0	0	0	0	0	0	0	0	0	0	0	0	0	53,269	0	0	0	0	53,269	53,269
Total intermediate	11,067	4,895	2,410	21,626	20,912	29,276	33,168	47,576	22,081	47,638	60,876	41,182	88,652	0	36,201	19,781	487,339	328,229	137,832	78,316	2,995	192,816	740,188	1,227,527
Imports	1,630	989	425	10,639	7,613	15,965	8,827	30,336	3,612	5,151	3,532	4,895	3,949	0	2,960	19	100,541	52,021	9,995	28,174	1,563	2,494	94,248	194,789
Duty on imports	34	6	5	136	101	214	171	405	48	66	51	26	2	0	9	0	1,273	547	91	382	20	32	1,073	2,346
VAT	0	0	0	0	0	0	0	0	0	0	0	218	3,259	0	1,181	0	4,658	33,257	3,915	3,731	0	0	40,902	45,561
Duties and levies	211	2	103	1,175	344	176	460	331	1,378	130	1,275	2,026	896	0	344	36	8,887	22,713	434	0	0	0	23,147	32,034
Other taxes and subsidies	-265	-25	-10	-50	-53	-46	-1,454	-212	-10	-34	-443	-404	-409	0	-186	-6	-3,607	4,559	-577	-45	4	-556	3,384	-223
Value added – Labour	7,143	1,409	1,822	10,151	15,790	18,529	9,691	36,483	5,492	29,947	61,877	35,191	70,149	60,316	69,067	0	433,059	0	0	0	0	0	0	433,059
Value added – Gross profits etc	4,388	10,428	738	8,432	4,786	9,536	6,250	11,074	9,118	1,505	27,820	15,406	44,549	3,527	4,381	33,440	195,376	0	0	0	0	0	0	195,376
Total inputs	24,	17,	5,	52,	49,	73,	57,	125,	41,	84,	154,	98,	211,	63,	113,	53,	1,227,	441,	151,	110,	4,	194,	902,	2,130,
	208	704	493	108	493	649	114	992	719	404	987	540	047	843	957	269	526	325	691	558	582	786	942	468

Source: ONS, Input-Output Tables of the United Kingdom, 1995.

Table A3

Industry by Industry Import Use Matrix for the UK economy 1995

(in millions of fs)

I x I Domestic Use Matrix	*Agricul-ture*	*Extrac-tion*	*Other-Mining*	*Chemi-cals*	*Metals*	*Engine-ering*	*Food, drink*	*Other Manuf.*	*Utili-ties*	*Constru-ction*	*Distri-bution*	*Trans-port*	*Finan-cial*	*Pub-lic Ad-min*	*Educ. Health.*	*Hous-ing*	*Total interme diate*	*Consu-mers' expen-diture*	*GG FC*	*GDF CF*	*Stocks*	*Exports*	*Total final demand*	*Total*
Agriculture	462	0	0	2	0	0	2,342	394	0	0	546	9	0	0	0	0	3,755	1,471	0	0	0	46	1,517	5,272
Extraction	0	133	0	1,532	0	0	0	0	1,613	0	0	0	0	0	0	0	3,278	0	0	0	0	0	0	3,278
Other Mining	0	0	68	359	540	31	4	50	312	540	0	0	0	0	0	0	1,905	29	3	0	0	2,003	2,035	3,941
Chemicals	802	11	142	7,931	1,028	1,274	844	7,476	382	196	165	609	22	0	299	0	21,182	2,259	873	0	199	165	3,495	24,677
Metals	26	180	57	222	5,249	2,251	378	1,745	0	1,690	64	0	0	0	0	0	11,863	0	0	3	220	0	222	12,085
Engineering	45	161	61	13	286	11,980	22	2,177	855	770	46	791	78	0	119	0	17,403	6,220	3,123	22,859	148	164	32,513	49,916
Food, drink	291	0	0	275	0	0	4,641	36	0	0	936	53	0	0	0	0	6,232	8,812	348	0	18	19	9,198	15,430
Other Manuf.	0	0	79	300	478	369	565	18,399	12	1,900	1,206	641	60	0	357	0	24,365	24,075	2,893	5,312	979	98	33,357	57,722
Utilities	0	0	0	3	4	1	2	3	432	0	0	0	0	0	0	0	446	0	0	0	0	0	0	446
Construction	0	0	0	0	0	0	0	0	0	44	0	0	0	0	0	0	44	0	0	0	0	0	0	44
Distribution	0	0	0	0	0	0	0	0	0	0	0	0	0	0	0	0	0	3,518	0	0	0	0	3,518	3,518
Transport	0	504	11	0	5	0	4	0	0	2	530	2,720	375	0	60	0	4,211	4,036	342	0	0	0	4,378	8,590
Financial	4	1	8	0	20	50	22	0	4	10	35	33	3,369	0	886	19	4,463	0	1,328	0	0	0	1,328	5,791
Public Admin	0	0	0	0	0	0	0	0	0	0	0	0	0	0	0	0	0	0	416	0	0	0	416	416
Educ. Health,	0	0	0	1	3	8	2	55	2	0	3	38	45	0	1,238	0	1,395	1,035	669	0	0	0	1,704	3,099
Housing	0	0	0	0	0	0	0	0	0	0	0	0	0	0	0	0	0	566	0	0	0	0	566	566
Total Imports	1,630	989	425	10,639	7,613	15,965	8,827	30,336	3,612	5,151	3,532	4,895	3,949	0	2,960	19	100,541	52,021	9,995	28,174	1,563	2,494	94,248	194,789

Source: Siddorn (1999) using ONS, Input-Output Tables of the United Kingdom, 1995.

Figure A1
Utility functions nesting in the UK model

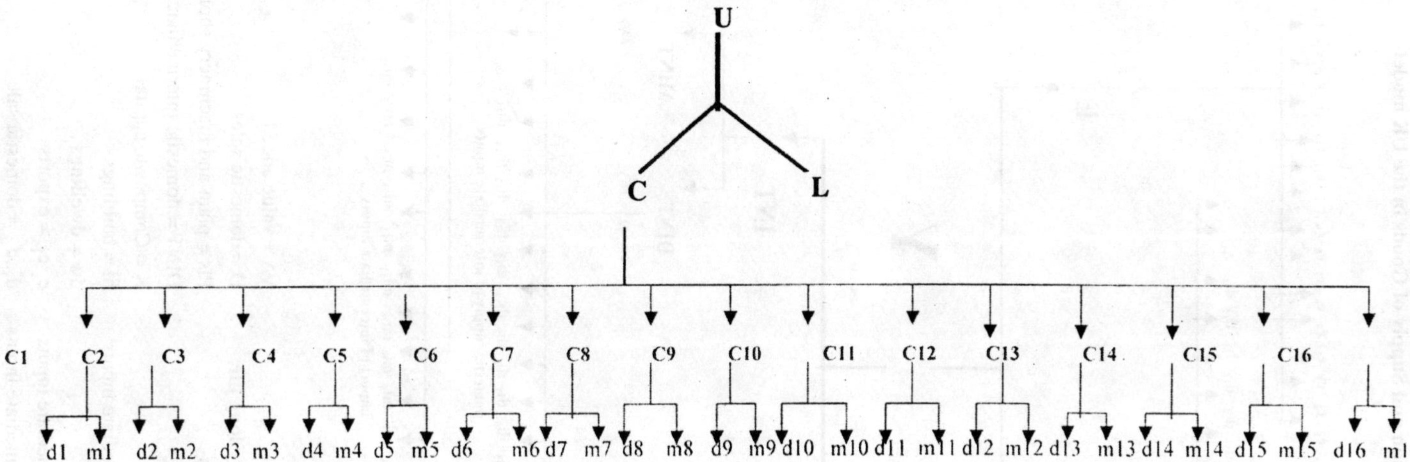

Legend: U = Utility
C = Composite consumption good
L = Leisure
C1..C16 = Sectoral composite
d1..d16 = domestic supply for consumption
m1..m16 = imports for consumption

Figure A2
Structure in Production and Supply of Goods in the UK model

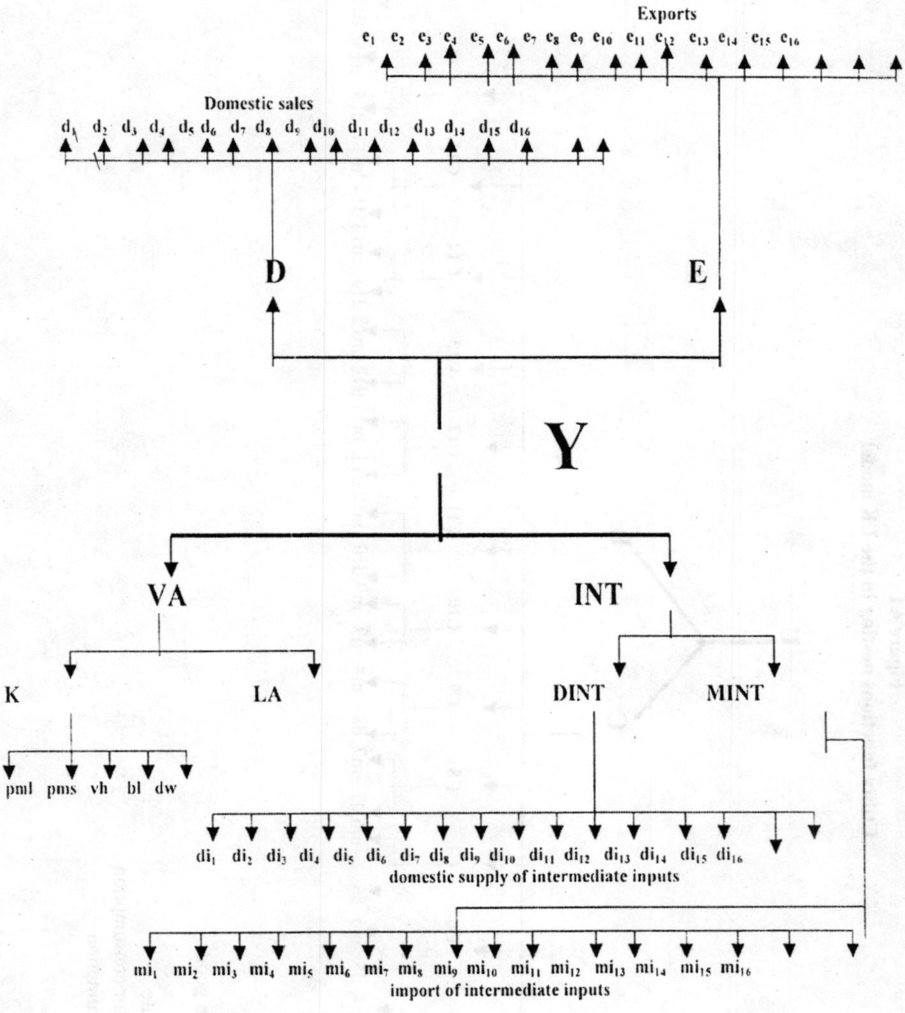

Legend:

Y = output	VA = value added
Pml = plant and machinery long life	D = domestic sales
INT = intermediate inputs	Pls = plant and machinery short life
E = Exports	DINT = domestic intermediate inputs
vh = vehicles	K = Composite capital
MINT = Import of intermediate inputs	bl = buildings
LA = labour	dw = dwellings
$di_1..di_{16}$ = domestic intermediate inputs	$e_{1..}e_{16}$ = exports
$mi_{1..}\ mi_{16}$ = imported intermediate inputs	$d_1..d_{16}$ = domestic sale

PART - III

GLOBAL GENERAL EQUILIBRIUM TRADE MODEL FROM UK PERSPECTIVE

8

WELFARE GAINS TO UK FROM A GLOBAL FREE TRADE[3]

BACKGROUND

The global trade model presented in this paper explicitly models the UK economy, which is linked to other economies through trade and investment. The UK is part of the wider world economy, where key regions and countries (such as the UK, the EU, USA, Japan, China, Canada-Australia and New Zealand, Africa and other Rest of the World economies) are modelled as separate but linked economies with substantial detail in the representation of production and consumption. Considering a little over 55 percent of the UK's international trade occurs within the EU (see Table 3 below), it is important to illustrate a model which explains the trading relations between the UK and the EU and then between the EU and other trading blocks in the global economy. Here the UK economy is modelled alongside other ten different regions in the global economy.

The GTAP4 data (Hertel (1997)) allows us to build a global model reating the UK as a separate region trading with the EU, the USA, other trading blocks and the rest of the world. This global model enables policy makers to examine the specific impacts of international trade policies pursued at the European level, at a level of various other trading blocks, and at a global level. It also allows for trade policy evaluation on a bilateral as well as on a multilateral basis.

The sectoral structure of the global model presented here is the same as for the open economy model presented in a parallel paper (Bhattarai (2000)). The only difference between these two models is that the global model consists of interdependent economies grouped in one of eleven trading blocks, namely, UK, Europe, USA, Canada-Australia and New Zealand, Japan, China, Asia, Central Europe, Former Soviet Union, oil exporting countries, and the rest of the world, whereas only the UK economy was considered in the small open economy model. Each of the trading regions in the global model has 15 production sectors, a representative household and a government, which collects taxes from factor incomes and domestically supplied or imported consumption goods and imports and redistributes this revenue through transfers. Goods are differentiated by

3. An earlier version of this chapter has been published in the European Research Studies Journal IV (3-4), 55-72, 2001.

location of production, i.e. the same good produced in the UK is different from that produced in the USA.

As discussed for the small open economy model, a representative household in each trading region maximises utility subject to a budget constraint, and producers maximise profit subject to technology constraints even in the global model. Households buy both domestic and foreign goods and producers produce for both domestic and foreign markets. Both the utility of households and production by firms are described by standard constant elasticity of substitution (CES) functions; they are concave, monotonic, homothetic and continuous. Equilibrium conditions in each region and at a global level imply that markets for goods and capital clear, competitive firms earn zero economic profit, the income and expenditure of a representative household are equal and trade is balanced. Labour market clears at the regional level in the model. The multi-regional equilibrium model is closed by allowing quantities, prices and income to adjust at global as well as regional level until all excess demand functions are zero and equilibrium conditions are satisfied. We use these market clearing conditions for simplicity and also following the tradition set in Arrow-Debreu general equilibrium models (1954).

The capital inflow or outflow, if any, is allowed to clear any imbalance in international trade. Capital will flow into and out of regions until real returns are equalised across among all regions and sectors. The governments in each region are allowed to carry out their own fiscal and trade policies in order to enhance bilateral and multi-lateral trades. This model explicitly specifies interdependency in global markets, and is an appropriate framework for the evaluation of the effects of various trade and investment promoting measures being pursued by members of the trading community grouped in various trading blocks (See Hartel (1997), Perroni and Whalley (1996), Whalley and Hamilton (1996), Will and Winters (1996) for more discussion on global trade).

THE STRUCTURE OF THE GLOBAL TRADE MODEL

Each region in the global model is endowed with primary factors of production, land, capital, skilled and unskilled labour and natural resources. These non-labour primary factors are either used in producing goods in the same region where these factors are located, or are permitted to move to other regions in response to factor price changes. Labour is mobile across sectors only at the regional level. Production in sector i in region r uses intermediate inputs, and labour and capital from its own region as well as from all other regions.

$$Y_{i,r} = \min\left(\frac{INT_{j,i,r}}{a_{i,j,r}}, \left(K_{i,r}^{\beta_r} L_{i,r}^{1-\beta_r}\right)\right) \tag{1}$$

Here $Y_{i,r}$ is output of the sector i good in region r, $K_{i,r}$ is capital services originating in region r but used to produce the good i in region r, $L_{i,r}$ are labour services originating in region r but used to produce the sector i good in region r, $INT_{j,i,r}$ is an intermediate input originating in sector j of region r but used to produce the sector i good in region r, $a_{j,i,r}$ is a coefficient that gives the amount of the sector j intermediate input of region r used to produce the sector i good in region r, and b_r is the share of capital income in sectoral output in region r. Land and natural resources are additional inputs in case of agriculture sector.

The output of good a particular region i, $Y_{i,r}$, is either supplied to the home region or exported to other regions. This is represented by a constant elasticity of transformation (CET) function:

$$Y_{i,r} = \left(\delta_{i,r} YD_{i,r}^{\eta_{i,r}} + (1-\delta_{i,r}) X_{i,r}^{\eta_{i,r}}\right)^{\frac{1}{\eta_{i,r}}} \tag{2}$$

where $YD_{i,r}$ is domestic sales of output of good i in region r, $X_{i,r}$ is exports of good i from a region r, $d_{i,r}$ is the share of domestic sales of gross output, $Y_{i,r}$, and $h_{i,r}$ is the elasticity of transformation between domestic sales and exports.

Total domestic supplies comes from domestic sales plus imports. Thus absorption of region, r is given by a CES aggregation of imports and domestic supplies

$$A_{i,r} = \left(\mu_{i,r} YD_{i,r}^{\sigma_{i,r}} + (1-\mu_{i,r}) M_{i,r}^{\sigma_{i,r}}\right)^{\frac{1}{\sigma_{i,r}}} \tag{3}$$

Here $A_{i,r}$, is Armington aggregation of domestic and imported goods, $\sigma_{i,r}$ is the elasticity of substitution between imported and domestic products, $m_{i,r}$ is the share of domestic production in the Armington product and $M_{i,r}$ is imports of good i to region r. The value of imports of goods into regions r are equal to value of exports of other region to that region plus transportation costs from the origin to the destination.

Transportation services are proportional to trade:

$$T_{i,r,s} = \tau_{i,r,s} M_{i,r,s} \tag{4}$$

Here $T_{i,r,s}$ transportation services, $\tau_{i,r,s}$ is transport cost per unit of traded goods $M_{i,r,s}$ amount of good i traded from region r to s.

These international transport services are produced using transport goods supplied by each region.

For simplicity, we represent the utility function in each region by a CES or Cobb-Douglas aggregation of final consumption goods supplied by each region. The total domestic demand is divided between household and government consumption. Household consumption is a Cobb-Douglas aggregation of sector i commodities over all r regions.

$$U_r = \prod_{i,r} C_{i,r}^{\gamma} \tag{5}$$

Households receive factor income from all regions and transfers from their own government. The income of the representative household in each region is

$$I_r = \sum_i w_r L_{i,r} + \sum_r r_r K_{i,r} + RV_r \tag{7}$$

where I_r is income, w_r is wage rate and r_r is the interest rate and RV_r is the transfer received by a representative household in region r.

Government consumption demand reflects a Cobb-Douglas aggregate of all sector i commodities over all r regions.

$$G_r = \prod_{i,r} GD_{i,r}^{\gamma} \tag{8}$$

$GD_{i,r}^{g}$ is the government consumption of good i in region r. The government in each region collects taxes from factors income, intermediate inputs, imports and domestic sales.

$$G_r = \tau_k r_r \overline{K}_r + \tau_w w_r \overline{L}_r + \tau_{i,r} P_{i,r} Y_{i,r} + \tau_{N,r} P_{i,r} INT_{j,i,r} \tag{9}$$

Here G_r is total government revenue, $i_{k,r}$ is tax rate on capital income, $i_{w,rr}$ is tax rate on labour income, $i_{w,r}$ is tax rate in wage income, $i_{i,r}$ is tax rate on intermediate income, $i_{N,r}$ is tax rate on intermediate input.

A competitive equilibrium in this global economy is such that, given the prices of commodities and factors, demands for good and supply of goods are equal at the regional as well as the global level; factor market clears for each region and at the world level; consumers of each region maximise their utility subject to their income constraints; and the government budget and trade are balanced for each region.

In this global model a competitive equilibrium is given by prices of consumption goods, $P_{i,r}$; the prices of capital; a wage rate for labour, w_r levels of gross output, $Y_{i,r}$; capital use, $K_{i,r}$; sectoral use of labour, $L_{i,r}$; and income I_r such that, given these prices and quantities:

(i) households in each region maximise utility subject to their budget constraints;

(ii) firms in each region maximise profits subject to technology constraints;

(iii) labour market clears at the regional level;

(iv) the markets for goods and services and capital clear in each region and at the global level;

(v) the government budget constraint is satisfied for each region, and

(vi) the trade-balance condition is satisfied at the regional and global level.

More specifically, the market clearing condition for the goods market is given by

$$Y_{i,r} = \sum_{r} C_{i,r} + \sum_{rr,j} a_{i,j,r} INT_{i,j,r} \tag{10}$$

The global capital market clearing condition implies

$$\sum_{r} \bar{K}_r = \sum_{i,r} K_{r,ri} \tag{11}$$

and labour market clears at the regional level:

$$LS_r = \sum_{i} LS_{i,r} \tag{12}$$

When there are *r.n* different markets in the economy, relative prices that clear *rn*-1 markets also clear the *rn*th market as well (Walras (1954)).

Model parameters are calibrated using information on international trade flows and production and consumption flows in each region reported in the GTAP4 data base for 1995 compiled by the Global Trade Analysis Project (GTAP) of the Purdue University in Indiana in the USA. This data base contains data on 50 sector input-output tables and national account series for 45 different regions in the global economy. We follow the GTAP in GAMS approach used by Rutherford (1998, GAMS/MPSGE (1997)) in formulating the model equations. MPSGE (Mathematical Programme for System of General Equilibrium Models) is a programming language with interface to the GAMS (General Algebraic Modelling System) software[1].

DATA SOURCES AND CALIBRATION PROCEDURE IN THE GLOBAL TRADE MODEL

The global trade model presented above requires data on output, imports, exports, consumption and government demand, employment of labour and capital, intermediate inputs, and base year prices for each sector and region included in the model. It also needs tax and tariff rates for each product. We use GTAP4.

The GTAP4 data has been prepared by the Center for Global Trade Analysis, Purdue University (McDougall (1998), Hertel (1997)) for implementing a global trade model from the UK's perspective. This data base consists of 50 GTAP sectors and 45 GTAP regions. We use the GTAP aggregation software of Rutherford (1998)[2] that maps data from the GLOBAL.HAR file of the GTAP4 data base to a GAMS readable data file, GTAP4001.gms. We also take basic features of Rutherford's (1998) regional model structure for implementing the global model.

Table 1
Regional Concordance of Global Trade Model with GTAP Regions

Model Regions	GTAP Regions
UK	United Kingdom, Channel Islands, Isle of Man
Europe (EUR)	Germany, Denmark, Sweden, FinlandRest of EU (Austria, Belgium, France, French Guiana, Gibraltar, Greece, Gaudeloupe, Holy See, Ireland, Italy, Luxembourg, Martinique, Monaco, Netherlands, Portugal, Reunion, Saint Pierre and Miquelon, San Marino, Spain) European Free Trade Area (Iceland, Leichtenstein, Norway, Svalbard and Jan Mayen Is, Switzerland)
Central and Eastern Europe (CEA)	Bulgaria, Czech Republic, Hungary, Poland, Romania, Slovakia, Slovenia
USA	American Samoa, Gaum, Northern Mariana Islands, Puerto Rico, United States Vergin Islands, United States of America
Japan (JPN)	Japan
ACN	Canada, Australia, New Zealand
China	China, Hong Kong, Taiwan
Asia	Malaysia, Singapore, Thailand, Philippines, Vietnam, Korea, India, Sri Lanka, Rest of Asia (Bangladesh, Bhutan, Maldives, Nepal, Pakistan)
Former Soviet Union	Armenia, Azerbaijan, Belarus, Estonia, Georgia, Kazakhstan, Kyrgyzstan, Latvia, Lithuania, Moldova, Russian Federation, Tajikistan, Turkmenistan, Ukraine, Uzbekistan
Major Oil Producers (MOP)	Mexico, Indonesia, Rest of the Middle East (Bahrain, Iran, Iraq, Isreal, Jordan, Kuwait, Lebanon, Oman, Qatar, Saudi Arabia, Syria, United Arab Emirates, Yemen, Yemen Democratic) Rest of North Africa (Algeria, Egypt, Libya, Tunisia)
Rest of the World	Morocco, Western Sahara, Turkey, Venezuela, Columbia, Argentina, Brazil, Chile, Uruguay Rest of Andean Pact (Bolivia, Ecuador, Peru)Central America and Caribbean (Anguila, Antigua and Barbuda, Aruba, Bahamas, Barbados, Belize, British Virgin Islands, Cayman Islands, Costa Rica, Cuba, Dominica, Dominican Republic, El Salvador, Grenada, Guatemala, Haiti, Honduras, Jamaica, Montserrat, Netherlands Antilles, Nicaragua, Panama, Saint Christopher and Nevis, Saint Lucia, Saint Vincent and the Grenadines, Trinidad and Tobago, Turks and Caicos Isl.)Rest of the South America (Guyana, Paraguay, Surinam)South Africa Customs Union (Botswana, Lesotho, Namibia, South Africa, Swaziland)Rest of South Africa (Angola, Malawi, Mauritius, Mozambique, Tanzania, Zambia, Zimbabwe)Rest of sub-Saharan Africa (Benin, Burkina Faso, Burundi, Cameroon, Cape Verde, Central African Republic, Chad, Comoros, Congo, Cote d'Ivoire, Djibouti, Equatorial Guinea, Eritrea, Ethiopia, Gabon, Gambia, Ghana, Guinea, Guinea-Bissau, Kenya, Liberia, Madagascar, Mali, Mauritania, Mayotte, Niger, Nigeria, Rwanda, Sao Tome and Principe, Senegal, Seychelles, Sierra Leone, Somalia, Sudan, Togo, Uganda, Zaire)Rest of the World (Afghanistan, Albania, Andorra, Bermuda, Bosnia and Herzegovina, British Indian Ocean Territories, Brunei, Cambodia, Christmas Island, Cocos (Keeling) Islands, Cook Islands, Croatia, Cyprus, Falkland Islands, Faroe Islands, Fiji, French Polynesia, Greenland, Johnston Island Kiribati, Laos, Macao, Macedonia- former Yugoslav Republic, Malta, Marshall Islands, Federation State of Micronesia, Mongolia, Myanmar, Nauru, New Caledonia, Niue, North Korea, Pacific Islands, Palau, Papua New Guinea, Pitcairn Islands, Saint Helena, Solomon Islands, Tokelau, Tonga, Tuvalu, Vanuatu, Wake Island, Wallis and Futura Isl., Western Samoa, Yugoslavia)

We have aggregated the 45 GTAP regions into eleven model regions to represent the global market. These regions are UK, Europe, USA, Canada-Australia and New Zealand, Japan, China, Asia, Central Europe, Former Soviet Union, Major Oil Producers, and the Rest of the World. Countries included in each region are listed in Table 1. This regional classification is made according to the degree of UK's trade linkage in the global economy. Europe region, which consists of continental Europe, Scandinavian economies and other economies in the European Free Trade Area, is the major trading partner of the UK. We treat the UK as a separate region to make this model to represent the UK perspective in the global trade issues. GTAP4 data set provides us the benchmark data set required for the calibration of the regional model.

Table 2
Concordance of sectors in the Global Trade Model with GTAP sectors

Model Sectors	Commodities
Agriculture	Paddy, wheat, grains, non-grain crops, wool, other livestock, fisheries, forestry
Extraction	Coal, Oil, Gas
Other mining	Other minerals, non-metallic mineral products,
Food and drink	Processed rice, meat products, milk products, other food products, beverage and tobacco,
Other Manufacturing	textiles, wearing apparel, leather etc., lumber, pulp, paper, etc.
Chemical	chemicals, rubbers, and plastic
Metal	primary ferrous metals
Engineering	fabricated metal products, machinery and equipment
Utilities	Electricity, gas and water
Construction	Construction
Trade and Transportation	Whole sale and retail trade, hotel and restaurants, railways highways subways transport, freight transport, inland and ocean transport, air transport, storage and warehousing, communication
Private services	Monetary and financial services, real estates, accounting, data processing, engineering and technical services, advertising, radio and TV broadcasting, amusement, repairs domestic services, photographic, personal services, business services
Public services	Public administration, health,education, veterinary, welfare and religious organisations, social and related community services, International and extra-territorial bodies
Housing	Dwellings

We aggregate 50 GTAP sectors into fifteen global model sectors in Table 2 consistent with the classification in the small open economy model of the UK. These sectors are agriculture, extraction, other mining, food and drink, other manufacturing, chemical, metal, engineering, utilities, construction, trade and transportation, private services, public services and housing. These sectors closely relate to the classification desired by the Inland Revenue (Bhattarai (1999b)).

GTAP draws on various national and international data sources in creating the global trade database. It takes macroeconomic data on GDP and GDP components and population data from the Bank Economics and Social Database

(BESD) of the International Economics Department of the World Bank. A large number of the input output tables were inherited from the Australian Industry Commission's SALTER project (McDougall (1998)). Input output tables for 12 European countries relies on the Central Statistical Offices of those countries, and Eurostat data base which contains input-output tables harmonised in accordance with the European System of Integrated National Accounts (ESA). The UK data in GTAP is drawn from the input-output table 1995 and business and agricultural statistics published by the Central Statistics Office in London.

Bilateral trade flows are based on the United Nation's COMTRADE database. GTAP's information on tariffs was drawn from UNCTAD's Trade Control Measures Database (TCMD) as well as from the WTO Integrated Database (IDB). TCMD is the most comprehensive database covering tariffs that is currently available. It covers all OECD member countries as well as a number of non-OECD countries. At the global level there are still many countries/regions which do not have input-output tables or other data sources. GTAP applies the proper regional average technique to fill data gaps in the absence of original data sources[3].

Table 3
Bilateral trade composition for 1995 (in percentage terms)
(From a region in the column to various regions in the row)

	USA	*JPN*	*EUR*	*UK*	*ACN*	*CHN*	*FSU*	*CEA*	*ASI*	*MOP*	ROW
USA	0.0	27.1	7.4	13.9	55.7	22.7	8.0	4.2	19.5	28.9	19.3
JPN	11.8	0.0	2.6	3.1	12.4	15.3	9.4	4.9	15.2	16.5	7.8
EUR	22.6	14.1	58.0	55.0	7.2	16.8	40.6	53.2	14.0	20.5	30.6
UK	5.6	3.3	8.1	0.0	2.4	2.9	3.2	3.3	3.6	2.3	4.9
CAN	19.2	4.7	1.5	3.6	3.5	3.9	0.9	0.8	3.2	2.3	2.0
CHN	7.0	16.9	2.6	2.8	4.9	16.7	6.9	3.4	12.6	3.6	3.7
FSU	1.0	0.5	1.8	1.4	0.3	0.7	4.3	5.2	1.2	0.4	1.5
CEA	0.7	0.4	3.2	1.8	0.2	0.7	9.1	11.5	0.7	0.6	1.3
ASI	11.6	23.4	4.1	6.2	7.1	11.8	7.7	2.7	18.2	13.8	6.3
MOP	11.2	5.3	4.8	5.9	3.0	3.6	2.7	3.8	5.9	4.2	4.8
ROW	9.3	4.3	5.8	6.3	3.2	5.0	7.2	7.0	5.9	6.7	17.8
Total%	100	100	100	100	100	100	100	100	100	100	100

Source: GTAP data base version 4, 1998; see Table 1 for countries included in above regions.

Flows of trade from one region to other regions reflect the comparative advantage enjoyed by an exporting region over importing regions and the production and consumption structure among trading regions. We present the structure of total volume of trade from one region to another in percentage terms in Table 3. Figures in this table show the volume of trade, in percentage terms, originating from a region on each row to other regions listed in columns. About 55 per cent of the UK's trade occurs with the European countries, followed by another 14 per cent with the United States, and remaining 30 per cent spread among other regions. The intra-regional trade is very important in the European region where 58 per cent of trade takes place among the member countries themselves. Also note that European region is the most integrated with other regions as reflected its dominance of trade link with other region in the global economy. Asian and the United States follow Europe in the degree of trade integration.

Volume of the global trade in value terms are given in Table 4 below, which shows that the value of global trade stood around 5.6 trillion us dollars in 1995. This implies the openness of the global economy of around 22 per cent in that year. Row sum in this table shows imports and column sum represents exports. In this benchmark data USA, UK, CEA, Asia and ROW regions had deficit in trade accounts whereas Japan, Europe, ACN, China, FSU and MOP regions had surpluses in the trade account. Intra-regional trade in Europe alone had more than 2 trillion US dollars.

Also note that the North-North trade volume is significantly larger than South-South or South-North trade. Rich countries in the North trade more among themselves than with developing countries in the South. The reason for the small share of South-South trade compared to North-South trade lies in predominance of imports of machinery and high-tech manufactured products by developing countries from the rich industrialised countries in the North. The South regions supplies the North only with cheap primary products. For instance, the USA, Japan and European regions were the major trading partners for the Asia and ROW regions. Asia exported more to Europe, USA and the ACN regions than to the ROW or to Asia itself.

Table 4
Volume of bilateral trade for 1995 (in billion of US $s)
(Imports across the column and exports down the column)

	USA	*JPN*	*EUR*	*UK*	*ACN*	*CHN*	*FSU*	*CEA*	*ASI*	*MOP*	*ROW*	*Global*
USA		131	159	38	154	94	7	4	96	93	64	842
JPN	83		56	9	34	64	8	5	75	53	26	413
EUR	159	68	1244	152	20	69	36	57	69	66	101	2041
UK	39	16	174		7	12	3	4	17	7	16	295
ACN	134	23	33	10	10	16	1	1	16	7	7	257
CHN	49	82	56	8	14	69	6	4	62	12	12	373
FSU	7	3	39	4	1	3	4	6	6	1	5	78
CEA	5	2	69	5	1	3	8	12	3	2	4	114
ASI	82	113	87	17	20	49	7	3	89	45	21	533
MOP	78	26	103	16	8	15	2	4	29	14	16	312
ROW	65	21	125	17	9	21	6	7	29	22	59	381
Global	701	484	2145	276	277	414	89	107	491	322	331	5638

Source: GTAP data base version 4, 1998; see Table 1 for countries included in above regions.

The North-North and South-North trade pattern observed above in aggregate trade flows is also apparent at the sectoral level. We present sectoral trade flows in the appendix A1. For instance, 71 per cent of total exports of European agricultural products are sold within the European region, while intra-regional trade for agricultural products is 19 per cent in the Asia region. About 54 per cent of CEA's agricultural products are exported to Europe compared to 15 per cent intra-regional flows.

The composition of regional exports and imports are presented in Table 5 and Table 6. The row sum in Table 5 and 6 show the percentage of sectoral imports and exports in the global economy. Most global trade occurs in the engineering sector which comprised about 34 per cent of global trade followed by other manufacturing, chemical and transport sectors. This global trade trend applied also to the UK economy. The columns for individual regions in table 5 and 6 represent sectoral share of imports and exports in each regions respectively. These regional aggregations on trade flows by goods and regions are obtained by aggregating the bilateral flows of GTAP countries. More details on their derivation and various consistency conditions checked for reconciling bilateral trade flows are presented in detail in McDougall (Chapter 3 and 16).

Subsidies and tariff rates are the most important means of protecting domestic industries against foreign competition. The GTAP reports trade-weighted average tariff rates from tariff lines of 6000 to 10,000 commodities. GTAP concordance procedure converts non-tariff distortions into tariff equivalent distortions for the effective tariff rates for year 1995 for the agriculture, energy, manufacturing and transport sectors as presented in Tables A2 and A3 in the appendix. Similarly producer subsidy equivalent (PSE) calculations are made to arrive at effective export taxes/ subsidies for all eight model sectors in Table A3.

Table 5
Sectoral composition of imports by regions for 1995
(gross of tariff in billions of US $s)

	USA	*JPN*	*EUR*	*UK*	*ACN*	*CHN*	*FSU*	*CEA*	*ASI*	*MOP*	*ROW*	*Global (%)*
AGR	2.1	9.5	4.1	3.4	2.1	4.3	4.1	3.6	4.2	5.0	4.0	4.2
EXT	7.0	11.6	4.7	3.1	3.1	2.3	1.9	7.1	7.4	2.4	6.7	5.5
OMI	2.1	3.3	2.8	2.6	1.9	2.3	1.7	3.0	2.8	3.5	2.1	2.6
FDR	2.7	9.7	6.1	6.4	3.4	3.7	15.6	5.4	4.1	6.8	6.9	5.6
OMA	16.6	13.9	14.6	15.0	12.6	17.5	14.6	16.8	8.9	13.1	13.5	14.3
CHM	7.0	5.7	12.0	10.3	10.3	11.7	7.9	13.2	10.1	10.2	12.6	10.3
MTL	5.4	4.6	7.5	5.9	5.6	7.7	3.2	7.2	8.0	7.6	5.8	6.7
ENG	42.8	17.7	30.3	35.6	44.2	38.2	25.3	30.8	41.5	34.8	33.7	34.2
UTI	0.1	0.0	0.2	0.2	0.0	0.1	0.2	0.1	0.0	0.0	0.1	0.1
CON	0.0	0.0	0.3	0.0	0.0	0.8	0.8	1.5	0.0	1.5	0.8	0.4
TRN	6.5	18.2	7.8	10.5	10.4	5.6	12.0	8.6	5.7	9.2	9.8	8.6
PRS	5.9	5.7	6.8	2.5	5.6	3.5	11.5	2.7	4.5	3.7	2.3	5.3
PUB	1.8	0.1	2.7	4.3	0.8	2.2	1.1	0.1	2.7	2.2	1.7	2.1
Global (%)	100	100	100	100	100	100	100	100	100	100	100	100
Total Value	904.2	474.3	2167	316.1	275.9	438.1	85.05	126.3	627.2	347.7	448	6210

Source: GTAP data base version 4, 1998; see Table 1 for countries included in above regions.

Figures in the rows in appendix A2 show tariff rates applied to commodities imported by one region from other regions. Agriculture is the most heavily protected sector among all sectors, followed by manufacturing. For instance, agricultural products from the USA were subject to a 165 per cent tariff rate in

Japan, 59 per cent in Asia, and 34 per cent in China. Food and drink sector also is subject to heavy import duties among regions.

Table 6
Sectoral composition of exports by regions for 1995
(gross of export taxes in billions of US $s)

	USA	*JPN*	*EUR*	*UK*	*ACN*	*CHN*	*FSU*	*CEA*	*ASI*	*MOP*	*ROW*	*Global (%)*
AGR	5.1	0.1	2.5	1.3	6.5	1.4	6.1	2.9	3.0	3.3	12.2	3.4
EXT	1.2	0.4	2.1	4.5	8.8	0.9	19.2	3.3	2.8	39.0	12.2	5.3
OMI	1.2	1.2	2.4	2.8	3.6	1.7	2.8	3.0	2.3	3.4	6.5	2.5
FDR	3.8	0.4	6.6	5.1	6.8	2.5	3.8	4.7	5.9	2.1	9.9	5.2
OMA	8.1	6.1	12.5	8.5	14.7	31.8	6.8	19.5	17.8	11.1	13.9	13.2
CHM	9.6	7.5	12.6	12.1	6.8	7.2	11.0	9.3	6.3	6.5	6.1	9.7
MTL	3.6	5.8	7.1	5.8	7.8	6.0	25.4	13.2	3.6	3.7	8.9	6.5
ENG	39.7	63.7	32.9	33.7	28.7	30.1	3.8	19.2	37.2	16.3	7.4	33.2
UTI	0.0	0.0	0.3	0.0	0.3	0.1	0.3	0.3	0.0	0.0	0.0	0.1
CON	0.0	0.0	0.6	0.0	0.0	0.2	0.4	4.9	0.3	0.0	0.0	0.4
TRN	14.0	11.4	11.2	15.7	10.9	14.3	13.1	15.9	15.8	10.6	16.1	12.8
PRS	10.4	3.4	6.9	6.1	3.2	2.7	5.3	2.7	3.0	1.4	3.1	5.5
PUB	3.3	0.1	2.3	4.3	1.8	0.9	1.9	1.2	2.1	2.4	3.7	2.3
Global (%)	100	100	100	100	100	100	100	100	100	100	100	100
Total Value	736	503	2224	291	287	422	93	112	518	334	349	5867

Source: GTAP data base version 4, 1998; see Table 1 for countries included in above regions.

From the export taxes (and subsidies) presented in A3, we again see that agriculture receives the highest rate of export subsidy or is subject to the highest export tax rates among these various sectors. Export subsidies on agricultural products from Europe range from 1 per cent for exports to the UK to 37 per cent for exports to major oil producers. Export subsidy rates were relatively lower in the UK.

WELFARE IMPACTS OF TARIFF REFORMS IN THE GLOBAL TRADE MODEL

We use our global trade model to compute welfare gains to various trading blocks from global free trade for a selected values of substitution elasticity among factors of production (σ), elasticity of substitution between domestic supplies and imports in consumption (σ^m) and transformation elasticity for domestic supplies and exports (σ^d). The results are displayed in Table 7.

The elimination of tariffs increases global trade. Almost all trading communities/regions in the model experience welfare gains from liberalisation. Altogether these gains add up to around 323 billion dollars for 1995. Gains from free trade at the global level is about 1.3 per cent of the global GDP. This gain varies significantly from one region to another. Japan gains most by global free trade, which was equivalent to 91 billions dollars (1.93 per cent of the Japanese GDP). Europe gains 67 billion but only 0.95 per cent of European GDP. UK gains 11 billion dollars. As a per cent of GDP China gains the most, about 3.8 per cent of GDP. This is not surprising considering the export-led growth process that is undergoing in the Chinese economy over last two decades. Major oil producing countries lose form global trade liberalisation. These welfare figures are very similar to those found in the literature (Whalley (1985), Harrison-Rutherford-Tarr (1997), Ghosh and Whalley (1997)).

Table 7

Hicksian EV by region from global trade liberalization (Benchmark 1995, for σ = 0.75; $σ^d$ =4; and $σ^m$ =6)

Trading blocks or model regions	*Welfare gains from free trade as a per cent of GDP*	*Welfare gains in billion of 1995 US dollars*
USA	0.825	54
Japan (JPN)	1.932	91
Europe (EUR)	0.949	67
UK	1.054	11
Australia-Canada and New Zealand (CAN)	3.035	27
China (CHN)	3.723	34
Former Soviet Union (FSU)	0.149	1
Central and East Asia (CEA)	2.143	6
Asia (ASI)	1.849	20
OPEC Countries (MOP)	-0.346	-3
Rest of the World (ROW)	0.886	17
Global gain	1.300	323

See Table 1 for countries included in above regions.

Table 8

Sensitivity of welfare to production and substitution elasticities in the global model (Welfare gain % of GDP from moving to the global free trade in 1995)

	Substitution elasticities in production, imports and exports									
Scenario	*S1*	*S2*	*S3*	*S4*	*S5*	*S6*	*S7*	*S8*	*S9*	*S10*
s	0.75	1.00	1.25	1.50	1.75	2.00	2.25	2.50	2.75	3.00
s^d	2.25	2.50	2.75	3.00	3.25	3.50	3.75	4.00	4.25	4.50
s^m	3.25	3.50	3.75	4.00	4.25	4.50	4.75	5.00	5.25	5.50

	Welfare gains % of GDP from moving to the global free trade in 1995 (by region and by the range of values for the elasticity of substituion)									
Scenario	*S1*	*S2*	*S3*	*S4*	*S5*	*S6*	*S7*	*S8*	*S9*	*S10*
USA	0.693	0.715	0.737	0.759	0.781	0.801	0.82	0.838	0.855	0.871
JPN	1.049	1.179	1.317	1.464	1.618	1.779	1.944	2.112	2.282	2.451
EUR	0.824	0.854	0.883	0.911	0.939	0.967	0.996	1.026	1.059	1.093
UK	0.623	0.679	0.737	0.796	0.858	0.921	0.987	1.054	1.124	1.195
CAN	1.437	1.54	1.647	1.761	1.887	2.031	2.195	2.388	2.616	2.894
CHN	1.598	1.786	1.978	2.176	2.382	2.598	2.826	3.069	3.329	3.611
FSU	-0.595	-0.548	-0.498	-0.445	-0.388	-0.328	-0.263	-0.191	-0.111	-0.021
CEA	1.177	1.208	1.247	1.295	1.351	1.421	1.506	1.614	1.748	1.917
ASI	0.164	0.344	0.526	0.712	0.9	1.093	1.291	1.494	1.704	1.92
MOP	-1.331	-1.209	-1.09	-0.973	-0.853	-0.729	-0.599	-0.463	-0.322	-0.175
ROW	-0.088	-0.008	0.075	0.161	0.251	0.344	0.442	0.544	0.652	0.765

See Table 1 for countries included in above regions.

We conduct a sensitivity analysis around key elasticity parameters in the production and utility functions to check the robustness of the results presented above. We make a ten step grid of three key substitution elasticities: substitution elasticity among factors of production (σ), elasticity of substitution between domestic supplies and imports in consumption (σ^m) and transformation elasticity for domestic supplies and exports (σ^d). Welfare gains as a per centage of base year GDP from global free trade are presented in Table 8, which shows welfare improving with increase in the elasticity in all regions except in Former Soviet Union (FSU) Region and major oil producers (MOP) region. Every regions may experience gains from global trade in case of higher values of elasticities.

Welfare gains from the liberalisation of the global trade as reported above are based on the comparative static analysis. It can only describe steady state situation, it requires a fully specified dynamic global trade model to track transitional dynamics of policy reform which we have left as an exercise for the next phase of research. It is more encouraging that some work has been already started to this direction (Diao and Somwaru (2002)).

CONCLUSION

This paper reports on a 11 region 15 sector global trade model including the UK as a separate region. The UK is modelled as part of the wider world economy, where key regions and countries (such as the UK, the EU, USA, Japan, China, Canada-Australia and New Zealand, Africa and other Rest of the World economies) are treated as separate but linked economies with substantial detail in the representation of production and consumption. A representative household in each trading region maximises utility subject to a budget constraint, and producers maximise profit subject to technology constraints even in the global model. Households buy both domestic and foreign goods and producers produce for both domestic and foreign markets. Equilibrium conditions in each region and at the global level imply that markets for goods, labour and capital clear, competitive firms earn zero economic profit, the income and expenditure of a representative household are equal, trade is balanced and all government revenue is transferred to a household. Model parameters are calibrated using information on international trade flows and production and consumption flows in each region reported in the GTAP4 data base for 1995.

This model shows that an elimination of tariffs increases the volume of trade at the global level. Almost all trading communities/regions in our model experience gains from liberalization. Gains from free trade at the global level are 1.3 per cent of the global GDP, roughly about 325 billion dollars in 1995. In absolute Japan gains most followed by Europe and the USA. UK gains about 11 billion dollars (6.8 billion pounds) from the multilateral trade liberalisation compared to 3 billion dollar gains from a unilateral liberalisation. The gain occurring to the China is much larger as a share of GDP than any other region included in the model. OPEC economies loose from global scale liberalization. This is mainly due to the removal of subsidies on their imports from developed countries and a significant amount of distortions prevalent in the domestic markets of these economies.

We carry out sensitivity analysis around major model parameters in the production and consumption functions of the model. The results show that the welfare gains reported are sensitive to values of substitution elasticities. It is possible to show much larger gains with higher values of production and trade elasticities. In general, model results show significant welfare gains to the UK economy from the removal of tariffs on international trade.

NOTES

1. The program used is presented in appendix II can be made available upon request for people with access to the GTAP4 data set.
2. See the detailed description of GTAP aggregation in http://nash.colorado.edu/tomruth/gtapingams.html/gtapgams.html.
3. See Whalley and Yeung (1983), Whalley (1985) more discussion on microconsistent data set required for regional trade models

REFERENCES

Arrow, J. K. and G. Debreu (1954), "Existence of an Equilibrium for a Competitive Economy" *Econometrica* 22, 265-90.

Bhagwati, J. N. and T. N. Srinivasan (1992), *Lectures on International Trade,* MIT Press.

Bhattarai, K. (2000), Efficiency and Factor Reallocation Effects and Marginal Excess Burden of Taxes in the UK Economy, Hull Economics Research Paper no. 7.

Bhattarai, K. and J. Whalley (1998), "The Division and Size of Gains from Liberalizaiton of Service Networks" NBER Working Paper No. 6712, August

Bhattarai, K., M. Ghosh and J. Whalley (1999), "On Some Properties of Widely Used Trade Closure", Economics Letters, Vol.62, no.1, pp. 13-21.

Bhattarai, K., M. Ghosh and J. Whalley (1998), "More on Trade Closure", in G. Ranis and K. Raut ed. *Trade, Growth and Development: Essays in Honor of Professor T.N. Srinivasan,* Yale University.

Brook, A. D. Kendrick, A. Meeraus (1992), *GAMS: Users's Guide,* release 2.25, TheScientific Press, San Fransisco, CA. Gerard, D. (1954), *The Theory of Value,* Yale University Press, New Haven.

Diao X. and Somwaru A. (2000), "An Inquiry on General Equilibrium Effects of MERCOSUR – An Intertemporal World Model", Journal of Policy Modelling 22(5):557-588.

Dirkse, S. P. and M. C. Ferris (1995), "CCPLIB: A collection of nonlinear mixed complementarity problems" *Optimization Methods and Software*. 5:319-345.

Dervis, Kamal, De Melo Jaime, and Robinson, Sherman, 1985: *General Equilibrium Models for Development Policy,* CUP, New York.

Ghosh, M. and J. Whalley (1997), "The Value of MFN Treatment", *manuscript*, University of Western Ontario.

Goulder, L. H., and L.H. Summers (1989), "Tax Policy, Asset Prices, and Growth: A General Equilibrium Analysis", *Journal of Public Economics*, 38:265-296, North Holland.

Harrison, G.W., T.F. Rutherford and D.G. Tarr (1997), "Quantifying the Uruaguy Round", *Economic Journal* vol. 107 no. 444, September, pp.1405-1430,

Hertel, T. (1997), *Global Trade Analysis: Modeling and Applications* Cambridge University Press.

Mansur, A. and J. Whalley (1984), "Numerical Specification of Applied General Equilibrium Models: Estimation, Calibration and Data", in Scarf Herbert E and Shoven John B. (1984) *Applied General Equilibrium Analysis,* CUP.

Will, M. and L. A.Winters (1996), The Uruguay Round and the developing countries, Cambridge University Press.

McDougall, R. A. (1998), *Global Trade Assistance and Protection:* The GTAP Data Base 4, Global Trade Analysis Project, Purdue University.

Office for National Statistics (ONS (1995)), *Input Output:* Tables for the United Kingdom, HMSO, London.

———(1992), *United Kingdom National Accounts:* Sources and Methods.

———(1996), *United Kingdom National Accounts:* the Blue Book.

Office for National Statistics (ONS (1995)), *Family Spending:* A report on the 1994-95 Expenditure Survey.

Perroni, C. and J. Whalley (1996), "How Severe is Global Retaliation Risk under Increasing Regionalism", *AER Papers and Proceedings*, vol.86. no. 2, May.

Piggott J. and J.Whalley (1985), *UK Tax Polcy and Applied General Equilibrium Analysis,* Cambridge University Press.

Rutherford, T. F. (1997), *The GAMS/ MPSGE and GAMS/MILES user notes,* GAMS Development Corporation, Washington D.C.

Rutherford, T. F. (1997), "GTAPinGAMS:The Dataset and Static Models", mimio, University of Colorado, Boulder *(http://nash.Colorado.edu/tomruth/gtapingams/html/gtapgams.html)*

Rutherford, T. F. and D. Tarr (1998), "Regional Trading Arrangements for Chile: Do The Results Differ with a Dynamic Model?", a paper presented at the Dynamic CGE Conference in Denmark.

St-Hilaire, F. and J. Whalley (1983), A microconsistent equilibrium data set for Canada for use in tax policy analysis, *Review Income and Wealth*, 29, 175-204.

Shoven, J. B. and J.Whalley (1992), *Applying General Equilibrium,* CUP, 1992.

Shoven, J. B. and J.Whalley (1984), "Applied General-Equilibrium Models of Taxation and International Trade: An Introduction and Survey", *Journal of Economic Literature*, vol. XXII, Sept,1984, pp.1007-1051.

Taylor, L. (Ed.) (1990), *Socially Relevant Policy Analysis: Structuralist Computable General Equilibrium Models for the Developing World,* MIT Press, Cambridge 1990.

Walras, L. *Elements of Pure Economics,* Allen and Unwin, London, 1954.

Whalley, J. and C. Hamilton (1996), *The Trading System: After the Uruguay Round,* Institute for International Economics, Washington D.C.

Whalley, J. (1985), *Trade Liberalization Among Major World Trading Areas,* MIT Press, Cambridge.

Whalley J. and B. Yeung (1983), "External Sector `Closing' Rules in Applied General Equilibrium Models" *Journal of International Economics*, 15, pp. 1-16.

APPENDIX A

Appendix 1

Trade distortions by import tariff and export taxes: illustration in case of agriculture sector

GTAP Import Tariff Rates by Sector for the year 1995 (in %)

	Agriculture										
	USA	*JPN*	*EUR*	*UK*	*CAN*	*CHN*	*FSU*	*CEA*	*ASI*	*MOP*	ROW
USA		165	13	17		34	-3	6	59	4	3
JPN	1		6	20	4	4	8	6	13	7	10
EUR	5	27	3		1	1	5	10	46	9	15
UK	1	27	2			-2	-1	10	6	11	27
ACN	1	116	5	5	3	2	2	4	27	4	8
CHN	3	11	5	4	1	3	8	2	24	10	19
FSU	2	1	18	13		17	6	8	13	7	23
CEA	32	6	29	2	1	11	2	-3	30	6	11
ASI	3	9	10	15	2	8		4	21	11	10
MOP	1	6	11	11	1	10	3	6	22	13	20
ROW	8	20	8	22	2	7	1	8	31	14	8

Source: GTAP data base version 4, 1998 see; see Table 1 for countries included in above regions. Tariff rates for other sectors are available upon request.

Appendix 2

GTAP Export Tax Rates on Net Basis by Sectors for 1995 (in %)

	Agriculture										
	USA	*JPN*	*EUR*	*UK*	*CAN*	*CHN*	*FSU*	*CEA*	*ASI*	*MOP*	ROW
USA		1	1	1	1		-1				
JPN	-7		-3	-9	-6	-13	-38	-35	-15	-29	-37
EUR	-9	-8	-1	-1	-6	-15	-7	-8	-14	-25	-19
UK	-21	-37			-9	-18	-9	-9	-14	-29	-17
ACN	-1	-1	-2	-2	-2	-1	-2	-1	-3	-1	-3
CHN	7	6	11	11	11	6	11	10	-9	-21	9
FSU	1	5	2	1		1	2	2	1	1	1
CEA	-2	-7	-3	-4	-1	-9	11	5	-5	9	8
ASI	3	4	3	2	5	3	1	4	4	2	4
MOP	3	2	2	1		1	1	3	3		3
ROW	3	4	6	5	3	3	2	8	4	2	7

Source: GTAP data base version 4, 1998; see Table 1 for countries included in above regions. Export tax rates for other sectors are available upon request.

Table A1

Sectoral Composition of Exports 1995 (Total volume in million of US $s)

	Agriculture												
	USA	*JPN*	*EUR*	*UK*	*CAN*	*CHN*	*FSU*	*CEA*	*ASI*	*MOP*	*ROW*	*Total*	*Total vol.*
USA	0.00	0.23	0.14	0.02	0.07	0.14	0.01	0.00	0.16	0.14	0.09	1.00	37670
JPN	0.08	0.00	0.06	0.02	0.06	0.49	0.00	0.01	0.17	0.03	0.07	1.00	680
EUR	0.02	0.02	0.71	0.07	0.00	0.02	0.02	0.03	0.01	0.04	0.05	1.00	56582
UK	0.02	0.04	0.65	0.00	0.02	0.03	0.01	0.01	0.04	0.10	0.07	1.00	3849

Contd...

	Agriculture												
	USA	*JPN*	*EUR*	*UK*	*CAN*	*CHN*	*FSU*	*CEA*	*ASI*	*MOP*	*ROW*	*Total*	*Total vol.*
ACN	0.17	0.16	0.13	0.02	0.03	0.15	0.00	0.00	0.15	0.12	0.06	1.00	18616
CHN	0.05	0.31	0.12	0.01	0.02	0.16	0.02	0.00	0.18	0.09	0.05	1.00	6104
FSU	0.00	0.11	0.44	0.01	0.00	0.07	0.05	0.10	0.11	0.02	0.10	1.00	5690
CEA	0.01	0.02	0.54	0.02	0.00	0.00	0.08	0.15	0.01	0.07	0.10	1.00	3206
ASI	0.11	0.20	0.15	0.03	0.02	0.14	0.03	0.02	0.19	0.07	0.05	1.00	15498
MOP	0.37	0.06	0.22	0.03	0.02	0.03	0.01	0.01	0.09	0.10	0.05	1.00	11170
ROW	0.14	0.06	0.40	0.06	0.02	0.04	0.01	0.02	0.07	0.06	0.12	1.00	42390
Total	16486	21603	77418	8746	5199	15124	3163	3939	18318	15840	15619		201455

Source: GTAP4 data set 1995.

	Extraction												
	USA	*JPN*	*EUR*	*UK*	*CAN*	*CHN*	*FSU*	*CEA*	*ASI*	*MOP*	*ROW*	*Total*	*Total vol.*
USA	0.00	0.10	0.22	0.03	0.14	0.04	0.00	0.02	0.09	0.16	0.21	1.00	8617
JPN	0.10	0.00	0.03	0.00	0.01	0.31	0.01	0.00	0.49	0.02	0.02	1.00	2080
EUR	0.05	0.00	0.64	0.15	0.03	0.00	0.01	0.02	0.01	0.02	0.05	1.00	46802
UK	0.20	0.00	0.67	0.00	0.02	0.00	0.00	0.02	0.01	0.00	0.06	1.00	13038
ACN	0.58	0.21	0.04	0.01	0.01	0.03	0.00	0.00	0.07	0.01	0.03	1.00	25192
CHN	0.09	0.37	0.09	0.01	0.00	0.07	0.00	0.00	0.24	0.04	0.09	1.00	3947
FSU	0.01	0.01	0.58	0.01	0.00	0.01	0.03	0.27	0.01	0.00	0.06	1.00	17785
CEA	0.02	0.00	0.49	0.02	0.00	0.00	0.10	0.26	0.01	0.02	0.07	1.00	3706
ASI	0.01	0.29	0.01	0.00	0.04	0.14	0.00	0.00	0.42	0.06	0.02	1.00	14419.06
MOP	0.14	0.27	0.24	0.01	0.02	0.03	0.00	0.01	0.20	0.02	0.07	1.00	130105.7
ROW	0.45	0.05	0.18	0.01	0.03	0.02	0.00	0.01	0.06	0.01	0.18	1.00	42546
Total	57340	49457	93745	9180	7511	8686	1504	8259	40370	7217	24969	3E+05	201455

Source: GTAP4 data set 1995.

	Other Mining												
	USA	*JPN*	*EUR*	*UK*	*CAN*	*CHN*	*FSU*	*CEA*	*ASI*	*MOP*	*ROW*	*Total*	*Total vol.*
USA	0.00	0.12	0.24	0.05	0.26	0.08	0.01	0.00	0.09	0.08	0.07	1.00	8832
JPN	0.18	0.00	0.11	0.02	0.03	0.24	0.00	0.00	0.36	0.03	0.02	1.00	5776
EUR	0.09	0.03	0.52	0.07	0.01	0.03	0.01	0.03	0.08	0.10	0.04	1.00	53356
UK	0.08	0.02	0.59	0.00	0.02	0.03	0.00	0.01	0.14	0.08	0.03	1.00	8241
ACN	0.20	0.24	0.23	0.06	0.01	0.08	0.00	0.00	0.11	0.03	0.03	1.00	10318
CHN	0.20	0.19	0.14	0.02	0.04	0.13	0.01	0.01	0.15	0.05	0.06	1.00	7301
FSU	0.06	0.02	0.42	0.02	0.01	0.02	0.04	0.25	0.03	0.09	0.02	1.00	2566
CEA	0.05	0.01	0.58	0.03	0.01	0.01	0.04	0.14	0.01	0.05	0.07	1.00	3330
ASI	0.18	0.24	0.19	0.01	0.02	0.13	0.00	0.00	0.15	0.05	0.03	1.00	11922
MOP	0:28	0.19	0.18	0.03	0.02	0.06	0.01	0.00	0.13	0.07	0.04	1.00	11502
ROW	0.09	0.13	0.42	0.09	0.02	0.04	0.01	0.02	0.05	0.04	0.10	1.00	22588
Total	17547	14576	55263	7730	4746	8899	1231	3224	15139	9931	7446		145732

Source: GTAP4 data set 1995.

	Food and Drink												
	USA	*JPN*	*EUR*	*UK*	*CAN*	*CHN*	*FSU*	*CEA*	*ASI*	*MOP*	*ROW*	*Total*	*Total vol.*
USA	0.00	0.30	0.10	0.02	0.13	0.07	0.05	0.00	0.07	0.14	0.12	1.00	27898
JPN	0.16	0.00	0.04	0.01	0.04	0.35	0.00	0.00	0.31	0.05	0.04	1.00	1930.19
EUR	0.04	0.03	0.60	0.08	0.01	0.01	0.05	0.03	0.02	0.07	0.06	1.00	147794
UK	0.06	0.03	0.59	0.00	0.02	0.03	0.02	0.01	0.06	0.07	0.12	1.00	14879
ACN	0.30	0.22	0.06	0.05	0.06	0.07	0.01	0.00	0.13	0.05	0.05	1.00	19631
CHN	0.08	0.48	0.05	0.01	0.02	0.15	0.03	0.00	0.14	0.02	0.04	1.00	10695
FSU	0.06	0.38	0.20	0.02	0.02	0.05	0.13	0.05	0.07	0.01	0.02	1.00	3549
CEA	0.03	0.01	0.42	0.02	0.01	0.00	0.22	0.15	0.02	0.03	0.09	1.00	5333
ASI	0.10	0.20	0.10	0.02	0.03	0.13	0.01	0.00	0.19	0.13	0.09	1.00	30355
MOP	0.23	0.16	0.24	0.02	0.02	0.05	0.02	0.01	0.08	0.12	0.06	1.00	7050
ROW	0.10	0.08	0.30	0.06	0.02	0.06	0.04	0.02	0.05	0.08	0.20	1.00	34554
Total	22204	34098	1E+05	17152	8635	14371	12426	6019	18569	23847	26304		303668.2

Source: GTAP4 data set 1995.

	Other Manufacturing Sector												
	USA	*JPN*	*EUR*	*UK*	*CAN*	*CHN*	*FSU*	*CEA*	*ASI*	*MOP*	*ROW*	*Total*	*Total vol.*
USA	0.00	0.13	0.16	0.05	0.21	0.06	0.00	0.00	0.09	0.14	0.15	1.00	59243
JPN	0.22	0.00	0.14	0.03	0.03	0.29	0.00	0.00	0.21	0.05	0.02	1.00	30482
EUR	0.05	0.03	0.63	0.09	0.01	0.02	0.02	0.05	0.02	0.04	0.04	1.00	278152
UK	0.11	0.03	0.62	0.00	0.04	0.03	0.01	0.02	0.04	0.04	0.07	1.00	24679
ACN	0.62	0.11	0.08	0.02	0.04	0.04	0.00	0.00	0.04	0.02	0.03	1.00	42310
CHN	0.25	0.18	0.16	0.03	0.04	0.16	0.01	0.01	0.08	0.03	0.05	1.00	133871
FSU	0.06	0.03	0.50	0.07	0.00	0.02	0.08	0.05	0.05	0.06	0.08	1.00	6344
CEA	0.03	0.00	0.74	0.03	0.01	0.00	0.05	0.08	0.01	0.02	0.04	1.00	21932
ASI	0.22	0.11	0.17	0.05	0.03	0.14	0.01	0.01	0.12	0.08	0.06	1.00	92032
MOP	0.35	0.09	0.24	0.05	0.03	0.06	0.00	0.00	0.08	0.06	0.04	1.00	36931
ROW	0.28	0.03	0.35	0.06	0.02	0.03	0.02	0.02	0.03	0.03	0.13	1.00	48598
Total	1E+05	59764	3E+05	43488	30274	59045	10738	18725	45532	38391	46609		774574

Source: GTAP4 data set 1995.

	Chemical Sector												
	USA	*JPN*	*EUR*	*UK*	*CAN*	*CHN*	*FSU*	*CEA*	*ASI*	*MOP*	*ROW*	*Total*	*Total vol.*
USA	0.00	0.09	0.21	0.04	0.20	0.10	0.00	0.00	0.10	0.11	0.14	1.00	70893
JPN	0.18	0.00	0.14	0.02	0.03	0.25	0.00	0.00	0.27	0.06	0.03	1.00	37462
EUR	0.06	0.03	0.62	0.08	0.02	0.02	0.01	0.04	0.03	0.04	0.06	1.00	280501
UK	0.11	0.03	0.63	0.00	0.04	0.02	0.01	0.02	0.04	0.05	0.06	1.00	35266
ACN	0.64	0.04	0.05	0.01	0.07	0.05	0.00	0.00	0.07	0.03	0.03	1.00	19606
CHN	0.16	0.10	0.14	0.03	0.04	0.26	0.00	0.00	0.17	0.05	0.05	1.00	30401
FSU	0.10	0.02	0.38	0.04	0.01	0.17	0.05	0.06	0.08	0.02	0.09	1.00	10213
CEA	0.04	0.01	0.45	0.03	0.01	0.02	0.08	0.23	0.03	0.02	0.09	1.00	10513
ASI	0.10	0.08	0.10	0.03	0.03	0.23	0.01	0.00	0.25	0.08	0.08	1.00	32443
MOP	0.18	0.06	0.22	0.02	0.02	0.07	0.01	0.01	0.24	0.08	0.11	1.00	21757
ROW	0.19	0.02	0.21	0.02	0.02	0.02	0.01	0.01	0.05	0.05	0.39	1.00	21112
Total	56697	24545	2E+05	30220	25834	42833	6051	14644	49475	30985	47151		570167

Source: GTAP4 data set 1995.

	Metal												
	USA	*JPN*	*EUR*	*UK*	*CAN*	*CHN*	*FSU*	*CEA*	*ASI*	*MOP*	*ROW*	*Total*	*Total vol.*
USA	0.00	0.09	0.12	0.06	0.29	0.08	0.00	0.00	0.12	0.16	0.09	1.00	26483
JPN	0.15	0.00	0.05	0.02	0.03	0.29	0.00	0.00	0.35	0.07	0.03	1.00	29215
EUR	0.05	0.01	0.67	0.07	0.01	0.02	0.01	0.03	0.03	0.04	0.05	1.00	158195
UK	0.08	0.02	0.66	0.00	0.03	0.04	0.01	0.01	0.06	0.05	0.05	1.00	16802
ACN	0.56	0.09	0.06	0.02	0.03	0.07	0.00	0.00	0.11	0.03	0.02	1.00	22474
CHN	0.18	0.15	0.13	0.02	0.04	0.18	0.00	0.00	0.20	0.05	0.04	1.00	25225
FSU	0.14	0.09	0.37	0.03	0.01	0.09	0.01	0.02	0.14	0.04	0.06	1.00	23550
CEA	0.02	0.01	0.57	0.04	0.00	0.03	0.02	0.15	0.05	0.05	0.06	1.00	14837
ASI	0.11	0.18	0.06	0.02	0.03	0.18	0.00	0.00	0.27	0.08	0.05	1.00	18487
MOP	0.30	0.10	0.15	0.02	0.01	0.05	0.00	0.00	0.17	0.13	0.06	1.00	12234
ROW	0.17	0.13	0.21	0.03	0.02	0.08	0.00	0.00	0.13	0.07	0.17	1.00	30947
Total	45241	20764	2E+05	17718	14352	29223	2399	8191	41929	22797	22058		378449

Source: GTAP4 data set 1995.

	Engineering												
	USA	*JPN*	*EUR*	*UK*	*CAN*	*CHN*	*FSU*	*CEA*	*ASI*	*MOP*	*ROW*	*Total*	*Total vol.*
USA	0.00	0.10	0.19	0.06	0.23	0.07	0.01	0.00	0.14	0.12	0.09	1.00	292467
JPN	0.31	0.00	0.14	0.03	0.04	0.14	0.00	0.00	0.22	0.05	0.05	1.00	320151
EUR	0.08	0.02	0.54	0.09	0.02	0.04	0.02	0.04	0.05	0.05	0.07	1.00	731215
UK	0.12	0.03	0.58	0.00	0.03	0.03	0.01	0.02	0.06	0.05	0.06	1.00	97994
ACN	0.81	0.01	0.04	0.02	0.02	0.02	0.00	0.00	0.03	0.02	0.03	1.00	82369
CHN	0.27	0.10	0.19	0.03	0.04	0.15	0.00	0.01	0.14	0.03	0.05	1.00	127017
FSU	0.03	0.00	0.26	0.03	0.01	0.13	0.21	0.09	0.08	0.02	0.13	1.00	3522
CEA	0.03	0.00	0.62	0.04	0.01	0.01	0.06	0.12	0.02	0.03	0.06	1.00	21630
ASI	0.27	0.09	0.13	0.04	0.03	0.11	0.01	0.01	0.22	0.04	0.05	1.00	192815
MOP	0.72	0.01	0.07	0.03	0.04	0.02	0.00	0.00	0.05	0.02	0.04	1.00	54433
ROW	0.15	0.00	0.25	0.04	0.02	0.02	0.02	0.01	0.06	0.05	0.39	1.00	25889
Total	4E+05	80334	6E+05	1E+05	1E+05	1E+05	19562	34858	2E+05	1E+05	1E+05		1949502

Source: GTAP4 data set 1995.

	Private Services												
	USA	*JPN*	*EUR*	*UK*	*CAN*	*CHN*	*FSU*	*CEA*	*ASI*	*MOP*	*ROW*	*Total*	*Total vol.*
USA	0.00	0.11	0.48	0.04	0.12	0.04	0.02	0.01	0.09	0.05	0.03	1.00	76427
JPN	0.25	0.00	0.14	0.01	0.06	0.15	0.03	0.01	0.29	0.04	0.03	1.00	17042
EUR	0.20	0.03	0.56	0.02	0.02	0.03	0.03	0.01	0.05	0.03	0.02	1.00	152688
UK	0.37	0.04	0.28	0.00	0.04	0.04	0.05	0.02	0.09	0.05	0.03	1.00	17843
ACN	0.35	0.27	0.11	0.01	0.03	0.04	0.02	0.01	0.10	0.03	0.02	1.00	9108
CHN	0.16	0.18	0.27	0.02	0.03	0.08	0.04	0.01	0.13	0.04	0.04	1.00	11510
FSU	0.15	0.17	0.36	0.02	0.02	0.08	0.03	0.01	0.07	0.03	0.05	1.00	4870
CEA	0.15	0.16	0.35	0.02	0.02	0.08	0.03	0.01	0.08	0.03	0.06	1.00	2984
ASI	0.13	0.23	0.23	0.01	0.03	0.11	0.04	0.02	0.10	0.05	0.05	1.00	15611
MOP	0.26	0.15	0.29	0.02	0.02	0.06	0.03	0.01	0.07	0.03	0.07	1.00	4747
ROW	0.13	0.15	0.35	0.02	0.02	0.06	0.03	0.01	0.08	0.04	0.11	1.00	10740
Total	52955	25457	1E+05	7509	15405	14747	9434	3365	27376	12639	9875		323570

Source: GTAP4 data set 1995.

	Public Services												
	USA	*JPN*	*EUR*	*UK*	*CAN*	*CHN*	*FSU*	*CEA*	*ASI*	*MOP*	*ROW*	*Total*	*Total vol.*
USA	0.00	0.00	0.45	0.19	0.04	0.10	0.00	0.00	0.13	0.04	0.03	1.00	24653
JPN	0.14	0.00	0.14	0.02	0.02	0.30	0.01	0.00	0.29	0.05	0.03	1.00	499.1201
EUR	0.13	0.00	0.54	0.10	0.01	0.04	0.01	0.00	0.09	0.05	0.04	1.00	50655
UK	0.29	0.00	0.35	0.00	0.02	0.04	0.01	0.00	0.14	0.09	0.06	1.00	12568
ACN	0.19	0.02	0.14	0.06	0.02	0.16	0.01	0.00	0.29	0.06	0.04	1.00	5193
CHN	0.14	0.01	0.31	0.07	0.02	0.10	0.01	0.00	0.20	0.07	0.07	1.00	3963
FSU	0.12	0.01	0.36	0.10	0.01	0.08	0.01	0.00	0.12	0.06	0.12	1.00	1749
CEA	0.12	0.01	0.36	0.10	0.01	0.08	0.01	0.00	0.13	0.07	0.12	1.00	1319
ASI	0.11	0.01	0.29	0.09	0.02	0.14	0.01	0.00	0.16	0.09	0.08	1.00	10649
MOP	0.13	0.01	0.38	0.11	0.01	0.08	0.01	0.00	0.12	0.06	0.11	1.00	8058
ROW	0.11	0.01	0.38	0.10	0.01	0.07	0.01	0.00	0.13	0.07	0.11	1.00	12934
Total	16125	590	57172	13605	2192	9652	962	82.12	16545	7726	7589		132240.1

Source: GTAP4 data set 1995.

	Utilities								
	USA	*EUR*	*UK*	*CHN*	*FSU*	*CEA*	*ROW*	*Total*	*Total vol.*
EUR	0.00	0.86	0.11	0.00	0.00	0.01	0.02	1.00	5901
ACN	1.00	0.00	0.00	0.00	0.00	0.00	0.00	1.00	856
CHN	0.00	0.00	0.00	0.98	0.00	0.00	0.02	1.00	623
FSU	0.00	0.42	0.00	0.01	0.46	0.11	0.00	1.00	274
CEA	0.00	0.58	0.00	0.00	0.00	0.12	0.30	1.00	297
MOP	0.90	0.00	0.00	0.00	0.00	0.00	0.10	1.00	86
ROW	0.00	0.04	0.00	0.00	0.00	0.14	0.81	1.00	113
Total	933	5353	668	612	127	156	301		8150

Source: GTAP4 data set 1995.

	Construction									
	EUR	*ACN*	*CHN*	*FSU*	*CEA*	*ASI*	*MOP*	*ROW*	*Total*	*Total vol.*
EUR	0.42	0.00	0.06	0.03	0.09	0.01	0.24	0.15	1.00	13958
ACN		0.50					0.33	0.17	1.00	6
CHN	0.09	0.00	0.03	0.06	0.15	0.02	0.40	0.26	1.00	761
FSU	0.21	0.00	0.32	0.03	0.07	0.01	0.20	0.15	1.00	402
CEA	0.22	0.00	0.33	0.03	0.07	0.01	0.20	0.14	1.00	5521
ASI	0.13	0.00	0.35	0.03	0.08	0.01	0.24	0.15	1.00	1429
ROW	0.17		0.30	0.03	0.07	0.03	0.21	0.18	1.00	126
Total	7464	60	3301	696	1880	215	5199	3388		22203

Source: GTAP4 data set 1995.

Table A2

GTAP Import Tariff Rates by Sector for the year 1995 (in %)

Agriculture

	USA	*JPN*	*EUR*	*UK*	*ACN*	*CHN*	*FSU*	*CEA*	*ASI*	*MOP*	ROW
USA		165	13	17		34	-3	6	59	4	3
JPN	1		6	20	4	4	8	6	13	7	10
EUR	5	27	3		1	1	5	10	46	9	15
UK	1	27	2			-2	-1	10	6	11	27
ACN	1	116	5	5	3	2	2	4	27	4	8
CHN	3	11	5	4	1	3	8	2	24	10	19
FSU	2	1	18	13		17	6	8	13	7	23
CEA	32	6	29	2	1	11	2	-3	30	6	11
ASI	3	9	10	15	2	8		4	21	11	10
MOP	1	6	11	11	1	10	3	6	22	13	20
ROW	8	20	8	22	2	7	1	8	31	14	8

Extraction

	USA	*JPN*	*EUR*	*UK*	*ACN*	*CHN*	*FSU*	*CEA*	*ASI*	*MOP*	ROW
USA						6	8	1	6	2	8
JPN			1	1		5	5	4	8	8	2
EUR	2	3			8	7	5	6	28	12	18
UK	1	1			9	7	9	6	24	11	11
ACN						3			5	4	10
CHN	1	2	1		2	1	5	2	5	5	20
FSU	2				9	5	5	1	3	6	6
CEA	1		1		1	8	5	4		4	13
ASI	2	1	1	1		4	5	1	9	4	25
MOP	1	1			3	4	5	2	6	6	10
ROW	1	1		1	4	3	6	2	3	6	12

Other Mining

	USA	*JPN*	*EUR*	*UK*	*ACN*	*CHN*	*FSU*	*CEA*	*ASI*	*MOP*	ROW
USA			1	1		9	10	9	10	3	10
JPN	6		4	5	7	9	16	12	9	10	15
EUR	5	1			6	10	16	8	6	13	15
UK	4	3			8	5	18	8	4	12	14
ACN						1	31	3	4	7	7
CHN	6	1	4	5	6	12	11	3	17	13	20
FSU				1		3	13		11	16	7
CEA	8	1	4	4	3	1	18	6	14	20	22
ASI	1		1	2	5	3	22	8	12	10	34
MOP					2	3	43	2	6	11	10
ROW	1				1	3	9	2	5	10	8

Source: GTAP data base version 4, 1998.

	Food and Drink										
	USA	*JPN*	*EUR*	*UK*	*ACN*	*CHN*	*FSU*	*CEA*	*ASI*	*MOP*	ROW
USA		27	30	14	6	12	12	15	33	12	25
JPN	9		23	36	4	21	14	27	30	17	49
EUR	17	42	3	1	11	21	12	19	42	16	26
UK	9	42	1		7	32	18	31	41	45	30
ACN	7	62	64	81	3	18	4	22	46	14	23
CHN	4	33	21	20	5	12	14	14	34	16	98
FSU	3	21	22	17	2	24	10	16	17	11	31
CEA	15	45	31	29	17	13	16	22	70	20	42
ASI	4	16	17	13	2	9	9	6	39	15	45
MOP	2	10	8	14	3	7	9	15	35	21	42
ROW	13	17	25	54	4	15	9	16	35	10	11

	Other Manufacturing										
	USA	*JPN*	*EUR*	*UK*	*ACN*	*CHN*	*FSU*	*CEA*	*ASI*	*MOP*	ROW
USA		3	4	4	1	10	15	8	12	3	17
JPN	3		5	5	9	30	13	14	12	12	32
EUR	6	8			12	13	13	9	14	15	27
UK	3	6			7	8	17	10	17	14	28
ACN		1	2	2	1	8	16	8	10	7	13
CHN	8	5	8	8	12	31	18	9	19	18	27
FSU	8	4	5	3	14	14	14	8	20	14	12
CEA	8	3	5	6	16	26	17	7	32	14	45
ASI	9	3	7	7	14	24	18	5	20	14	29
MOP	3	1	7	7	11	13	18	10	13	16	22
ROW	9	2	7	7	13	13	18	8	11	14	15

	Chemical										
	USA	*JPN*	*EUR*	*UK*	*ACN*	*CHN*	*FSU*	*CEA*	*ASI*	*MOP*	ROW
USA		2	4	4	1	8	10	10	14	2	9
JPN	3		5	5	8	11	8	8	13	10	13
EUR	3	2			6	8	9	8	19	10	11
UK	3	2			6	8	11	7	21	8	12
ACN		1	3	3	1	8	13	11	12	10	16
CHN	9	3	6	6	13	23	16	8	17	11	15
FSU		2	5	5	4	6	10	11	26	12	8
CEA	1	1	3	3	5	7	11	7	17	12	17
ASI	5	1	4	4	9	12	13	10	22	11	15
MOP	3	2	3	3	7	9	13	10	29	10	9
ROW	1		4	4	2	8	13	8	35	10	9

Source: GTAP data base version 4, 1998.

	Metal										
	USA	*JPN*	*EUR*	*UK*	*ACN*	*CHN*	*FSU*	*CEA*	*ASI*	*MOP*	ROW
USA		1	3	3		9	23	7	10	3	10
JPN	4		4	4	7	11	18	6	13	11	14
EUR	4	1			8	10	12	6	22	14	12
UK	3	1			8	6	15	6	21	13	14
ACN			2	2	1	5	19	6	11	8	16
CHN	4	1	4	4	9	16	14	8	10	11	18
FSU	2		2	2	3	9	13	6	11	10	6
CEA	3	1	3	3	5	8	15	5	13	13	15
ASI	3	2	4	4	8	11	17	7	18	11	23
MOP		1	3	3	3	7	15	8	16	13	11
ROW	1		3	3	3	5	16	6	13	11	9

	Engineering										
	USA	*JPN*	*EUR*	*UK*	*ACN*	*CHN*	*FSU*	*CEA*	*ASI*	*MOP*	ROW
USA		1	3	3	1	9	11	11	9	4	12
JPN	3		5	5	8	15	13	13	12	12	18
EUR	3				7	20	8	8	15	13	14
UK	3	1			7	7	11	7	19	13	12
ACN		1	3	4	2	8	7	12	11	9	15
CHN	3		5	5	6	15	9	11	9	11	14
FSU	1		5	6	6	15	9	12	37	15	10
CEA			4	4	6	27	10	8	30	14	23
ASI	1		4	4	5	8	17	13	9	13	16
MOP			4	3	1	4	7	13	11	15	15
ROW			4	4	6	42	13	11	8	16	14

	Utility		
	CHN	*FSU*	ROW
EUR			1
CHN			1
FSU	1	4	
CEA			1

	Construction
	ROW
EUR	1
ACN	1
CHN	1
FSU	1
CEA	1
ASI	1
ROW	1

Source: GTAP data base version 4, 1998.

	Transport JPN	FSU
USA	3	2
JPN		2
EUR	3	2
UK	3	2
ACN	3	2
CHN	3	2
FSU	3	2
CEA	3	2
ASI	3	2
MOP	3	2
ROW	3	2

	JPN	*Private Services* *CHN*	*FSU*	*ROW*
USA	3	1	2	
JPN		1	2	1
EUR	3	3	2	1
UK	3	3	2	1
ACN	3	2	2	1
CHN	3	1	2	1
FSU	3	1	2	
CEA	3	1	2	
ASI	3	1	2	1
MOP	3	1	2	
ROW	3	1	2	

	Public Services *JPN*	FSU
USA	2	2
JPN		2
EUR	2	2
UK	2	2
ACN	2	2
CHN	2	1
FSU	2	1
CEA	2	1
ASI	2	2
MOP	2	1
ROW	2	1

Source: GTAP data base version 4, 1998.

Table A3

GTAP Export Tax Rates on Net Basis by Sectors for 1995 (in %)

Agriculture

	USA	*JPN*	*EUR*	*UK*	*ACN*	*CHN*	*FSU*	*CEA*	*ASI*	*MOP*	ROW
USA		1	1	1	1		-1				
JPN	-7		-3	-9	-6	-13	-38	-35	-15	-29	-37
EUR	-9	-8	-1	-1	-6	-15	-7	-8	-14	-25	-19
UK	-21	-37			-9	-18	-9	-9	-14	-29	-17
ACN	-1	-1	-2	-2	-2	-1	-2	-1	-3	-1	-3
CHN	7	6	11	11	11	6	11	10	-9	-21	9
FSU	1	5	2	1		1	2	2	1	1	1
CEA	-2	-7	-3	-4	-1	-9	11	5	-5	9	8
ASI	3	4	3	2	5	3	1	4	4	2	4
MOP	3	2	2	1		1	1	3	3		3
ROW	3	4	6	5	3	3	2	8	4	2	7

Extraction

	USA	*JPN*	*EUR*	*UK*	*ACN*	*CHN*	*FSU*	*CEA*	*ASI*	*MOP*	ROW
USA		8	8	9	1	8	7	9	7	2	7
EUR		1				1	1	1	1	1	1
ACN		1	1	1		2		1	3	2	3
CHN	28	32	-3	-4	3		7	-3	12	27	14
FSU	4	1	3	3	2	6	3	2	2	1	2
ASI	3	7	1	1	4	2		1	5	2	2
MOP			1	1				1			
ROW	8	2	8	6	4	8	3	4	6	7	2

Other Mining

	USA	*JPN*	*EUR*	*UK*	*ACN*	*CHN*	*FSU*	*CEA*	*ASI*	*MOP*	ROW
USA		4	4	4		3	4	2	3	1	2
EUR	1	1			1	1	1	1	1	1	1
CHN	-14	-14	-12	-12	-15	-9	-10	-6	-13	-17	-17
ASI	1	1	1	1	2	1	1		3	1	2
MOP	1	1	2	2	1	2	2	3	1		1
ROW	1			-4	1	-1	-2	-1	1	1	1

Source: GTAP data base version 4, 1998.

Food and Drinking

	USA	*JPN*	*EUR*	*UK*	*ACN*	*CHN*	*FSU*	*CEA*	*ASI*	*MOP*	ROW
USA		3	1	3	-1		-3	1		-3	-1
JPN	-2		-7	-7	-4	-3	-19	-32	-9	-40	-2
EUR	-11	-12	-2	-1	-13	-12	-19	-14	-26	-37	-26
UK	-3	-11			-2	-12	-4	-9	-5	-19	-16
ACN	-1	-2	-4	-2	-1	-3	-2	-3	-7	-11	-4
CHN	-3	1	4	-3	-3	1	30	13	-1	-10	-3
FSU	6	3	3	4	3	3	8	1	3	1	2
CEA	-10	-7	-12	-4	-4	-8	-5	-7	-16	-13	-10
ASI	-4	-5	-5	-4	-4	-16	-4	-18	-5	-15	-17
MOP	1	1	1				1	-1			1
ROW	2	1	4	-1	4	4	6	7	5	3	3

Other Manufacturing

	USA	JPN	EUR	UK	ACN	CHN	FSU	CEA	ASI	MOP	ROW
USA		1	1	1		1	1	1	1		1
EUR	1	1			1	1			1	1	1
CHN	10		9	9	8	-1	-3	1	1	2	2
FSU		1		1						1	
ASI	7	3	4	4	5	2	1	1	4	1	1
MOP			-1	-2				-1		-1	-1
ROW	1		1		1	-2					

Chemical

	USA	JPN	EUR	UK	ACN	CHN	FSU	CEA	ASI	MOP	ROW
USA		2	2	2		2	2	2	2		2
EUR										1	1
CHN	-8	-8	-9	-9	-8	-2	-12	-9	-6	-7	-8
ASI	4	2	3	3	2	1	1	1	2	1	1
MOP			1	1			1			1	
ROW	1	5	2	2	1	2	1	2	3	2	2

Metal

	USA	JPN	EUR	UK	ACN	CHN	FSU	CEA	ASI	MOP	ROW
USA		1	1	1		1	1	1	1		1
EUR										1	1
CHN	-4	-5	-6	-5	-4	-3	-9	-6	-4	-5	-7
ASI	1	1	2	2	2	1		2	3	2	1
MOP			1							1	
ROW								1	-1		

Source: GTAP data base version 4, 1998.

Engineering

	USA	JPN	EUR	UK	CAN	CHN	FSU	CEA	ASI	MOP	ROW
USA		1	1	1		1	1	1	1		1
EUR										1	1
ACN		1	1						1	1	1
CHN	-2	-3	-3	-2	-3	-1	-6	-2	-2	-3	-3
ASI	3	3	2	4	3	2		2	4	2	1
MOP						1				1	
ROW	2	2	1	1	2	1					

Utilities

	EUR	CHN	FSU	CEA	ROW
EUR					1
CHN		-9			-11
FSU	-1	-1	-1	-1	
CEA	-1			-1	-1
MOP					4

	Construction							
	EUR	*ACN*	*CHN*	*FSU*	*CEA*	*ASI*	*MOP*	ROW
EUR		1	1	1	1	1	1	1
ACN	475		475	475	475	475	475	475
FSU	1	1	1	1	1	1	1	1
ROW	1	1	1	1	1	1	1	1

	Transportation										
	USA	*JPN*	*EUR*	*UK*	*ACN*	*CHN*	*FSU*	*CEA*	*ASI*	*MOP*	ROW
USA		12	12	12	2	12	12	12	12	7	12
EUR	1	1			1	1	1	1	1	1	1
ASI	1	2	3	2	1	1	2	2	2	2	3
MOP	1	3	3	3	2	4	2	2	3	2	3
ROW	2	1	1	1	1	1	1	1	1	1	1

	Private Services										
	USA	*JPN*	*EUR*	*UK*	*CAN*	*CHN*	*FSU*	*CEA*	*ASI*	*MOP*	ROW
USA		8	8	8	1	8	8	8	8	3	8
EUR	1	1			1	1	1	1	1	1	1
FSU	2	2	2	2	2	2	2	2	2	2	2
ASI	1		1	1	1	1		1	1	1	2
ROW	1	2	1	1	1	1	1	1	1	1	1

	Public Services										
	USA	*JPN*	*EUR*	*UK*	*CAN*	*CHN*	*FSU*	*CEA*	*ASI*	*MOP*	ROW
ASI			1	1			1	1	1	1	1
MOP	8	8	8	8	8	8	7	6	8	8	8
ROW	1	1	1	1	1	1	1	1	1	1	1

Source: GTAP data base version 4, 1998.

APPENDIX B

$Title UK Dataset for the global trade model of the UK economy

SET I Sectors/

agr	Agriculture
ext	Extraction
omi	Other mining
fdr	Food and drink
oma	Other Manufacturing
chm	Chemical
MTL	Metals-related Industry(IRONSTL & NONFERR)
eng	Engineering
uti	Utility
con	Construction
trn	Transport distribution and communication
prs	Private services
pub	Public service
hsn	Housing
CGD	Savings good /;

SET R Aggregated Regions /

USA	United States
JPN	Japan
EUR	Europe
UK	United Kingdom
ACN	Australia Canada and New Zealand
CHN	China
FSU	Former Soviet Union
CEA	Central European Associates
ASI	Other Asia
MPC	Mexico Plus OPEC
ROW	Other Countries /;

SET F Factors of Production/

LND	Land,
SKL	Skilled labor,
LAB	Unskilled labor,
CAP	Capital,
RES	Natural resources/

$TITLE UK Dataset Mapping from GTAP version 4 to 10 regions and 10 goods
$SETGLOBAL source gtap 4001

Set Mapi Mapping for Sectors and Goods/

PDR.agr	Paddy Rice,
WHT.agr	Wheat,
GRO.agr	Grains (other than rice and wheat),
V_F.agr	Vegetable Fruit Nuts
OSD.agr	Oil seeds
C_B.agr	Sugar Cane and Beet
PFB.agr	Plant-based Fibers
OCR.agr	Crops n.e.c.
CTL.agr	Bovine Cattle - sheep and Goats - horse
OAP.agr	Animal Products n.e.c.
RMK.agr	Raw milk
WOL.agr	Wool,
FRS.agr	Forestry,
FSH.agr	Fishing,
COL.ext	Coal,
OIL.ext	Oil,
GAS.ext	Natural Gas,
OMN.omi	Other Minerals,
CMT.fdr	Bovine Cattle Meat Products
OMT.fdr	Meat Products n.e.c.
VOL.fdr	Vegetable Oils
MIL.fdr	Dairy Products
PCR.fdr	Processed Rice,
SGR.fdr	Sugar
OFD.fdr	Other Food Products
B_T.fdr	Beverages and Tobacco,
TEX.oma	Textiles,
WAP.oma	Wearing Apparel,
LEA.oma	Leather Goods,
LUM.oma	Lumber and Wood,

```
    PPP.oma        Pulp and Paper,
    P_C.ext        Petroleum and Coal Products,
    CRP.chm        Chemicals Rubber and Plastics,
    NMM.omi        Non-metallic Mineral Products,
    I_S.mtl        Primary Ferrous Metals,
    NFM.mtl        Non-ferrous Metals,
    FMP.mtl        Fabricated Metal Products,
    MVH.eng        Motor Vehicles
    OTN.eng        Other Transport Equipment
    ELE.eng        Electronic Equipment
    OME.eng        Machinery and Equipment,
    OMF.oma        Other Manufacturing Products,
    ELY.uti        Electricity
    GDT.uti        Gas Manufacturing and Distribution,
    WTR.uti        Water
    CNS.con        Construction,
    T_T.trn        Trade and Transport,
    OSP.prs        Other Services (Private),
    OSG.pub        Other Services (Public),
    DWE.hsn        Dwellings,
    CGD.cgd        Savings good/;
SET MAPR mapping GTAP regions /
    AUS.ACN        Australia
    NZL.ACN        New Zealand
    JPN.JPN        Japan
    KOR.ASI        Republic of Korea
    IDN.MPC        Indonesia
    MYS.ASI        Malaysia
    PHL.ASI        Philippines
    SGP.ASI        Singapore
    THA.ASI        Thailand
    VNM.ASI        Vietnam
    CHN.CHN        China
    HKG.CHN        Hong Kong
    TWN.CHN        Taiwan
    IND.ASI        India
    LKA.ASI        Sri Lanka
    RAS.ASI        Rest of South Asia
    CAN.ACN        Canada
    USA.USA        United States of America
    MEX.MPC        Mexico
    CAM.ROW        Central America and Caribbean
    VEN.ROW        Venezuela
    COL.ROW        Columbia
    RAP.ROW        Rest of Andean Pact
    ARG.ROW        Argentina
    BRA.ROW        Brazil
    CHL.ROW        Chile
    URY.ROW        Uruguay
    RSM.ROW        Rest of South America
    GBR.UK         United Kingdom
    DEU.EUR        Germany
    DNK.EUR        Denmark
```

```
SWE.EUR      Sweden
FIN.EUR      Finland
REU.EUR      Rest of EU,
EFT.EUR      European Free Trade Area
CEA.CEA      Central European Associates
FSU.FSU      Former Soviet Union
TUR.ROW      Turkey
RME.MPC      Rest of Middle East
MAR.ROW      Morocco
RNF.MPC      Rest of North Africa
SAF.ROW      South Africa
RSA.ROW      Rest of South Africa
RSS.ROW      Rest of Sub-Saharan Africa
ROW.ROW      Rest of World /;
```

$TITLE UKGTAPinGAMS — Global Economy Model from UK Perspective

```
*   Note:
*   This is the model implemented in MPSGE.
*   This implementation accomodates both constant-elasticity of
*   Transformation between production for domestic and export
*   Markets (eta < +INF), and perfect substitution between
*   Those markets (eta=+INF).
*   Variables, equations and GAMS keywords are in UPPER case.
*   Sets and parameters are in lower case.
*   Read the dataset using the standard routine:

$SETGLOBAL dataset uk
$IF EXIST dataset $INCLUDE dataset
$INCLUDE..\inclib\mrtdata
SCALAR
    eta      Elasticity of Transformation - domestic vs. exports    / +inf /,
    esubdm   Elasticity of Substitution - domestic vs. imports       / 4 /,
    esubmm   Elasticity of Substitution - imports                    / 8 /
    sigmap   Elasticity of Substitution - imports                    /0.75/;
    display  vim;

$ONTEXT
$MODEL:uk
```

$SECTORS:

```
    C(r)                 ! Private consumption
    G(r)                 ! Public provision
    Y(i,r)$vom(i,r)      ! Output
    M(i,r)$vim(i,r)      ! Import aggregation
    A(d,i,r)$va(d,i,r)   ! Armington aggregation of domestic and imports
    YT                   ! Transport
```

$COMMODITIES:

```
    C(r)                 ! Private consumption
    PC(r)                ! Private demand
    PG(r)                ! Public provision
```

```
PY(i,r)$(vom(i,r) and (1/eta=0))        ! Output price
PD(i,r)$(vdm(i,r) and 1/ETA)            ! Domestic price
PX(i,r)$(vxm(i,r) and 1/ETA)            ! Export price
PM(i,r)$vim(i,r)                        ! Import price
PA(d,i,r)$va(d,i,r)                     ! Armington composite price
PF(f,r)$evoa(f,r)                       ! Factor price
PT                                      ! Transport services
$CONSUMERS:
RA(r)                                   ! Representative agent
```

* **Production:**

```
$PROD:Y(i,r)$(vom(i,r)>0 and 1/eta>0) S:0 T:eta va:sigmap
O:PD(i,r)          Q:vdm(i,r) A:RA(r) T:ty(i,r)
O:PX(i,r)          Q:vxm(i,r) A:RA(r) T:ty(i,r)
I:PA("i",j,r)      Q:vafm(J,i,r) A:RA(r) T:ti(j,i,r)
I:PF(f,r)          Q:vfm(f,i,r) P:pf0(f,i,r) A:RA(r) T:tf(f,i,r) va:
$PROD:Y(i,r)$(vom(i,r)>0 and 1/eta=0) S:0 va:sigmap
O:PY(i,r)          Q:vom(i,r) A:RA(r) T:ty(i,r)
I:PA("i",j,r)      Q:vafm(J,i,r) A:RA(r) T:ti(j,i,r)
I:PF(f,r)          Q:vfm(f,i,r) P:pf0(f,i,r) A:RA(r) T:tf(f,i,r) va:
$REPORT:
V:FD(f,i,r) I:PF(f,r) PROD:Y(i,r)
V:YD(i,r)$(1/eta>0) O:PD(i,r) PROD:Y(i,r)
V:YX(i,r)$(1/eta>0) O:PX(i,r) PROD:Y(i,r)
```

* **Armington aggregation over domestic versus imports:**

```
$PROD:A(d,i,r)$va(d,i,r) S:esubdm
O:PA(d,i,r)            Q:va(d,i,r)
I:PD(i,r)$(1/eta>0)    Q:vd(d,i,r)
I:PY(i,r)$(1/eta=0)    Q:vd(d,i,r)
I:PM(i,r)              Q:vm(d,i,r)
```

* **Armington aggregation across imports from different countries:**

```
$PROD:M(i,r)$(vim(i,r)>0 and 1/eta>0) S:esubmm s.TL:0
O:PM(i,r)              Q:vim(i,r)
I:PX(i,s)              Q:vxmd(i,s,r) P:pmx0(i,s,r)
+          A:RA(S) T:TX(i,s,r) A:RA(r) T:(tm(i,s,r)*(1+tx(i,s,r))) s.TL:
I:PT#(s)               Q:vtwr(i,s,r) P:pmt0(i,s,r)s.TL:
+          A:RA(r) T:tm(i,s,r)
$PROD:M(i,r)$(vim(i,r)>0 and 1/eta=0) S:esubmm s.TL:0
O:PM(i,r)              Q:vim(i,r)
I:PY(i,s)              Q:vxmd(i,s,r) P:pmx0(i,s,r)
+          A:RA(S) T:TX(i,s,r) A:RA(r) T:(tm(i,s,r)*(1+tx(i,s,r))) s.TL:
I:PT#(s)               Q:vtwr(i,s,r) P:pmt0(i,s,r)s.TL:
+          A:RA(r) T:tm(i,s,r)
```

* **Demand for public output:**

```
O:PG(r)                Q:vg(r)
I:PA("g",i,r)          Q:vgm(i,r) P:pg0(i,r) A:RA(r) T:tg(i,r)
```

* **Private consumption:**

```
$PROD:C(r) S:1
O:PC(r)                Q:vp(r)
I:PA("c",i,r)          Q:vpm(i,r) P:pc0(i,r) A:RA(r) T:tp(i,r)
```

```
*      Inter-national transport services (Cobb-Douglas):

       $PROD:YT S:1
       O:PT                    Q:vt
       I:PX(i,r)$(1/eta>0)  Q:vst(i,r)
       I:PY(i,r)$(1/eta=0)  Q:vst(i,r)

*      Final demand over consumption, savings and government

*      Services (Cobb-Douglas):

       $DEMAND:RA(r)
       E:PF(f,r)                    Q:evoa(f,r)
       E:PC(num)                    Q:vb(r)
       E:PD(cgd,r)$(1/eta>0)  Q:-vi(r)
       E:PY(cgd,r)$(1/eta=0)  Q:-vi(r)
       E:PG(r)                      Q:-vg(r)
       D:PC(r)                      Q:vp(r)
       $OFFTEXT
       $SYSINCLUDE mpsgeset uk

*      Check the benchmark:

       uk.ITERLIM = 0;
       $INCLUDE uk.GEN
       SOLVE uk USING MCP;

*      Fix a numeraire to permit comparison with MCP:

       RA.FX(num) = RA.L(num);

*      Do a cleanup calculation:

       uk.ITERLIM = 8000;
       $INCLUDE uk.GEN
       SOLVE uk USING MCP;
       $TITLE   Test calculation with the MGEUK model (and MCP solver)
       $INCLUDE mrtuk
       alias (r,rr), (s,ss);
       PARAMETER
       TMRATE import tariff rate
       TXRATE export tax rate
       imports value of import of good i, from region s to region r
       exports value of exports of good i, from region s to region r
             impsum
             trdcomp
               trdsum
             glblgain


TMRATE(I,S,R) = ROUND(100 * TM(I,S,R));
OPTION TMRATE:0:1:1; DISPLAY TMRATE;

TXRATE(I,S,R) = ROUND(100 * TX(I,S,R));
OPTION TXRATE:0:1:1; DISPLAY TXRATE;
       imports(i,r,s)          = 10000*vxmd(i,r,s);
       impsum(s,r)             = sum(i, vxmd(i,r,s));
       trdcomp(s,r)            = impsum(s,r)/sum(ss,impsum(ss,r));
```

```
      trdsum(r)              = sum(s,trdcomp(s,r));
      option imports:0:1:1;
      display imports, impsum, vxm,vim, txrate, tmrate;
      display imports, vxm,vim, trdcomp,txrate, tmrate,trdsum,impsum, imports;
      esubdm=4;
      esubmm=6;
      ty(i,r) = 0;
      ti(j,i,r) = 0;
      tf(f,i,r) = 0;
      tx(i,s,r) = 0;
      tm(i,s,r) = 0;
      tg(i,r)= 0;
      tp(i,r) = 0;

$INCLUDE uk.GEN
SOLVE uk USING MCP;
      parameter     prices      Equilibrium consumer prices;
      prices(r,"mge")     = pc.l(r);
      Parameter welfare(r), wdoller;
      welfare(r)          = 100*(C.l(r) -1);
      display welfare;
      wdoller(r,"wefare") = welfare(r);
      wdoller(r,"gains")  = (welfare(r)*sum((f,i),10*(vfm(f,i,r))))/100;
      glblgain            = 100*sum(r,wdoller(r,"gains"))/sum(rr, sum((f,i),10*(vfm(f,i,rr))));
      display wdoller, sigmap, esubdm, esubmm, glblgain;
      $exit
      parameter ep,epp,welfarr,sigg,sigm,sigd;
      sigmap = 0.75;
      set steps /s1*s10/;
      ep(steps) = 0.25;
      epp(steps) =0.25;
      esubdm =2;
      esubmm =3;
      loop(steps,
      ep(steps+1)              = ep(steps);
      epp(steps+1)             = epp(steps);
      sigmap                   = sigmap +ep(steps);
      esubdm                   = esubdm +epp(steps);
      esubmm                   = esubmm +epp(steps);

$INCLUDE uk.GEN
SOLVE uk USING MCP;
      welfare(r)               = 100*(C.l(r) -1);
      welfarr(r,steps)         = welfare(r);
      sigg(steps)              = sigmap;
      sigm(steps)              = esubmm;
      sigd(steps)              = esubdm;
  );

display imports, vxm,vim, trdcomp,txrate, tmrate,trdsum,impsum, imports;
display       welfare,              welfarr,             sigg,          sigm,          sigd;
```

9

CONCLUSIONS AND RECOMMENDATIONS

We have covered specification, calibration, replication and application of a 16 sector general equilibrium tax policy model of the UK economy using a benchmark data set for the year 1995. To our knowledge this is the first attempt, after Piggott and Whalley (1985), to use a large scale GE tax policy model of the UK economy. This model uses data assembled by the Economics Unit of the Inland Revenue and evaluates within the model the efficiency effects of equal yield tax reform in the UK economy using the year 1995 as its benchmark. The sectoral classification as well as the tax structure built into the model reflects modelling needs of the Unit.

The basic ingredients of the model are the same as those found in standard GE models in an Arrow-Debreu economy (Arrow and Hahn (1971)). Households maximise utility subject to their budget constraints. Their consumption and labour supply decisions influence producers' decisions, aimed at maximising profits subject to technology constraints. This model fulfils all of the standard equilibrium conditions that are characteristics of an applied general equilibrium model in the tradition of the BFSW model (Ballard, Fullerton, Shoven and Whalley (1985)). These equilibrium conditions imply that the markets for goods, labour and capital clear, firms receive zero profits in equilibrium, income is equal to expenditure for households, investors and government, and the value of exports equals the value of imports. The government collects direct and indirect taxes from households on their income and consumption, production and capital income taxes from corporations, and import duties from traders. It spends revenue on public consumption or redistributes it as transfers to households.

The GE tax model considered here includes five types of taxes existing in the UK in 1995. These taxes were: 1) capital income tax applied to five different categories of capital assets – buildings, plant and machinery with short and long life, vehicles and dwellings; 2) labour income tax; 3) value added taxes on public and private consumption and investment; 4) production taxes on use of intermediate inputs, and 5) tariffs on imports. We calibrate the model to the 1995 data set and assure consistency by replicating the benchmark data as model solutions.

The tax rates used in the model reflect the tax law in the UK in 1995. Specifically, capital tax rates are differentiated by asset and sector; tax rates on income from building services and housing services are generally between 40 and 51 percent. Similarly, income from vehicles is taxed at between 15 and 21 percent, while tax rates on plant and machinery of short life range from 12 percent to 16 percent across sectors. Besides capital income taxes the model used a 38 percent marginal income tax rate on household labour income.

Compound VAT rates on intermediate and final demands are computed by taking account of the cascading of one indirect tax upon another. Tariffs and subsidies are imposed on net of tax prices of commodities. Then levies and duties are applied to the gross of tariffs and subsidies price basis. Finally the VAT rates apply gross of all other taxes. A substantial difference existed in compound VAT rates on public and private consumption and investment, and on intermediate inputs. Generally indirect taxes on consumption were higher than those rate on investment or government consumption. Tariff rates vary between 0 and 4 percent in the data set.

The model has mainly been used for equal yield capital income tax policy reforms after replicating the benchmark economy. For each tax policy scenario, we compute changes in total money metric aggregate welfare by summing up money metric equivalent variations for households, investors and government. The money metric equivalent variations measure the amount of money required to compensate agents in the new equilibrium rather than leaving them in the old equilibrium, with goods evaluated in terms of new prices. A positive equivalent variation represents a gain compared to the old equilibrium and a negative equivalent variation represents a loss. To be comprehensive, we take changes in total money metric equivalent variation in response to tax changes as a percentage of UK GDP for various alternative tax policies. Then we check the robustness of the model results by computing the sensitivity of the EV/GDP ratio to moving to a set of relevant substitution elasticities.

Firms use capital services and labour services in production. Following convention in general equilibrium analysis, before tax prices of these factors are set to unity in the benchmark. Producers, or users of these inputs, however, pay the gross of tax prices to the owners of these factors. In this model, capital income taxes are collected at the sectoral level. There are no labour income taxes at the firm level, but they are collected from households. Agents pay indirect taxes in the form of higher commodity prices.

While the major advantage of a large scale multi-sectoral general equilibrium tax model, such as the present one, lies in its ability to provide answers relating to the impact of tax changes at a very specific level of disaggregation, such as individual sectors or households, readers should be aware that there are some serious disadvantages of large scale general equilibrium models. These models are quite often labelled as black boxes which take a large set of inputs and generate a very long list of output. The very complex structure of the model often makes it difficult to trace out detailed consequences of certain experiments. The results should not be accepted unless they follow through economic logic and intuition. Besides this general limitation, the current model cannot provide answers to many other policy questions. A full employment general equilibrium model is not suitable for studying issues relating to unemployment in labour markets and capacity under-utilization in capital markets. Similarly, inflationary issues are outside the scope of such models where money is neutral. This model assumes perfect competition in both commodity and factor markets where each economic agent has perfect information about the world and, being very small compared to the size of the market, cannot have any impact on market activities. Thus market power of monopolistic firms is ruled out in this model. At the moment the model includes only one representative household, along with the government and investors in the economy. It is not capable of providing answers to intra-household income distribution. This is a static model and is useful for comparative static analysis between two equilibria. It cannot provide any answer to the transition process from one equilibrium to another. Each of these limitations needs to be borne in mind while interpreting the model results. Plenty of scope remains for extending the model in the future.

Despite these limitations, this model is still useful and provides a consistent framework for looking at the impacts of tax policy changes. Consumption and production decisions are optimal given the resource constraints in the UK economy. We use the model mainly to assess the impacts of five different taxes included in the model: capital income taxes, value added taxes, production taxes, household income taxes and tariffs.

The major findings from our study using the model are the following:

1. We show welfare gains when capital income tax rates existing in 1995 are replaced by a uniform yield preserving 26.5 percent rate across sectors and assets for a low labour supply elasticity. In the central case, we find an improvement in efficiency by 0.035 percent of UK GDP (£217 million). The improvement is 0.022 percent of UK GDP (£140 million) in the case of unit elasticity specification.
2. The efficiency gain from replacing existing taxes by uniform capital income tax rates in the no equal yield capital tax reform was about 0.281 percent of UK GDP for the low labour supply elasticity case and 0.283 for high elasticity case. The size of the government is allowed change in these cases and government consumption also is one component of aggregate welfare.
3. The computed efficiency gain from replacing capital income tax by yield preserving lump-sum taxes was 0.3 percent of UK GDP.
4. We check the robustness of the welfare results by means of sensitivity analysis. The welfare impacts of moving to a yield preserving capital income tax from a set of existing taxes is positive and almost linear in the values of substitution elasticities among assets (s_k) for a particular set of elasticities of substitution between labour and capital assets (s_v). Similarly,

it is also linear in the values of substitution elasticities between capital and labour for any particular value of substitution elasticities among capital assets. When both $s_{\blacktriangledown}$ and s_k are very high, each assuming a value of 5.0, the welfare impact of switching to a uniform tax rate was about 0.11 percent of UK GDP, which amounts to nearly £729 million.

5. Changes in the relative prices of capital assets across sectors compared to the benchmark following the yield preserving capital income tax reform leads to a reallocation of capital assets across sectors. The equal yield uniform tax reform reduces the inter-sectoral and inter-asset differences in the relative user cost of capital in the counterfactual scenarios. Consequently we see a significant reallocation, up to a 20 percent increase or up to a 10 percent reduction in the use of capital assets in a low labour supply elasticity case and changes in the use of labour resources of between –5 and 5 percent across sectors, occurring in comparison to the base year. Both capital and labour reallocation effects are robust with respect to labour supply elasticity.
6. When capital inputs become relatively cheaper than labour input, producers tend to substitute capital for labour; this happens in the agriculture, finance, public administration, and education sectors. Capital becomes relatively expensive in manufacturing sectors, after a uniform tax reform. We see substitution of capital by labour in these sectors. The effect of the reduction in capital assets is however not completely compensated for by increased use of labour. Therefore output levels decrease in most of the manufacturing sectors, though not by as much as would have been warranted by the reduction in the use of capital in these sectors.
7. The effects of tax changes are different in am open capital market to in the closed capital market. We open up the capital market by fixing the net of tax return at the benchmark level, assuming the UK to be a small open economy compared to the global market. The gap between the sum of endowments of capital assets and use of these assets is met by inflows and outflows of assets in the open capital market economy. When the existing capital income taxes are replaced by uniform yield preserving capital income taxes, we find inflows of assets, such as building services, for which the user cost of capital has reduced, and outflows of assets, such as short and long lived plant and machinery and vehicles, for which the user cost had increased. The pure effect of opening up the capital market ranges from 0.03 percent of base year capital stock in the education sector to 5.6 percent in the engineering sector.
8. The marginal excess burden (MEB) of taxes is computed as a ratio of loss in welfare to a net change in government revenue. It varies according to the tax instruments in use for raising the additional pound of revenue. For the low labour supply elasticity case, the MEB ranges from 35 pence

in case of capital income taxes to 54 pence per pound of additional revenue from production taxes. The effects of other taxes lie between these two numbers. If MEB figures reflect the degree of distortion for the tax instrument used to raise the additional revenue, production taxes in intermediate goods and indirect taxes on investment goods seem to be the most distortionary tax instruments in the UK economy. MEB figures are higher for higher values of labour supply elasticities compared to corresponding numbers for lower labour supply elasticities. These MEB figures are comparable to rates available in the literature (BFSW(1985)).

REFERENCES

Arrow, K. J. and F. H. Hahn (1971), *General Competitive Analysis*, San Franscisco:Holden-Day.

Arrow, K. J. and G. Debreu (1954), "Existence of an Equilibrium for a Competitive Economy" *Econometrica* 22, 265-90.

Adelman, I. and S. Robinson (1978), *Income Distribution Policy in Developing Countries: A Case of South Korea*, Stanford University Press, Stanford, California.

Aurbach, A. J. and L. J. Kotlikoff (1987), *Dynamic Fiscal Policy*. Cambridge University Press.

Ballard, C. L., D. Fullerton , J. B. Shoven and J. Whalley (1985), *A General Equilibrium Model for Tax Policy Evaluation*, University of Chicago Press, Chicago.

Bhattarai, K. and J. Whalley (1999), "Role of Labor Demand Elasticities in Tax Incidence Analysis with Heterogeneous Labour Model" Empirical Economics, 24(4) November.

Bhattarai, K. and J. Whalley (1998), "General Equilibrium Modelling of UK Tax Policy" *forthcoming in* Sean Holly and Martin Weale (eds.) *Econometric Modelling: Technique and Applications*, Cambridge University Press.

Bhattarai, K. and J. Whalley (1998), "The Division and Size of Gains from Liberalisation of Service Networks" *NBER Working paper* 6712, August 1998.

Bhattarai, K (1999), "A Global Trade Model from a UK Perspective" *mimeo*, University of Warwick, July.

Bhattarai, K (1999), "Small Open Economy Model of UK" *mimeo*, University of Warwick, July.

Bhattarai, K. and J. Whalley (1997), "A Standard Static General Equilibrium Model of the UK economy" (mimeo, August 1997).

Bhattarai, K. and J. Whalley (1997), "Redistributive Effects of Transfers", *NBER Working Paper* No. 6281, November.

Bhattarai, K. and J. Whalley (1997), "Discreteness and welfare cost of labour supply tax distortions", *NBER working paper* no. 6280, November.

Bhattarai, K. M. Ghosh and J.Whalley (1999), "On some properties of a trade closure widely used in numerical modelling", *Economics Letters* 62 13-21.

Bhattarai, K. M. Ghosh and J.Whalley (1999), "More on Trade Closure", forthcoming in *Trade, Growth and Development: Essays in Honor of Professor T.N. Srinivasan*, North-Holland.

Brook, A. K. D. Kendtrick, A. Meeraus (1992), *GAMS: Users's Guide*, release 2.25, The Scientific Press, San Francisco, CA.

Browning, E. K. (1987), "On the Marginal Cost of Taxation", *American Economic Review*, 77(1), March, pp. 11-23.

Browning, E. K. and Johnson, W. R. (1984), "The Trade-off between Equality and Efficiency", *Journal of Political Economy*, 1984 vol. 92. no. 21 pp. 175-203.

Central Statistical Office (CSO (1995)), *Family Spending*: A report on the 1994-95 Expenditure Survey.

Debreu, G. (1954), *The Theory of Value*, Yale University Press, New Haven.

Dervis, K., J. De Melo, and S. Robinson (1985), *General Equilibrium Models for Development Policy*, CUP, New York.

Devarajan, S., J. D. Lewis, S. Robinson (1996), *A Bibliography of Computable General Equilibrium Models Applied to Developing Countries*, Harvard Institute of International Development, DDP No. 224.

Dirkse, S. P. and M. C. Ferris (1995), "CCPLIB: A collection of nonlinear mixed complementarity problems" *Optimization Methods and Software*. 5:319-345.

Dirkse, S. P. and M. C. Ferris (1996) "A pathsearch damped Newton method for computing general equilibria" *Annals of Operations Research*, 1996.

Ferris, M. C. and J. S. Pang (1997), "Engineering and economic applications of complementarity problems" *SIAM Review*, 39:669—713. Financial Markets Group, LSE "How to Use P-Tax" and Manual for Turbo P-tax.

Fleming, M.J. (1962), "Domestic Financial Policies Under Fixed and Under Floating Exchange Rates", IMF Staff Papers 9, 3, 369-379.

Fullerton, D. and D. L. Rogers (1993), *Who Bears the Lifetime Tax Burden?* Brookings Institution, Washington D. C.

Giles, C. and P. Johnson (1994) "Tax Reform in the UK and Changes in the Progressivity of the Tax System, 1985-95", *Fiscal Studies*, vol. 15, no. 3, pp. 64-86.

Goulder, L. H., J. Shoven and J. Whalley (1983), "Domestic Tax Policy and Foreign Sector: The Importance of Alternative Foreign Sector Formulations to Results from a General Equilibrium Tax Analysis Model" in M. Feldstein ed. *Behavioral Simulation Methods in Tax Policy Analysis*, Chicago University Press.

Goulder, L. H., and L. H. Summers (1989), "Tax Policy, Asset Prices, and Growth: A General Equilibrium Analysis", *Journal of Public Economics*, 38:265-296, North Holland.

Hamermesh, D. S. (1993), *Labour Demand*, Princeton University Press, New Jersey.

Harberger, A. C. (1962), "The incidence of the corporation income tax" *Journal of Political Economy* 70 (June):215-40.

HMSO (1995) *New Earnings Survey*, London.

Inland Revenue (1991), "How to Use P-Tax", *memio*, Economics Unit, London.

Kehoe, T. J. (1991), "Computation and Multiplicity of Equilibria" in *Handbook of Mathematical Economics*, Volume IV, Elsevier Science Publishers B.V.

Killingsworth, M. (1983), *Labor Supply*, Cambridge University Press.

King, M. A. and D. Fullerton (1984), *The taxation of income from capital :a comparative study of the United States, the United Kingdom, Sweden and West Germany* Chicago University Press.

King, M. A. and M. H. Robson (1988), "Manual for Turbo P-tax", *LSE*, London.

Kotlikoff, L. (1998), "Two Decades of A-K Model", *NBER working Paper*, August.

Mansur, A. and J. Whalley (1984), "Numerical Specification of Applied General Equilibrium Models: Estimation, Calibration and Data", in Scarf Herbert E and Shoven John B. (1984) *Applied General Equilibrium Analysis*, CUP.

Mercenier, J. and Srinivasan, T. N. ed. (1994), *Applied General Equilibrium and Economic Development: Present Achievement and Future Trends*, University of Michigan Press, Ann Arbor.

Mundell, R.A. (1968), *International Economics*, Macmillan, New York.

Office of National Statistics (ONS (1995)), *Input Output :Tables for the United Kingdom*, HMSO, London.

———(1992), *United Kingdom National Accounts: Sources ana Methods.*

———(1996), *United Kingdom National Accounts:* the Blue Book.

———(1997), *Financial Statistics*, February.

Piggott, J. and J.Whalley (1985), *UK Tax Policy and Applied General Equilibrium Analysis*, Cambridge University Press.

Robinson, S. (1991), "Macroeconomics, Financial Variables, and Computable General Equilibrium Models" *World Development*, vol. 19, no.11, pp.1509-1523, Pergamon Press plc.

Rutherford, T. F. (1995), "Extension of GAMS for Complementary Problems Arising in applied Economic Analysis" *Journal of Economic Dynamics and Control* 19 1299-1324.

Rutherford, T. F. (1997), *The GAMS/ MPSGE and GAMS/MILES user notes*, GAMS Development Corporation, Washington D. C.

Scarf, H. E. (1986), The Computation of Equilibrium Prices, in Scarf H. E and Shoven John B. ed. *Applied General Equilibrium Analysis*, Cambridge University Press.

Siddorn, G. (1999), Derivation of 1995 Symmetric Use Matrices, *mimeo*, *Economics Unit*, Inland Revenue, F4 West Wing, Somerset House, Strand, London WC2R 1LB.

St-Hilaire F. and J. Whalley (1983), "A micro consistent equilibrium data set for Canada for use in tax policy analysis", *Review Income and Wealth*, 29, 175-204.

Shoven, J. B. and J. Whalley (1992), *Applying General Equilibrium*, Cambridge University Press, 1992.

Shoven, J. B. and J. Whalley (1973), "General Equilibrium with Taxes: A Computation Procedure and an Existence Proof" *Review of Economic Studies* 40, 475-90.

Shoven, J. B. and J. Whalley (1977) "Equal Yield Tax Alternatives: General Equilibrium Computational Techniques." *Journal of Public Economics* 8, 211-24.

Shoven, J. B. and J. Whalley (1984), "Applied General-Equilibrium Models of Taxation and International Trade: An Introduction and Survey", *Jorunal of Economic Literature*, vol. XXII, Sept,pp.1007-1051.

Taylor, L. ed. (1990), *Socially Relevant Policy Analysis: Structuralist Computable General Equilibrium Models for the Developing World*, MIT Press, Cambridge 1990.

Varian, H. R (1992), *Microeconomic Analysis*, 3rd edition, W. W. Norton and Company, New York.

Walras, L. *Elements of Pure Economics*, Allen and Unwin, London, 1954.

Whalley, J. (1985), *Trade Liberalization Among Major World Trading Areas*, MIT Press, Cambridge.

Whalley, J. and B. Yeung (1983), "External Sector `Closing' Rules in Applied General Equilibrium Models" *Journal of International Economics*, 15, pp.1-16.

INSTRUCTIONS FOR RUNNING THE MODEL

The modelling package discussed in this report runs in DOS or Windows versions of the GAMS software. For users who are beginners in using GAMS/MPSGE, the programme manuals of GAMS/MPSGE contain detailed information on how to install the programme in a machine and these manuals cover substantial instructions on syntax, solution procedure, output reporting and problem shooting. Recent versions of GAMS/MPSGE run efficiently on a Pentium machine. This model is formulated with the mixed complementarity format using PATH solver in GAMS. GAMS could be invoked from any directory if it is added to the path in the autoexec.bat file.

The model package contains basic programme files which may be executed to generate list files that contain reports of the solutions. Other batch files may be added as necessary. It is better to keep all these files in a separate directory such as UKCGE.

Inputs to the Programme

If the data set ranges in many columns and rows, data entry is easier in a tabular format generated from any spreadsheet programme that is readable by the GAMS programme. Data elements entered in these tables are then converted into parameters or base year values of variables by the assignment syntax in the model.

There are different styles of writing a code for a general equilibrium model. GAMS uses explicit declaration of model equations. MPSGE uses a set of codes for equation generators that allow one to be concise in model declarations and focus more on model results. The choice between these two types of syntax depends upon the preference of the user and the nature of the model. Many non-standard assumptions are difficult to incorporate in MPSGE, and a large dimensional model is more easily handled by MPSGE than by the GAMS algebra.

There are several ways to handle the output of a GAMS programme by display statement, by declaring a set of report parameters or by exporting outputs into a different files using the "put" facilities in GAMS that make output files readable by any spreadsheet programme. There are standard plotting facilities such as "gnuplot" that can be imbedded in the GAMS program. Similarly, standard tools exist to generate tables. These facilities are being added to and refined in the software continuously. There is much information on both GAMS and MPSGE modelling and several contact addresses are listed on the home page of the GAMS Corporation: http//www.gams.com.

```
***RAS Balance Procedure
Set K Industry/                                agric    agriculture forestry fishing 1-3
                                               extra    extraction oil and gas 5
                                               minin    mining & quarrying coal stone clay
metal ores and minerals 4 14 10
                                               chemi    chemicals coke nuclear fuels
organin inorganic paints 6 20-29
                                               metal    metal and mineral products iron
steel alum cementconcrete 11-13 15-19 30-34 37
                                               engin    engineering machine tractor tools
equipment electronic 35 35 38-52 57
                                               foodd    food drink and tobacco meat grain
sugar oil fat alcohol soft drink conf 58-70
                                               Othma    other manufacturing motor ship
aerospce hosiery textile leather 53-56 71-90
                                               power    electricity gas and water 7-9
                                               const    construction 91
                                               distr    distribution hotels etc. wholesale
retail hotel distribution 92-95
                                               trans    transport storage and
communication rail sea air road transprt postal 96-102
                                               finan    financial sector bank ins real
estate legal comput accnt advert R&D103-114 118
                                               pubad    public administration 115
                                               educa    education health and social work
recreation personaldom services 116 117 119-122
                                               house    housing services 123

;

alias (k,kk);
Table make make matric 1995
        Agric  Extra  Minin  Chemi  Metal  Engin  Foodd  Othma  Power  Const
Distr   Trans  Finan  Pubad  Educa  House
Agric   20693  0      0      0      0      0      0      0      0      0      0
        0      0      0      0      0
Extra   0      17499  0      0      0      0      0      0      0      0      0
        0      0      0      0      0
Minin   0      0      4991   30     177    0      0      0      0      0      0
        0      0      0      0      0
Chemi   0      0      0      50283  365    367    165    400    0      0      0
        0      0      0      0      0
Metal   2      0      154    544    41595  2358   0      1613   0      0      0
        0      0      0      0      0
Engin   0      0      0      286    1813   58747  1      1612   0      0      0
        0      0      0      0      0
Foodd   2      0      0      82     49     30     58347  2      0      0      0
        0      0      0      0      0
Othma   20     0      0      1152   2434   3012   6      106391 0      0      0
        0      0      0      0      0
Power   2      0      0      0      0      0      0      0      40430  0      0
        0      0      0      0      0
```

```
Const   165     0       28      728     147     156     103     335     1453    82864   0
        0       0       0       0       0
Distr   128     122     42      5411    1914    6491    5552    6072    700     975
        156424  566     1701    0       323     0
Trans   0       0       51      850     224     646     354     553     246     0       0
        93716   0       0       0       0
Finan   241     80      217     973     636     1608    870     8740    346     387     5799
        1836    201887  0       2980    0
Pubad   0       0       0       0       0       0       0       0       0       0       0
        0       0       63843   0       0
Educa   2       0       0       0       0       0       0       0       0       0       0
        0       0       0       109177  0
House   76      3       11      83      124     212     171     233     23      150     1164
        169     7459    0       238     52199
```

Table rctotal Row Colum Total

```
          Agric   Extra   Minin   Chemi   Metal   Engin   Foodd   Othma   Power   Const
          Distr   Trans   Finan   Pubad   Educa   House
Coltot            21332   17704   5493    60422   49477   73626   65569   125952
          43198   84377   163387          96287   211047          63843   112452
          52199
Rowtot            20693   17499   5198    51579   46267   62459   58513   113015
          40432   85978   186421          96640   226599          63843   109179
          62315
Target            20694   17499   5096    56823   47345   68656   63293   115557
          40431   84570   176615          96228   223945          63843   109179
          56591

;

parameter
        abar(k,kk)
        coltot(kk)
        rowtot(k)
        target(kk);

abar(k,kk) = make(k,kk);

coltot(kk) = rctotal( "coltot",KK);
rowtot(k) =rctotal("rowtot",k);
target(kk) = rctotal("target",kk);

parameter csum, rsum;

csum =sum(kk,target(kk));
rsum = sum(k,rowtot(k));

display abar, coltot, rowtot, target, rsum,csum;

variables
        aa(k,kk)
        cell(k,kk)
        rowt(k)
        colt(kk)
        zob
```

***RAS procedure**

```
parameters
        ahat(k,kk)        after row adjustment
        ahatt(k,kk)       after column adjustment
        targetr(kk)
        targetc(kk)
        resultr(kk)
        resultc(kk)

targetr(kk) = target(kk)- sum(k, abar(k,kk)$(ord(k) eq ord(kk)));
targetc(kk) = coltot(kk)- sum(k, abar(k,kk)$(ord(k) eq ord(kk)));
ahat(k,kk) = abar(k,kk);
ahat(k,kk)$(ord(k) eq ord(kk)) = abar(k,kk)$(ord(k) eq ord(kk));
resultc(kk) =sum(k, ahat(k,kk)$(ord(k) ne ord(kk)));

ahatt(k,kk) = ahat(k,kk);

*resultr(kk)=sum(k, ahatt(k,kk)$(ord(k) ne ord(kk)));
*ahat(k,kk)$resultr(kk) = (targetr(kk)/resultr(kk))*ahatt(k,kk);
*resultc(kk) =sum(k, ahat(k,kk)$(ord(k) ne ord(kk)));
*display ahat, resultr, resultc;

set iter /s1*s15/;

loop(iter,
ahat(k,kk)$(ord(k) eq ord(kk)) = abar(k,kk)$(ord(k) eq ord(kk));
ahatt(k,kk)$((ord(k) ne ord(kk)) and (resultc(kk) ne 0)) = ((targetc(kk)/resultc(kk))*ahat(k,kk));
resultr(k) =sum(kk, ahatt(k,kk)$(ord(k) ne ord(kk)));
ahat(k,kk)$((ord(k) ne ord(kk)) and (resultr(k) ne 0)) = (targetr(k)/resultr(k))*ahatt(k,kk);
resultc(kk) =sum(k, ahat(k,kk)$(ord(k) ne ord(kk)));

);

parameters rowsum, colsum;

rowsum(k) = sum(kk, ahat(k,kk));
colsum(kk) = sum(k, ahat(k,kk));
display ahat, resultr, resultc, rowsum, colsum;
```

*****P-Tax model**

```
$TITLE reformulation of P-Tax in GAMS

SET          J          Asset          / build          buildings
                                         pmlon          p&m long life
                                         pmsho          p&m short life
                                         vehic          vehicles
                                         dwell          dwellings
```

```
K        Industry                 / agric   agriculture forestry fishing 1-3
                                  extra     extraction oil and gas 5
                                  power     electricity gas and water 7-9
                                  minin     mining & quarrying coal stone clay
metal ores and minerals 4 14 10
                                  chemi     chemicals coke nuclear fuels
organin inorganic paints 6 20-29
                                  metal     metal and mineral products iron
steel alum cementconcrete 11-13 15-19 30-34 37
                                  engin     engineering machine tractor tools
equipment electronic 35 35 38-52 57
                                  foodd     food drink and tobacco meat grain
sugar oil fat alcohol soft drink conf 58-70
                                  othma     other manufacturing motor ship
aerospce hosiery textile leather 53-56 71-90
                                  power     electricity gas and water 7-9
                                  const     construction 91
                                  distr     distribution hotels etc. wholesale
retail hotel distribution 92-95
                                  trans     transport storage and
communication rail sea air road transprt postal 96-102
                                  finan     financial sector bank ins real
estate legal comput accnt advert R & D103-114 118
                                  pubad     public administration 115
                                  educa     education health and social work
recreation personaldom services 116 117 119-122
                                  house     housing services 123
                                  /
      L        Finance            / debt    debt
                                  nshr      new share
                                  rtearn    retained Earning
                                  /
      M        Owner              / hhs     households
                                  tex       tax exempt
                                  ins       insurance company
                                  /

alias (j,jj), (k, kk), (l,ll), (m,mm);

parameter
F1(J,K)          writing down allowance
F2(J,K)          first year capital allowance
F3(J,K)          cash grants (proportion of cost of an asset)
G(J,K)           rate of cash grant on purchase of an asset
ASS(J,K)         tax depreciation rate on db basis
TD(J,K)          0-db 1-sl 2-soyd 3-from db to sl 4-from db to soyd
AL(J,K)          rate of tax depreciation for sl or soyd basis
DEP(J,K)         economic depreciation rate(exponential)
CAP(J,K)         proportion of net capital stock
own(l,m)         share of ownership by owner and source of finance
RM(L,M)          rate of personal income tax to owners of capital
```

TABLE BASE(*,*,K) **Basic parameters**

	agric	extra	minin	chemi	metal	engin	foodd	othma
F1.build	0.96	0.96	0.96	0.96	0.96	0.96	0.96	0.96
F1.pmlon	0.75	0.75	0.75	0.75	0.75	0.75	0.75	0.75
F1.pmsho	0.75	0.75	0.75	0.75	0.75	0.75	0.75	0.75
F1.vehic	0.75	0.75	0.75	0.75	0.75	0.75	0.75	0.75
F1.dwell	0	0	0	0	0	0	0	0
F2.build	0.04	0.04	0.04	0.04	0.04	0.04	0.04	0.04
F2.pmlon	0.25	0.25	0.25	0.25	0.25	0.25	0.25	0.25
F2.pmsho	0.25	0.25	0.25	0.25	0.25	0.25	0.25	0.25
F2.vehic	0.25	0.25	0.25	0.25	0.25	0.25	0.25	0.25
F2.dwell	0	0	0	0	0	0	0	0
F3.build	0	0	0	0	0	0	0	0
F3.pmlon	0	0	0	0	0	0	0	0
F3.pmsho	0	0	0	0	0	0	0	0
F3.vehic	0	0	0	0	0	0	0	0
F3.dwell	0	0	0	0	0	0	0	0
G.build	0	0	0	0	0	0	0	0
G.pmlon	0	0	0	0	0	0	0	0
G.pmsho	0	0	0	0	0	0	0	0
G.vehic	0	0	0	0	0	0	0	0
G.dwell	0	0	0	0	0	0	0	0
TD.build	1	1	1	1	1	1	1	1
TD.pmlon	0	0	0	0	0	0	0	0
TD.pmsho	0	0	0	0	0	0	0	0
TD.vehic	0	0	0	0	0	0	0	0
TD.dwell	0	0	0	0	0	0	0	0
ASS.build	0	0	0	0	0	0	0	0
ASS.pmlon	0.25	0.25	0.25	0.25	0.25	0.25	0.25	0.25
ASS.pmsho	0.25	0.25	0.25	0.25	0.25	0.25	0.25	0.25
ASS.vehic	0.25	0.25	0.25	0.25	0.25	0.25	0.25	0.25
ASS.dwell	0	0	0	0	0	0	0	0
AL.build	0.04	0.04	0.04	0.04	0.04	0.04	0.04	0.04
AL.pmlon	0	0	0	0	0	0	0	0
AL.pmsho	0	0	0	0	0	0	0	0
AL.vehic	0	0	0	0	0	0	0	0
AL.dwell	0	0	0	0	0	0	0	0
DEP.build	0.064	0.101	0.052	0.026	0.025	0.025	0.025	0.025
DEP.pmlon	0.050	0.061	0.050	0.037	0.029	0.029	0.032	0.036
DEP.pmsho	0.153	0.181	0.131	0.079	0.072	0.083	0.078	0.090
DEP.vehic	0.159	0.2	0.2	0.2	0.2	0.2	0.2	0.214
DEP.dwell	0	0	0	0	0	0	0	0
CAP.build	0.9772	0.0031	0.0702	0.7036	0.8344	0.9756	0.8435	1.5313
CAP.pmlon	0.0000	0.1851	0.000	0.4180	0.1634	0.0464	0.0572	0.3796
CAP.pmsho	0.1866	1.2491	0.1164	1.0819	1.1701	1.1628	0.8555	2.1434
CAP.vehic	0.0700	0.0177	0.0044	0.0306	0.0436	0.0662	0.0413	0.0977
CAP.dwell	0.0000	0.0000	0.0000	0.0000	0.0000	0.0000	0.0000	0.0000

+	power	const	distr	trans	finan	pubad	educa	house
F1.build	0.96	0.96	0.96	0.96	0.048	0.048	0.048	0.048
F1.pmlon	0.75	0.75	0.75	0.75	0.75	0.75	0.75	0.75
F1.pmsho	0.75	0.75	0.75	0.75	0.75	0.75	0.75	0.75
F1.vehic	0.75	0.75	0.75	0.75	0.75	0.75	0.75	0.75

```
F1.dwell    0       0       0       0       0       0       0       0
F2.build    0.04    0.04    0.04    0.04    0.002   0.002   0.002   0.002
F2.pmlon    0.25    0.25    0.25    0.25    0.25    0.25    0.25    0.25
F2.pmsho    0.25    0.25    0.25    0.25    0.25    0.25    0.25    0.25
F2.vehic    0.25    0.25    0.25    0.25    0.25    0.25    0.25    0.25
F2.dwell    0       0       0       0       0       0       0       0
F3.build    0       0       0       0       0       0       0       0
F3.pmlon    0       0       0       0       0       0       0       0
F3.pmsho    0       0       0       0       0       0       0       0
F3.vehic    0       0       0       0       0       0       0       0
F3.dwell    0       0       0       0       0       0       0       0
G.build     0       0       0       0       0       0       0       0
G.pmlon     0       0       0       0       0       0       0       0
G.pmsho     0       0       0       0       0       0       0       0
G.vehic     0       0       0       0       0       0       0       0
G.dwell     0       0       0       0       0       0       0       0
TD.build    0       0       0       0       0       0       0       0
TD.pmlon    0       0       0       0       0       0       0       0
TD.pmsho    0       0       0       0       0       0       0       0
TD.vehic    0       0       0       0       0       0       0       0
TD.dwell    0       0       0       0       0       0       0       0
ASS.build   0       0       0       0       0       0       0       0
ASS.pmlon   0.25    0.25    0.25    0.25    0.25    0.25    0.25    0.25
ASS.pmsho   0.25    0.25    0.25    0.25    0.25    0.25    0.25    0.25
ASS.vehic   0.25    0.25    0.25    0.25    0.25    0.25    0.25    0.25
ASS.dwell   0       0       0       0       0       0       0       0
AL.build    0.04    0.04    0.04    0.04    0.04    0.04    0.04    0.04
AL.pmlon    0       0       0       0       0       0       0       0
AL.pmsho    0       0       0       0       0       0       0       0
AL.vehic    0       0       0       0       0       0       0       0
AL.dwell    0       0       0       0       0       0       0       0
DEP.build   0.031   0.025   0.025   0.025   0.025   0.025   0.027   0.020
DEP.pmlon   0.042   0.050   0.040   0.066   0.040   0.040   0.04    0.020
DEP.pmsho   0.208   0.134   0.138   0.166   0.146   0.137   0.120   0.020
DEP.vehic   0.2     0.2     0.2     0.173   0.2     0.2     0.2     0.2
DEP.dwell   0       0       0       0       0       0       0       0
CAP.build   3.3923  0.2466  4.7905  3.1698  6.7226  3.1152  5.7320  0.000
CAP.pmlon   2.6261  0.0176  0.3979  1.3684  0.0604  0.1109  0.0000  0.000
CAP.pmsho   0.1496  0.1589  1.4610  0.8664  1.9487  0.4689  0.6362  0.000
CAP.vehic   0.0313  0.1069  0.4021  0.9618  1.1522  0.0658  0.0590  0.000
CAP.dwell 0 0 0 0 0 0 0 44.2552
;
```

TABLE BASE1(L,M) ownership of funds

```
         hhs     tex     ins
debt     0.766   0.16    0.074
nshr     0.271   0.621   0.109
rtearn   0.271   0.621   0.109
;
```

TABLE BASE2(L,M) tax rates on interest and divident

```
         hhs     tex     ins
debt     0.19    0.0     0.20
nshr     0.29    0.0     0.20
```

```
rtearn   0.29   0.0   0.20

parameter
      fin(l)   sources of finance
               /debt    0.241
               nshr     0.106
               rtearn   0.651/
      ZS(m)    Marginal capital gains tax rate
               /hhs     0.30
               tex      0.0
               ins      0.240/
      WP(m)    personal wealth tax rate
               /hhs     0.0
               tex      0.0
               ins      0.0/
      WC(J)    tax      rate on corporate wealth
               /build   0.019
               pmlon    0.006
               pmsho    0.006
               vehic    0.000
               dwell    0.000/;

F1(J,K)=BASE("F1",J,K);
F2(J,K)=BASE("F2",J,K);
F3(J,K)=BASE("F3",J,K);
G(J,K)=BASE("G",J,K);
ASS(J,K)=BASE("ASS",J,K);
TD(J,K)=BASE("TD",J,K);
AL(J,K)=BASE("AL",J,K);
DEP(J,K)=BASE("DEP",J,K);
CAP(J,K)=BASE("CAP",J,K);
own(l,m) =BASE1(L,M);
RM(L,M)=BASE2(L,M);

PARAMETER
A(L,M,J,K)       present value of depreciation allowance
AD(L,M,J,K)      depreciation allowances
P(L,M,J,K)       Pre-tax rate of return
PAFO(J,K)        Pre-tax rate of return averaged over all finance and owner groups
S(L,M)           Post tax real rate of return
SAFO             Post tax rate of return averaged over all finance and owner groups
TW(L,M,J,K)      Total tax wedge
TR(L,M,J,K)      Total tax rate
CTW(L,M,J,K)     Corporate tax wedge
CTR(L,M,J,K)     Corporate tax rate
PTW(L,M,J,K)     Personal tax wedge
PTR(L,M,J,K)     Personal tax rate
TRAFO(J,K)       Total tax rate averaged over all finance and owner groups
CTRAFO(J,K)      Corporate tax rate averaged over all finance and owner groups
PTRAFO(J,K)      Personal rate averaged over all finance and owner groups
I                nominal rate of interest
BES              1-business expansion scheme 0-otherwise
```

```
PIE          inflation rate
RFIX         real rate of interest (fixed)
TAU          corporate tax rate
THETA        opportunity cost of retained earning
sigma        imputation rate
BETA         proportion of interest payments deductible from CT base
D1           deductible proportion of WC from WC base
INDEXC       degree of indexation of capital gains
INDEXNE      degree of indexation of CAP GAIN OF NEW EQUITY
INDEXRE      degree of indexation of CAP GAIN OF RETAINED EARNINGS
INDEXD       degree of indexation of depreciation allowance
INDEXS       degree of indexation of in increases of value of inv
INDEXI       index of payments and receipts
VLAMDA       reciprocal of mean asset holding time
RHO(L,M)     discount rates (opportunity cost of capital)
Z(L,M)       effective rate of capital gains tax
;

RFIX        = 0.05;
PIE         = 0.02;
I           = RFIX + PIE;
BES         = 0;
TAU         = 0.33;
sigma       = 0.25;
THETA       = 1/(1-sigma);
BETA        = 1;
D1          = 1;
INDEXC      = 1;
INDEXNE     = 1;
INDEXRE     = 1;
INDEXI      = 0;
INDEXD      = 0;
INDEXS      = 0;
VLAMDA      = 1/7;
RHO(L,M)    = 0;
Z(L,M)      = 0;
```

***Post tax real rate of return**

```
S(L,M) = I*(1-RM("DEBT",M))-PIE-WP(M)+RM("DEBT",M)*PIE*INDEXI;
```

***Effective rate of capital gains tax**

```
Z(L,M) = (ZS(M)*VLAMDA)/(VLAMDA+S(L,M)+PIE);
```

***DISCOUNT RATES**

***debt**

```
RHO("DEBT",M) = I*(1-BETA*TAU) + BETA*TAU*PIE*INDEXI;
```

***new equity**

```
RHO("NSHR",M) = ((1-RM("NSHR",M)*BES)/(THETA*(1-RM("NSHR",M)))
 *(I*(1-RM("NSHR",M))+PIE*(RM("NSHR",M)*INDEXI
 -(Z("NSHR",M)*INDEXNE)/(1-(RM("NSHR",M)*BES)))));
```

```
*retained earnings
RHO("RTEARN",M) = ((1-RM("RTEARN",M)*BES)/(1-Z("RTEARN",M)))
*(I*(1-RM("RTEARN",M))+PIE*(RM("RTEARN",M)*INDEXI
-(Z("RTEARN",M)*INDEXRE)/(1-(RM("RTEARN",M)*BES))));

*depreciation allowances
*(a) declining balance method
AD(L,M,J,K)$(TD(J,K) EQ 0) =(TAU*ASS(J,K))/(ASS(J,K)+RHO(L,M)-PIE*INDEXD);

*(b) straight line method
AD(L,M,J,K)$(TD(J,K) EQ 1) = (TAU*AL(J,K)*(1-EXP(-(RHO(L,M)-PIE*INDEXD)*(F1(J,K)/
AL(J,K)))))
 /(F1(J,k)*(rho(l,m)-pie*INDEXD));

*(c) sum of the years digit method
set h /1*25/;
parameter n(j,k), nn(h),f(j,k), ff(h);
f(j,k) = 0;
n(j,k)$al(j,k) = 1/al(j,k);
ff(h) = 0;
loop(h,
f(j,k)$(f(j,k) gt 0) = n(j,k) -1;
ff(h+1) = ff(h)+1
);

AD(L,M,J,K)$(TD(J,K) EQ 2) = (tau/(al(j,k)*25*(rho(l,m)-pie*indexd)))
*(1-exp(-0.5*(rho(l,m)-pie*indexd))+sum(h$(card(h) le 25),
(exp(-(ord(h)-0.5)*(rho(l,m)-pie*indexd)) -
exp(-(ord(h)+0.5)*(rho(l,m)-pie*indexd)))
*(1-al(j,k)*(ord(h)-0.5))));

A(L,M,J,K) = F1(J,K)*AD(L,M,J,K)+F2(J,K)*TAU +F3(J,K)*G(J,K);

*pre-tax rate of return

P(L,M,J,K) = (((1-A(L,M,J,K))*(rho(l,m)+dep(j,k)-pie) + (1-d1*tau)*wc(j))
/ (1-tau)) - dep(j,k);

*total tax wedge
TW(L,M,J,K) = P(L,M,J,K) - S(L,M);

*total tax rate
TR(L,M,J,K) = TW(L,M,J,K)/P(L,M,J,K);

*corporate tax wedge, for debt
CTW("DEBT",M,J,K) = P("DEBT",M,J,K) - RFIX;

*corporate tax wedge, for new equity
CTW("NSHR",M,J,K) = P("NSHR",M,J,K) - (RHO("NSHR",M)*THETA - PIE);
```

```
*corporate tax wedge, for retained earnings
CTW("RTEARN",M,J,K) = P("RTEARN",M,J,K) - (RHO("RTEARN",M) - PIE);

*personal tax wedge
PTW(L,M,J,K) = TW(L,M,J,K) - CTW(L,M,J,K);

*corporate tax rate
CTR(L,M,J,K) = CTW(L,M,J,K)/P(L,M,J,K);

*personal tax rate
PTR(L,M,J,K) = PTW(L,M,J,K)/(P(L,M,J,K)-CTW(L,M,J,K));

*total tax rate averaged over all finance/owner groups
TRAFO(J,K) = SUM(L, SUM(M, TR(L,M,J,K) * OWN(L,M) * FIN(L)));

*corporate tax rate averaged over all finance/owner groups
CTRAFO(J,K) = SUM(L, SUM(M, CTR(L,M,J,K) * OWN(L,M) * FIN(L)));

*personal tax rate averaged over all finance/owner groups
PTRAFO(J,K) = SUM(L, SUM(M, PTR(L,M,J,K) * OWN(L,M) * FIN(L)));

*pre tax rate of return personal averaged over all finance/owner groups
PAFO(J,K) = SUM(L, SUM(M, P(L,M,J,K) * OWN(L,M) * FIN(L)));

*post tax rate of return averaged over all finance/owner groups
SAFO = SUM(L, SUM(M, S(L,M) * OWN(L,M) * FIN(L)));

*Set housing tax rates equal to zero
TRAFO(J,"HOUSE")=0;
Trafo ("dwell",k)=0;

DISPLAY TRAFO;
** Basic UK Model
$title multisecotral general equilibrium tax model of the uk economy Jan99
$include ptax.gms

SET
        HH Households and labor categories /
                H1 Household 1 /
        FD final demand /Cons
                GGFC
                GDFCF
                Stocks
                Exports/;
ALIAS (HH,lc);
```

TABLE IOF(K,KK) domestic intermediate demand (Input-output flows 1995)

	Agric	Extra	Minin	Chemi	Metal	Engin	Foodd	othma	Power	Const	Distr	Trans	Finan	Pubad	Educa	House
Agric	2096	0	14	27	7	5	12132	435	0	4	564	48	15	0	148	0
Extra	0	2439	0	4697	3	0	0	0	3622	0	0	0	0	0	0	0
Minin	20	0	353	218	846	26	45	130	1897	401	105	17	8	0	57	0
Chemi	1433	10	37	3899	433	546	571	1484	466	737	1299	1254	913	0	3204	19
Metal	110	162	192	1225	7249	6320	1831	5197	50	7074	503	389	5	0	84	0
Engin	0	576	317	682	1254	5705	528	2432	634	788	848	1808	1018	0	1567	36
Foodd	2797	52	25	356	82	120	6382	350	64	51	6589	650	1058	0	1796	4
othma	583	80	134	1781	1839	3005	2816	16404	474	4242	6702	4139	8242	0	3340	283
Power	279	0	160	1330	1596	1189	931	1980	12273	272	1201	857	1184	0	705	23
Const	172	0	122	109	32	56	0	31	0	21085	603	151	1985	0	146	3929
Distr	1005	200	206	1479	2489	4115	1647	3724	355	1371	4164	2470	2276	0	790	0
Trans	245	704	335	1232	2047	1415	1583	3614	183	887	14871	15642	17082	0	3175	198
Finan	1949	671	471	4070	2781	6194	4205	9177	1884	10483	22425	12387	50836	0	13435	15221
Pubad	0	0	0	0	0	0	0	0	0	0	0	0	0	0	0	0
Educa	378	1	41	520	253	581	496	2618	179	242	1001	1369	4031	0	7756	67
House	0	0	0	0	0	0	0	0	0	0	0	0	0	0	0	0

TABLE IOFM(K,KK) imports for intermediate demand

	Agric	Extra	Minin	Chemi	Metal	Engin	Foodd	othma	Power	Const	Distr	Trans	Finan	Pubad	Educa	House
Agric	462	0	0	2	0	0	2342	394	0	0	546	9	0	0	0	0
Extra	0	133	0	1532	0	0	0	0	1613	0	0	0	0	0	0	0
Minin	0	0	68	359	540	31	4	50	312	540	0	0	0	0	0	0
Chemi	802	11	142	7931	1028	1274	844	7476	382	196	165	609	22	0	299	0
Metal	26	180	57	222	5249	2251	378	1745	0	1690	64	0	0	0	0	0
Engin	45	161	61	13	286	11980	22	2177	855	770	46	791	78	0	119	0
Foodd	291	0	0	275	0	0	4641	36	0	0	936	53	0	0	0	0

othma	0	0	79	300	478	369	565	18399	12	1900	1206
	641	60	0	357	0						
Power	0	0	0	3	4	1	2	3	432	0	0 0
	0	0	0	0							
Const	0	0	0	0	0	0	0	0	0	44	0 0
	0	0	0	0							
Distr	0	0	0	0	0	0	0	0	0	0	0 0
	0	0	0	0							
Trans	0	504	11	0	5	0	4	0	0	2	530
	2720	375	0	60	0						
Finan	4	1	8	0	20	50	22	0	4	10	35
	33	3369	0	886	19						
Pubad	0	0	0	0	0	0	0	0	0	0	0 0
	0	0	0	0							
Educa	0	0	0	1	3	8	2	55	2	0	3 38
	45	0	1238	0							
House	0	0	0	0	0	0	0	0	0	0	0 0
	0	0	0	0							

;

Table asset(j,K) categories of capital asset in the year 1995

	Agric	Extra	Minin	Chemi	Metal	Engin	Foodd	othma	Power	Const	Distr
	Trans	Finan	Pubad	Educa	House						
Build	15672	50	1125	11284	13381	15646	13528	24558	54403	3955	76826
	50835	107812	49959	91925	0						
pmlon	0	2968	0	6703	2621	744	918	6088	42115	283	6381
	21945	968	1778	0	0						
pmsho	2993	20032	1867	17351	18766	18647	13721	34374	2399	2549	23430
	13894	31251	7519	10204	0						
vehic	1122	283	71	490	699	1062	662	1568	501	1715	6448
	15425	18478	1055	946	0						
dwell	0	0	0	0	0	0	0	0	0	0	0 0
	0	0	0	709731							

*source:Inland Revenue

;

TABLE ZZ(*,K) MISCELLANEOUS PARAMETERS AND INITIAL DATA

	Agric	Extra	Minin	Chemi	Metal	Engin	Foodd	othma	Power	Const	Distr
	Trans	Finan	Pubad	Educa	House						
XD	24208	17704	5493	52108	49493	73649	57114	125992		41719	
	84404	154987		98540	211047		63843	113957		53269	
Tariff		34	6	5	136	101	214	171	405	48	66
	51	26	2	0	9	0					
VAT	0	0	0	0	0	0	0	0	0	0	0 218
	3259	0	1181	0							
dtlv	211	2	103	1175	344	176	460	331	1378	130	
	1275	2026	896	0	344	36					
Othtxsb		-265	-25	-10	-50	-53	-46	-1454	-212	-10	-34
	-443	-404	-409	0	-186	-6					
Lb	7143	1409	1822	10151	15790	18529	9691	36483	5492	29947	
	61877	35191	70149	60316	69067	0					
ka	4388	10428	738	8432	4786	9536	6250	11074	9118	1505	
	27820	15406	44549	3527	4381	33440					

```
Kstock   19788   23333   3063   35827   35466
36099   28829   66588   99419   8502   113086
102099   158508   60311   103075   709731
Intdm    3755   3278   1905   21182   11863   17403   6232   24365   446   44   0
         4211   4463   0   1395   0
INTSD    15495   10762   4124   16304   30392   18192   20377   54064   23981   28420
         26289   63216   156189   0   19535   0
INTM     1630   989   425   10639   7613   15965   8827   30336   3612   5151
         3532   4895   3949   0   2960   19
INTD     11067   4895   2410   21626   20912   29276   33168   47576   22081   47638
         60876   41182   88652   0   36201   19781
TMFD     1517   0   2035   3495   222   32513   9198   33357   0   0
         3518   4378   1328   416   1704   566
TFIND    8713   6942   1369   35804   19101   55457   36737   71928   17738   55983
         128698   35324   54859   63843   94422   53269
Exports  1942   6942   983   28663   10230   50923   10270   39858   62   0
         13701   12194   12545   0   4504   0
rexpt    46   0   2003   165   0   164   19   98   0   0
         0   0   0   0   0   0
p0       1   1   1   1   1   1   1   1   1   1   1 1
         1   1   1
```

Table DF(*, k) domestic sales to final demand

```
         Agric    Extra   Minin   Chemi   Metal   Engin   Foodd   othma   Power   Const
         Distr    Trans   Finan   Pubad   Educa   House
Cons     6730     0       339     3764    346     0       25904   18082   16353   3521
         111181   19715   25373   0       43653   53269
GGFC     42       0       47      3116    588     1589    411     3872    1323    4414
         1229     2637    8458    63843   46265   0
GDFCF    0        0       0       0       7158    2613    0       8933    0       47764
         2586     779     8483    0       0       0
Stocks   0        0       0       261     779     332     153     1185    0       285   0
         0        0       0       0       0
Exports  1942     6942    983     28663   10230   50923   10270   39858   62      0
         13701    12194   12545   0       4504    0
expsub   -192     0       0       -25     -3      -9      0       -9      0       0     0
         -267     0       0       -48     -5
;
```

Table MF(*, k) imports to final demand

```
         Agric    Extra   Minin   Chemi   Metal   Engin   Foodd   othma   Power   Const
         Distr    Trans   Finan   Pubad   Educa   House
Cons     1471     0       29      2259    0       6220    8812    24075   0       0
         3518     4036    0       0       1035    566
GGFC     0        0       3       873     0       3123    348     2893    0       0     0
         342      1328    416     669     0
GDFCF    0        0       0       0       3       22859   0       5312    0       0     0
         0        0       0       0       0
Stocks   0        0       0       199     220     148     18      979     0       0     0
         0        0       0       0       0
Exports  46       0       2003    165     0       164     19      98      0       0     0
         0        0       0       0       0
```

```
Table VATTN(k,kk) value added tax on intermediate demand
        Agric  Extra  Minin  Chemi  Metal  Engin  Foodd  othma  Power  Const
        Distr  Trans  Finan  Pubad  Educa  House
Agric   0      0      0      0      0      0      0      0      0      0      0
        0      0      0      1      0
Extra   0      0      0      0      0      0      0      0      0      0      0
        0      0      0      0      0
Minin   0      0      0      0      0      0      0      0      0      0      0
        0      0      0      0      0
Chemi   0      0      0      0      0      0      0      0      0      0      0
        10     61     0      247    0
Metal   0      0      0      0      0      0      0      0      0      0      0
        3      1      0      0      0
Engin   0      0      0      0      0      0      0      0      0      0      0
        8      35     0      281    0
Foodd   0      0      0      0      0      0      0      0      0      0      0
        4      14     0      34     0
othma   0      0      0      0      0      0      0      0      0      0      0
        22     454    0      144    0
Power   0      0      0      0      0      0      0      0      0      0      0
        13     85     0      94     0
Const   0      0      0      0      0      0      0      0      0      0      0
        3      223    0      4      0
Distr   0      0      0      0      0      0      0      0      0      0      0
        32     206    0      16     0
Trans   0      0      0      0      0      0      0      0      0      0      0
        89     957    0      138    0
Finan   0      0      0      0      0      0      0      0      0      0      0
        33     1197   0      181    0
Pubad   0      0      0      0      0      0      0      0      0      0      0
        0      0      0      0      0
Educa   0      0      0      0      0      0      0      0      0      0      0
        3      26     0      41     0
House   0      0      0      0      0      0      0      0      0      0      0
        0      0      0      0      0
;

Table VATT(*, k) value added tax on final demand
        Agric  Extra  Minin  Chemi  Metal  Engin  Foodd  othma  Power  Const
        Distr  Trans  Finan  Pubad  Educa  House
Cons    83     0      20     2177   60     973    4272   6201   973    492
        14636  1667   0      0      1701   0
GGFC    1      0      8      209    103    793    13     741    177    753    97
        272    599    0      148    0
GDFCF   0      0      0      0      273    1358   0      895    0      1179   0
        2      23     0      0      0
Stocks  0      0      0      0      0      0      0      0      0      0      0
        0      0      0      0      0
Exports 0      0      0      0      0      0      0      0      0      0      0
        0      0      0      0      0
;
```

Table tarrif(k,kk) tariff on intermediate demand

	Agric	Extra	Minin	Chemi	Metal	Engin	Foodd	othma	Power	Const	Distr	Trans	Finan	Pubad	Educa	House
Agric	19	0	0	0	0	0	95	16	0	0	22	0	0	0	0	0
Extra	0	2	0	20	0	0	0	0	21	0	0	0	0	0	0	0
Minin	0	0	1	5	7	0	0	1	4	7	0	0	0	0	0	0
Chemi	11	0	2	100	13	16	11	95	5	2	2	7	0	0	3	0
Metal	0	2	1	3	71	30	5	24	0	22	1	0	0	0	0	0
Engin		2	1	0	4	162	0	30	12	10	1	10	1	0	1	0
Foodd	3	0	0	3	0	0	52	0	0	0	10	1	0	0	0	0
othma	0	0	1	4	6	4	7	239	0	24	15	8	1	0	4	0
Power	0	0	0	0	0	0	0	0	5	0	0	0	0	0	0	0
Const	0	0	0	0	0	0	0	0	0	0	0	0	0	0	0	0
Distr	0	0	0	0	0	0	0	0	0	0	0	0	0	0	0	0
Trans	0	0	0	0	0	0	0	0	0	0	0	0	0	0	0	0
Finan	0	0	0	0	0	0	0	0	0	0	0	0	0	0	0	0
Pubad	0	0	0	0	0	0	0	0	0	0	0	0	0	0	0	0
Educa	0	0	0	0	0	0	0	0	0	0	0	0	0	0	0	0
House	0	0	0	0	0	0	0	0	0	0	0	0	0	0	0	0

Table tariff(*,k) tariff on final demand

	Agric	Extra	Minin	Chemi	Metal	Engin	Foodd	othma	Power	Const	Distr	Trans	Finan	Pubad	Educa	House
Cons	55	0	0	27	0	80	91	294	0	0	0	0	0	0	0	0
GGFC	0	0	0	11	0	41	4	36	0	0	0	0	0	0	0	0
GDFCF	0	0	0	0	0	313	0	69	0	0	0	0	0	0	0	0
Stocks	0	0	0	3	3	2	0	13	0	0	0	0	0	0	0	0
Exports	2	0	25	2	0	2	0	1	0	0	0	0	0	0	0	0
rexpsub	2	0	25	2	0	2	0	1	0	0	0	0	0	0	0	0

Table duties(*,kk) duties and levies in intermediate demand

	Agric	Extra	Minin	Chemi	Metal	Engin	Foodd	othma	Power	Const	
	Distr	Trans	Finan	Pubad	Educa	House					
Agric	0	0	0	0	0	0	0	0	0	0	0
	0	0	0	0	0						
Extra	0	0	0	0	0	0	0	0	0	0	0
	0	0	0	0	0						
Minin	0	0	0	0	0	0	0	0	0	0	0
	0	0	0	0	0						
Chemi	190	0	94	1103	276	120	188	232	892	104	964
	1909	640	0	237	11						
Metal	0	0	0	0	0	0	0	0	0	0	0
	0	0	0	0	0						
Engin	0	0	0	0	0	0	0	0	0	0	0
	0	0	0	0	0						
Foodd	0	0	0	0	0	0	0	0	0	0	0
	0	0	0	0	0						
othma	0	0	0	0	0	0	0	0	0	0	0
	0	0	0	0	0						
Power	0	0	0	0	0	0	0	0	0	0	0
	0	0	0	0	0						
Const	0	0	0	0	0	0	0	0	0	0	0
	0	0	0	0	0						
Distr	0	0	0	0	0	0	0	0	0	0	0
	0	0	0	0	0						
Trans	0	0	0	0	0	0	0	0	0	0	0
	0	0	0	0	0						
Finan	7	0	1	6	7	8	5	15	5	10	49
	41	153	0	18	24						
Pubad	0	0	0	0	0	0	0	0	0	0	0
	0	0	0	0	0						
Educa	0	0	0	0	0	0	0	0	0	0	0
	0	0	0	0	0						
House	0	0	0	0	0	0	0	0	0	0	0
	0	0	0	0	0						

Table dutychitd(*,k) duties and levies in chemical and food

	Agric	Extra	Minin	Chemi	Metal	Engin	Foodd	othma	Power	Const
	Distr	Trans	Finan	Pubad	Educa	House				
tobacco	1	0	0	0	0	0	2	0	0	4
	152	26	29	0	22	0				
alcohol	2	1	0	18	3	2	196	4	0	1
	61	14	23	0	39	0				
sugar	0	0	0	1	0	0	38	0	0	0
	3	1	1	0	2	0				
fosfuel	10	0	7	43	53	42	29	75		
	435	10	43	33	47	0	24	1		
gas	0	0	0	4	6	4	3	5		
	47	0	3	2	3	0	3	0		

```
Table dutyf(*,*) duties and levies on final consumption
         Agric  Extra  Minin  Chemi  Metal  Engin  Foodd  othma  Power  Const
         Distr  Trans  Finan  Pubad  Educa  House
Cons     0      0      0      7727   0      0      12254  0      500    0      0
         351    286    0      1595   0
GGFC     0      0      0      386    0      0      2      0      46     0      0
         0      0      0      0      0
GDFCF    0      0      0      0      0      0      0      0      0      0      0
         0      0      0      0      0
Stocks          0      0      0      0      0      0      0      0      0      0
         0      0      0      0      0
Exports  0      0      0      0      0      0      0      0      0      0      0
         0      0      0      0      0
;

Table dutychfd(*,fd) levies and duties in chemical and food
         Cons   GGFC   GDFCF  Stocks Exports
tobacco         7136   0      0      0      0
alcohol         5110   1      0      0      0
sugar           8      1      0      0      0
fosfuel         425    41     0      0      0
gas             75     5      0      0      0
;

Table subsidy(*,k) Subsidies and other taxes on persons
         Agric  Extra  Minin  Chemi  Metal  Engin  Foodd  othma  Power  Const
         Distr  Trans  Finan  Pubad  Educa  House
Agric    -252   0      -1     -3     -1     -1     -1411  -85    0      0      -
         111    -6     -1     0      -14    0
Extra    0      0      0      0      0      0      0      0      0      0      0
         0      0      0      0      0
Minin    0      0      0      0      0      0      0      0      0      0      0
         0      0      0      0      0
Chemi    -2     0      0      -12    -2     -2     -2     -9     -2     -1     -2
         -4     -2     0      -3     0
Metal    0      0      0      0      -3     -2     -1     -2     0      -2     0
         0      0      0      0      0
Engin    0      0      0      0      0      -3     0      -1     0      0      0
         0      0      0      0      0
Foodd    0      0      0      0      0      0      0      0      0      0      0
         0      0      0      0      0
othma           0      0      -1     -1     -1     -1     -7     0      -1     -2
         -1     -2     0      -1     0
Power    0      0      0      0      0      0      0      0      0      0      0
         0      0      0      0      0
Const    0      0      0      0      0      0      0      0      0      -7     0
         0      -1     0      0      -1
Distr    0      0      0      0      0      0      0      0      0      0      0
         0      0      0      0      0
Trans    -6     -25    -7     -28    -44    -31    -34    -79    -6     -20    -317
         -378   -359   0      -67    -4
Finan    0      0      0      0      0      0      0      0      0      0      0
         0      0      0      0      0
```

```
Pubad    0     0     0     0     0     0     0     0     0     0     0
         0     0     0     0     0
Educa    -4    0     0     -6    -3    -6    -5    -29   -2    -3    -11
         -15   -44   0     -96   -1
House    0     0     0     0     0     0     0     0     0     0     0
         0     0     0     -4    0
;
```

Table subsidyf(*,k) Subsidies and other taxes on final demand

```
         Agric Extra Minin Chemi Metal Engin Foodd othma Power Const
         Distr Trans Finan Pubad Educa House
Cons     -799  0     0     -14   0     -1    0     -9    0     -1    0
         -496  0     0     -469  -1060
GGFC     -4    0     0     -4    0     -1    0     -2    0     -1    0
         -64   0     0     -499  -2
GDFCF    0     0     0     0     -2    -5    0     -3    0     -15   0
         -19   0     0     0     0
Stocks   5     0     0     0     0     0     0     -1    0     0     0
         0     0     0     0     0
Exports  -192  0     0     -25   -3    -9    0     -9    0     0     0
         -267  0     0     -48   -5
;
```

***Check for data**

```
parameter chk, chkk, chintd, chinm;

chk                  = sum(k, zz("lb",k));
chkk                 = sum(k, zz("ka",k));
chintd(k)            = sum(kk, iof(k,kk));
chinm(k)             = sum(kk, iofm(k,kk));

display chk, chkk, chintd,chinm;
```

Table income(*,hh) Sources of Income to the households

```
        h1
wage 433059
intr 195376
;

parameter subsum;

subsum(k) =sum(kk, subsidy(kk,k));

display subsum;
```

Parameter

```
vtintd     value added tax in intermediate inputs
vatcd(k)   value added tax in consumption
vatkd(k)   value added tax in investment
vatgd(k)   value added tax in public cons
vtint      value added tax rate in intermediate inputs
vatc(k)    value added tax rate in consumption
```

vatk(k)	value added tax rate in investment
vatg(k)	value added tax rate in public cons
vtint0	base year value added tax rate on int inputs
vatc0	base year value added tax rate on consumption
vatk0	base year value added tax rate on investment
vatg0	base year value added tax rate on gov consumption
dlintd	duties and levies in intermediate inputs
dlcd	duties and levies in consumption
dlkd	duties and leveis in investment
dlgd	duties and leveis rate in government consumption
dlint	duties and levies rate in intermediate inputs
dlc	duties and levies rate in consumption
dlg	duties and leveis rate in government consumption
dlk	
dlint0	base year levies and duties on int inputs
dlc0	base year levies and duties on consumption
dlk0	base year levies and duties on investment
dlg0	base year levies and duties on gov consumption
tarcd	tariff in final consumption
tarkd	tariff in investment
targd	tariff in government consumption
tarintd	tariff on intermediate input
tarc	tariff in final consumption
tark	tariff in investment
targ	tariff in government consumption
tarrexd	
tarc0	base year tariff on consumption
targ0	base year tariff on gov consumption
tark0	base year tariff on investment
tarint	tariff on intermediate input
tarint0	base year tariff on intermediate input
otxsbd	other taxes and subsidies
otxsb	other taxes and subsidy rates
otxsb0	other taxes and subsidies in the base
expsrt	export subsidy rate
expsrt0	
intdm	import for intermediate inputs
subintd	subsidy in intermediate inputs
subfdc	subsidy in consumption
subfdg	subsidy in government consumption
subfdk	subsidy in investment
subfde	subsidy in exorts
subint	subsidy in intermediate inputs
subfc	subsidy in consumption
subfg	subsidy in government consumption
subfk	subsidy in investment
subfe	subsidy in exorts
subint0	subsidy in intermediate inputs
subfc0	subsidy in consumption
subfg0	subsidy in government consumption
subfk0	subsidy in investment
subfe0	subsidy in exorts
sumtar	total tariff revenue
sumvat	total vat revenue

```
        sumdl     total duties and levies
        sumsub    total subsidies
;
parameter dutyfsfuel, dutygas, dutytobac, dutyalcohl, dutysugar, sumk;

* value added tax revenue
        vtintd(k,kk)          = vattn(k,kk);
        vatcd(k)              = vatt("cons",k);
        vatgd(k)              = vatt("GGFC",k);
        vatkd(k)              = vatt("GDFCF",k);
        sumvat                =sum(k, vatcd(k)+vatgd(k)+vatkd(k))+sum((k,kk),vtintd(k,kk));
        sumk(kk)              = vatcd(kk)+vatgd(kk)+vatkd(kk)+sum(k,vtintd(kk,k));

display sumk;
*dlcd(kk)+dlgd(kk)+ sum(k,dlintd(kk,k));
* revenue from duties and levies
        dutyfsfuel(k)         = dutychitd("fosfuel",k);
        dutygas(k)            = dutychitd("gas",k);
        dutytobac(k)          = dutychitd("tobacco",k);
        dutyalcohl(k)         = dutychitd("alcohol",k);
        dutysugar(k)          = dutychitd("sugar",k);
        dlintd(k,kk)          = duties(k,kk);
        dlintd("power",k)     = dutyfsfuel(k)+dutygas(k);
        dlintd("foodd",k)     = dutytobac(k)+dutyalcohl(k)+dutysugar(k);
        dlcd(k)               = dutyf("cons",k);
        dlgd(k)               = dutyf("GGFC",k);
        dlcd("power")         = dutychfd("fosfuel","cons")+dutychfd("gas","cons");
        dlcd("foodd")         = dutychfd("tobacco","cons")+dutychfd("alcohol","cons")
                                  +dutychfd("sugar","cons");
        dlgd("power")         = dutychfd("fosfuel","ggfc")+dutychfd("gas","ggfc");
        dlgd("foodd")         = dutychfd("tobacco","ggfc")+dutychfd("alcohol","ggfc")
                                  +dutychfd("sugar","ggfc");
        sumdl                 = sum(k, dlcd(k)+dlgd(k))+ sum((k,kk),dlintd(kk,k));
*revenue from tariffs
        tarintd(k,kk)         = tarrif(k,kk);
        tarcd(k)              = tariff("cons",k);
        targd(k)              = tariff("GGFC",k);
        tarkd(k)              = tariff("GDFCF",k)+tariff("stocks",k);
        tarrexd(k)            = tariff("rexpsub",k);
        sumtar                = sum(k,tarkd(k)+targd(k)+tarcd(k)+tarrexd(k))+sum((k,kk),
                                  tarintd(k,kk));
        subintd(k,kk)         = subsidy(k,kk);
        subfdc(k)             = subsidyf("cons",k);
        subfdg(k)             = subsidyf("GGFC",k);
        subfdk(k)             = subsidyf("GDFCF",k)+subsidyf("stocks",k);
        subfde(k)             = subsidyf("exports",k);
*revenue from other taxes and personal subsidies

display tarintd, tarcd, targd, tarkd, vtintd, vatcd, vatgd, vatkd, dlintd, dlcd, dlgd, sumtar, sumvat,
sumdl, sumk;
display vtintd, vatcd, vatgd, vatkd, subintd, subfdc, subfdg, subfdk, subfde;
```

Parameter

tid0	Total investment
id0(k)	domestic suplly of investment
id0m(k)	foreign supply of investment
stock(k)	change in stocks -domesti
stockm(k)	change in stock - import
G0(k)	government consumption -domestic
gm0(k)	government consumption -import
cc0(k)	consuption demand by households -domestic
ccm0(k)	consumption by households -imports
m0(k)	total imports
dd0(k)	total domestic demands
cch0(hh,k)	household demand for domestic goods
cchm0(hh,k)	household demand for imported goods
expt(k)	exports
rexp(k)	imports re-exported
expe(hh,k)	export earning to households
expem(hh,k)	re-export earning to households

;

Parameter

c0(hh)	consumption of goods and leisure
cap0(j,k)	capital stock type asset j for sector k
d0(hh,k)	households' final demand -domestic
d0m(hh,k)	households' final demand -imports
grev	government revenue
hit(hh)	labour income tax
hit0(hh)	base year labour income tax rate
incbal(*)	budget balance check
intr(j,hh)	gross capital income to households
iof(kk,k)	domestic intermediate demand
kt0(k)	aggregate capital income from sector k
k0(j,k)	capital income from asset j in sector k
kj0(j)	total of type j assets in the base year
l0(k)	labour income from sector K
leisure(hh)	leisure demand (value net of income tax)
mcf	marginal cost of public funds
mkt(*)	market cleance check for the base year
nettrn(hh)	net income transfer to households
netwage(hh)	wage income (net of income tax)
wages(hh)	wage income (gross of income tax)
p0(k)	consumer prices (gross of vat)
pindex	price index for marginal calculations
prf(kk)	zero profit condition
rk0(j,k)	base year return to capital (gross of tax)
tk(j,k)	capital tax rate by assets per sector: P-tax rates
tk0(j,k)	base year capital tax rate
y0(k)	sectoral output (gross of tax)
gsize	government size;

*** Extract some data:**

*** capital tax rates from Ptax:**

```
tk(j,k) = trafo(j,k);
tk("dwell",k) = 0;
tk("dwell","house") = trafo("dwell","house");
cap0(j,k) = asset(j,k);
kt0(k) = zz("ka",k);
tk(j,k) =0;
tk(j,k)$cap0(j,k) = trafo(j,k);
```

**** Split value added from capital by value of assets in the base year 1995**

```
k0(j,k) = zz("ka",k)*(cap0(j,k)/sum(jj,cap0(jj,K)));
```

**** allocation of capital income among assets accounting for different depreciation rates**

**** Asset with lower depreciation rate live longer and therefore, given less weight while**

**** decomposing value added from capital into different assets.**

```
k0(j,k) = zz("ka",k)*(pafo(j,k)+dep(j,k))*(cap0(j,k)
sum(jj,(pafo(j,k)+dep(j,k))*cap0(jj,K)));
kt0(k) = sum(j,k0(j,k)-tk(j,k)*k0(j,k));
kj0(j) =sum(k,k0(j,k));
k0(j,k) = k0(j,k)-tk(j,k)*k0(j,k);
L0(k) = zz("lb",k);
tk(j,k)$cap0(j,k) = trafo(j,k);

parameter ptaxr(k);

ptaxr(k) = sum(j,tk(j,k)*(k0(j,k)/(1-tk(j,k))));

display kt0, l0, ptaxr, k0;
```

***the patax rate in capital stock would increase gross of tax output**

***the elements of final demand are retrieved below**

```
y0(k)          = zz("xd",k);
id0(k)         = DF("GDFCF", k);
id0m(k)        = MF("GDFCF", k);
stock(k)       = DF("stocks", k);
stockm(k)      = MF("stocks", k);
g0(k)          = DF("GGFC", k);
gm0(k)         = MF("GGFC", k);
cc0(k)         = DF("cons", k);
ccm0(k)        = MF("cons", k);
expt(k)        = DF("exports",k);
rexp(k)        = MF("exports",k);
expe(hh,k)     = (1/card(hh))*expt(k);
expem(hh,k)    = (1/card(hh))*rexp(k);

alias (kk,kkk), (kkk,kkkk);
```

***total imports**

```
m0(k)          = sum(kk, iofm(K,kk))+id0m(k)+ ccm0(k)+gm0(k)+stockm(k);
intdm(k)       = zz("intdm",k);
```

```
        cch0(hh,k)          = cc0(k);
        cchm0(hh,k)         = ccm0(k);
```

***total final demand for domestic and imported products**

```
        d0(hh,k)            = y0(k)- sum(kk,iof(k,Kk))-ZZ("exports",k);
        d0m(hh,k)           = m0(k)- sum(kk,iofm(k,Kk))-ZZ("rexpt",k);

display k0,kt0, l0, cap0, d0, d0m;
```

***gross of capital tax price of assets in the benchmark**

```
        rk0(j,k)            = 1/(1-tk(j,k));

display tk, rk0;
```

***gross of tax wage and gross of tax captal income for households**

```
        wages(hh)           = sum(k,l0(k));
        intr(j,hh)          = sum(k, k0(j,k)/(1-tk(j,k)));

display l0, wages, intr;

parameters p0c, p0k, p0g;
```

*** compute tariff rates on intermediate and final demands**

```
        tarint(k,kk)$iofm(k,kk)             = (tarintd(k,kk)/iofm(k,kk)$iofm(k,kk));
        tarc(k)$ccm0(k)                     = tarcd(k)/ccm0(k);
        targ(k)$gm0(k)                      = targd(k)/gm0(k);
        tark(k)$(id0m(k)+stockm(k))         = tarkd(k)/(id0m(k)+stockm(k));
        tarint0(k,kk)$iofm(k,kk)            = tarint(k,kk);
        tarc0(k)                            = tarc(k);
        targ0(k)                            = targ(k);
        tark0(k)                            = tark(k);

*subsidy rates
        subint(k,kk)$(iof(k,kk))            = subintd(k,kk)/(iof(k,kk));
        subfc(k)$(cc0(k))                   = subfdc(k)/(cc0(k));
        subfg(k)$g0(k)                      = subfdg(k)/(g0(k));
        subfk(k)$(id0(k)+stock(k))          = subfdk(k)/(id0(k)+stock(k));
        subfe(k)$expt(k)                    = subfde(k)/(expt(k));
        subint0(k,kk)                       = subint(k,kk);
        subfc0(k)                           = subfc(k);
        subfg0(k)                           = subfg(k);
        subfk0(k)                           = subfk(k);
        subfe0(k)                           = subfe(k);
```

*** Impose duties and levies on intermediate and final consumption,investment and goverment consumption**

```
        dlint(k,kk)$(iof(k,kk)+iofm(k,kk))          =
dlintd(k,kk)/(iof(k,kk)*(1+subint(k,KK))+iofm(k,KK)*(1+tarint(k,KK)));
        dlc(k)$(cc0(k)+ccm0(k))                     =
dlcd(k)/(cc0(k)*(1+subfc(k))+ccm0(k)*(1+tarc(k)));
        dlg(k)$(g0(k)+gm0(k))                       =
dlgd(k)/(g0(k)*(1+subfg(k))+gm0(k)*(1+targ(k)));
```

```
        dlk(k)                          = 0;
        dlint0(k,kk)                    = dlint(k,kk);
        dlc0(k)                         = dlc(k);
        dlg0(k)                         = dlg(k);
```

*** Impose VAT on intermediate and final consumption,investment and goverment consumption**

```
        vtint(k,kk)$(iof(k,kk)+iofm(k,kk))              =
vtintd(k,kk)/((iof(k,kk)*(1+subint(k,KK))+iofm(k,KK)*(1+tarint(k,KK)))*(1+dlint(k,kk)));
        vatc(k)$(cc0(k)+ccm0(k))                        =
vatcd(k)/((cc0(k)*(1+subfc(k))+ccm0(k)*(1+tarc(k)))*(1+dlc(k)));
        vatg(k)$(g0(k)+gm0(k))                          =
vatgd(k)/((g0(k)*(1+subfg(k))+gm0(k)*(1+targ(k)))*(1+dlg(k)));
        vatk(k)$(id0(k)+stock(k)+id0m(k)+stockm(k)) =
vatkd(k)/(((id0(k)+stock(k))*(1+subfk(k))+(id0m(k)+stockm(k))*(1+tark(k)))*(1+dlk(k)));
        vtint0(k,kk)        = vtint(k,kk);
        vatc0(k)            = vatc(k);
        vatg0(k)            = vatg(k);
        vatk0(k)            = vatk(k);

        expsrt(k)$expt(k) = df("expsub",k)/expt(k);
        expsrt0(k) =expsrt(k);
display tarint,tarc,targ,tark, vtint,vatc, vatg,vatk,dlint,dlc,dlg, tk;
display tarintd,tarcd,targd,tarkd,vtintd,vatcd,vatgd,vatkd,dlintd, dlcd,dlgd,sumtar,sumvat, sumdl;
```

*** Impose a marginal income tax on labour income according to data:**

```
        hit(hh)             = 0.38;
        netwage(hh)         = (1-hit(hh)) * wages(hh);
```

*** Assume that 3/4 as much time is spent on leisure and**

*** home production for all households:**

```
        leisure(hh) =(3/4) * netwage(hh);
```

Parameter

```
        orev revenue from other taxes and subsidies in production
        trev revenue from tariff
        drev revenue from duties and levies
        vrev vat revenue
        lrev revenue from labour income tax
        krev revenue from capital income tax
;

parameter vrev1, vrev2, vrev3, vrev4;
parameter orev1, orev2, orev3, orev4, orev5;

        orev        = sum((k,kk),
subint(k,KK)*(iof(k,kk)))+sum((hh,k),(cch0(hh,k))*(subfc(k)))
                        +sum(k,(id0(k))*(subfk(k))) +sum(k,(g0(k))*subfg(k))
                        +sum(k,subfe(k)*expt(k));
        orev1(k) =sum(kk, subint(k,KK)*(iof(k,kk))) ;
        orev2(k) = sum(hh,(cch0(hh,k))*(subfc(k)));
```

```
        orev3(k) =(id0(k)+stock(k))*(subfk(k)) ;
        orev4(k) = (g0(k))*subfg(k);
        orev5(k) = subfe(k)*expt(k);
orev= sum(k,orev1(k)+orev2(k)+orev3(k)+orev4(k)+orev5(k));
display orev1, orev2, orev3, orev4, orev5;
        trev = sum((k,kk), tarint(k,KK)*iofm(k,KK))+sum(k,ccm0(k)*(tarc0(k)))
                 +sum(k,(id0m(k)+stockm(k))*(tark0(k))) +sum(k,gm0(k)*targ0(k))
                 +sum(k,tarrexd(k));

*       tarint(k,kk)$iofm(k,kk)         = (tarintd(k,kk)/iofm(k,kk)$iofm(k,kk));
*       tarc(k)$ccm0(k)                 = tarcd(k)/ccm0(k);
*       targ(k)$gm0(k)                  = targd(k)/gm0(k);
*       tark(k)$(id0m(k)+stockm(k)) = tarkd(k)/(id0m(k)+stockm(k));

        drev =
sum((k,kk),dlint(k,kk)*((iof(k,kk)*(1+subint(k,KK))+iofm(k,KK)*(1+tarint(k,KK)))))
        +sum(k, dlc(k)*((cc0(k)*(1+subfc(k))+ccm0(k)*(1+tarc(k)))))
        +sum(k,dlg(k)*((g0(k)*(1+subfg(k))+gm0(k)*(1+targ(k)))))
        +sum(k,dlk(k)*((id0(k)*(1+subfk(k))+id0m(k)*(1+tark(k)))));

        vrev1(k)= sum(kk,
vtint0(k,kk)*((iof(k,kk)*(1+subint(k,KK))+iofm(k,KK)*(1+tarint(k,KK)))*(1+dlint(k,kk))));
        vrev2(k)= vatc(k)*((cc0(k)*(1+subfc(k))+ccm0(k)*(1+tarc(k)))*(1+dlc(k)));
        vrev3(k)=vatk(k)*(((id0(k)+stock(k))*(1+subfk(k))+(id0m(k)+stockm(k))
*(1+tark(k)))*(1+dlk(k)));
        vrev4(k)= vatg(k)*((g0(k)*(1+subfg(k))+gm0(k)*(1+targ(k)))*(1+dlg(k)));
vrev = sum(k, vrev1(k)+vrev2(k)+vrev3(k)+vrev4(k));

        lrev = sum(hh, hit(hh)*wages(hh));
        krev = sum((j,k),tk(j,k)*(k0(j,k)/(1-tk(j,k))));

grev = orev+trev+drev+vrev+lrev+krev;

display orev,trev,drev,vrev,lrev,krev, grev;

display vrev1, vrev2, vrev3, vrev4;

parameter
gdc(hh,k) consumption of domestic goods gross of taxes
gmc(hh,k) consumption of imported goods gross of taxes
gid0 total investment gross of taxes
;

*total domestic demand
        gdc(hh,k) = cc0(k)*(1+subfc(k))*(1+dlc(k))*(1+vatc(k));
        gmc(hh,k) = ccm0(k)*(1+tarc(k))*(1+dlc(k))*(1+vatc(k));
        dd0(k) = sum(kk, iof(kk,k))+id0(k)+ cc0(k)+g0(k)+stock(k);
*total investment
        gid0 =sum(k,(id0(k)+stock(k))*(1+subfk(k))*(1+vatk(k)))
        +sum(k,(id0m(k)+stockm(k))*(1+tark(k))*(1+vatk(k)));
        display gdc,gmc,gid0;
```

*** The value of aggregate (extended) consumption:**

```
*        c0(hh) = sum(k, cch0(hh,k)+ cchm0(hh,k)) + leisure(hh);
         c0(hh) = sum(k, gdc(hh,k)+ gmc(hh,k)) + leisure(hh);
```

***check the trade balance condition**

```
parameter tbal, labtax,gsav, gsavh, vatrev;

         tbal = sum(k,m0(k)+rexp(k))-sum(k,
expt(k)+rexp(k)+tariff("rexpsub",k)+df("expsub",k));

display tbal;
```

*** Government tax revenue:**

```
k0(j,k) = zz("ka",k)*(pafo(j,k)+dep(j,k))*(cap0(j,k)/sum(jj,(pafo(j,k)+dep(j,k))*cap0(jj,K)));
         kt0(k) = sum(j,k0(j,k));
kt0(k) = zz("ka",k);
         k0(j,k) = k0(j,k)-tk(j,k)*k0(j,k);
```

*** Zero profit:**

```
prf(k) = y0(k) - sum(kk, iof(kk,k)) - sum(kk, iofm(kk,k))- l0(k)
         - sum(j, k0(j,k)/(1-tk(j,k)))-sum(kk,tarintd(kk,k))
         -sum(kk,vtintd(kk,k))-sum(kk,dlintd(kk,k))-sum(kk,subintd(kk,k));
```

parameter iofd, iomd, iotar,iovt,iodl;

```
         iofd(k)= sum(kk, iof(kk,k));
         iomd(k)= sum(kk, iofm(kk,k)) ;
         iotar(k)= sum(kk,tarintd(kk,k)) ;
         iovt(k)= sum(kk,vtintd(kk,k)) ;
         iodl(k)= sum(kk,dlintd(kk,k)) ;
display k0,kt0,prf;
```

***,y0,iofd, iomd, iotar,iovt,iodl;**

*** Market clearance:**

```
mkt(k) = y0(k) - sum(kk,iof(k,kk)) - cc0(k)-g0(k)-id0(k)-stock(k)-expt(k);
mkt("l") = sum(hh, wages(hh)) - sum(k, l0(k));
mkt("k") = sum((j,k), k0(j,k)/(1-tk(j,k))) - sum((j,hh),intr(j,hh));
display mkt, prf;
```

*** Assuming that the data satisfy zero profit and market**

*** clearance, use net transfers to balance income accounts:**

parameter

```
         tvald total value added
         ciof composite gross intermediate input
```

```
;

tvald(hh) = (sum(j,intr(j,hh)))+wages(hh);
ciof(kk,k) =
(iof(kk,k)*(1+subint(kk,k))+iofm(kk,k)*(1+tarint(kk,k)))*(1+dlint(kk,k))*(1+vtint(kk,k));

*+sum(k,prot(k)+tar(k))
display tvald;

parameter
        gbal            government balance
        grinv           gross investment
        pub             total public consumption
        netintr(hh)     netinterest income
        saving          household savigns
        incadj(hh)      income adjustment term
        pubshr


parameter ntrnrt;

pub=sum(k,(g0(k)*(1+subfg(k))*(1+dlg(k))*(1+vatg(k))))+sum(k,gm0(k)*(1+targ(k))*(1+dlg(k))*(1+vatg(k)));
gbal = grev -pub;
grinv(hh)= 1/card(hh)*gid0;
nettrn(hh) = sum(j,intr(j,hh))+(netwage(hh)+leisure(hh))-c0(hh)-sum((j,k),tk(j,k)*(k0(j,k)/(1-
tk(j,k))));
labtax(hh) =hit(hh)*wages(hh);
saving(hh) = nettrn(hh)+gbal;
incadj(hh) =grinv(hh) -saving(hh);
pubshr = pub/grev;
ntrnrt(hh) = nettrn(hh)/(sum(j,intr(j,hh))+(netwage(hh)+leisure(hh)));
display grev, pub,pubshr, gbal,saving,grinv, nettrn, incadj,ntrnrt;

hit0(hh) = hit(hh);
tk0(j,k) = tk(j,k);

gsize =1;

*elasticities of the model
```

TABLE elast(K,*) elasticities in central case

	SIGMAV	SIGMAK	SIGMAC	ETRAN
Agric	1.214	1.214	1.214	1.214
Extra	1.654	1.654	1.654	1.654
Minin	1.500	1.500	1.500	1.500
Chemi	1.654	1.654	1.654	1.654
Metal	1.612	1.612	1.612	1.612
Engin	1.500	1.500	1.500	1.500
Foodd	1.000	1.000	1.000	1.000
othma	0.900	0.900	0.900	0.900
Power	1.500	1.500	1.500	1.500
Const	1.000	1.000	1.000	1.000

Distr	1.600	1.600	1.600	1.600
Trans	1.600	1.600	1.600	1.600
Finan	1.600	1.600	1.600	1.600
Pubad	1.600	1.600	1.600	1.600
Educa	1.600	1.600	1.600	1.600
House	1.000	1.000	1.000	1.000

;

```
Parameters
        etran               transformation elsticity
        sigmav              subt. elasticity -labour and composite capital
         sigmak             substitution elasticity among assets
        sigmac              subt elasticity in consumption
        sigmau              sub elasticity- consumption and leisure
        sigmal              elasticity of substitution between labour and leisure
        lselas              labour supply elasticity
        etran0, sigmav0, sigmak0, sigmac0, sigmau0,sigmal0;

        sigmav(k)           = elast(k,"sigmav");
        sigmak(k)           = elast(k,"sigmak");
        sigmac(k)           = elast(k,"sigmac");
        sigmau(hh)          = 1.5;
        sigmal(hh)          = 1.5;
        etran(k)            = elast(k,"etran");

        etran0(k)           = etran(k);
        sigmav0(k)          = sigmav(k);
        sigmak0(k)          = sigmak(k);
        sigmac0(k)          = sigmac(k);
        sigmau0(hh)         = sigmau(hh);
        sigmal0(hh)         = sigmal(hh);

        sigmav(k)           = 1/1.5*sigmav0(k);
        sigmak(k)           = 1/1.5*sigmak0(k);
        sigmac(k)           = 1/1.5*sigmac0(k);
        sigmau(hh)          = .5;
        sigmal(hh)          = .5;
        etran(k)            = 2.5*etran0(k);
```

***reference prices**

```
parameter
        pint0               reference price for domestic intermediate input
        pmint0              reference price for imported intermediate input
        pdc0                reference price for domestic consumption goods
        pmc0                reference price for imported consumption goods
        pdk0                reference price for domestic investment goods
        pmk0                reference price for inported investment goods
        pdg0                reference price for government consumption goods
        pmg0                reference price for government consumption for imported goods
```

parameter

```
        vatdc composite tax on consumption of domestic goods
        vatmc composite tax on consumption of imported goods
```

```
        vatdk composite tax on investment of domesitc goods
        vatmk composite tax on investment of imported goods
        vatdg composite tax on public consumption of domestic goods
        vatmg composite tax on public consumption of imported goods
        vatdc0 composite tax on consumption of domestic goods
        vatmc0 composite tax on consumption of imported goods
        vatdk0 composite tax on investment of domestic goods
        vatmk0 composite tax on investment of imported goods
        vatdg0 composite tax on public consumption of domestic goods
        vatmg0 composite tax on consumption of imported goods
        alldint composite tax on domestic intermediate goods
        allmint composite tax on imported intermediate goods
        alldint0 composite tax on domestic intermediate goods
        allmint0 composite tax on imported intermediate goods
;

parameter crevfc,crevfk,crevfg, basetax, bsinttx;

vatdc(k) = (1+subfc(k))*(1+dlc(k))*(1+vatc(k))-1;
vatmc(k) = (1+tarc(k))*(1+dlc(k))*(1+vatc(k))-1;
vatdk(k)= (1+subfk(k))*(1+dlk(k))*(1+vatk(k))-1;
vatmk(k)= (1+tark(k))*(1+dlk(k))*(1+vatk(k))-1;
vatdg(k)= (1+subfg(k))*(1+dlg(k))*(1+vatg(k))-1;
vatmg(k)= (1+targ(k))*(1+dlg(k))*(1+vatg(k))-1;

crevfc = sum(k, (vatdc(k)*cc0(k))+vatmc(k)*ccm0(k));
crevfk = sum(k, (vatdk(k)*(id0(k)+stock(k)))+(vatmk(k)*(id0m(k)+stockm(k))));
crevfg = sum(k, (vatdg(k)*g0(k))+vatmg(k)*gm0(k));
display crevfc, crevfk,crevfg;

alldint(k,Kk) = (1+vtint(k,kk))*(1+dlint(k,kk))*(1+subint(k,kk))-1;
allmint(k,Kk) = (1+tarint(k,kk))*(1+dlint(k,kk))*(1+vtint(k,kk))-1;

alldint0(k,kk) = alldint(k,Kk);
allmint0(k,kk) = allmint(k,Kk);
vatdc0(k)= vatdc(k);
vatmc0(k)= vatmc(k);
vatdk0(k)= vatdk(k);
vatmk0(k)= vatmk(k);
vatdg0(k)= vatdg(k);
vatmg0(k)= vatmg(k);

basetax(k,"vatc_d") = vatdc0(k);
basetax(k,"vatc_m") = vatmc0(k);
basetax(k,"vatk_d") = vatdk(k);
basetax(k,"vatk_m") = vatmk(k);
basetax(k,"vatg_d") = vatdg0(k);
basetax(k,"vatg_m") = vatmg0(k);
bsinttx("dint",k,kk) =alldint(k,Kk);
bsinttx("mint",k,kk) =allmint(k,Kk);

Pint0(k,kk)=(1+alldint0(k,kk));
pmint0(k,kk)= (1+allmint0(k,kk));
pdc0(k)=(1+vatdc0(k));
```

```
pmc0(k)=(1+vatmc0(k));
pdk0(k)=(1+vatdk0(k));
pmk0(k)=(1+vatmk0(k));
pdg0(k)=(1+vatdg0(k));
pmg0(k)=(1+vatmg0(k));

display pint0, pmint0,pdc0,pmc0,pdk0,pmk0,pdg0,pmg0;
display alldint0,allmint0,vatdc0,vatmc0,vatdk0,
vatmk0,vatdg0,vatmg0, basetax,bsinttx;

$ONTEXT

$MODEL:UK
$ECHOP:.TRUE
*$FUNLOG:.TRUE
*$DATECH:.TRUE

$sectors:
        y(k)                    ! production
        ls(hh)                  ! labor supply
        c(hh)                   ! consumpion
        IM(K)$(m0(k))           ! imports
        inv                     ! investment
        go                      ! public good production
        x(k)$expt(k)            ! export
        u(hh)                   ! Utility
        intd(k,kk)$(iof(k,kk)+iofm(k,kk)) !composite intermediate input
        mint(k,kk)$(iofm(k,kk))!imported intermediate input
        dint(k,kk)$(iof(k,kk))!domestic intermediate input
        imf(k)$(ccm0(k)+gm0(k)+id0m(k)+stockm(k))      !imports for final demand

$commodities:
        pd(k)                                   ! domestic supply price
         PM(K)$m0(k)                            ! import price
        pfx                                     ! foreign price in terms of dom price
        px(k)$expt(k)                           ! export price
        rk(j)                                   ! capital rental rate
        pl                                      ! wage rate
        ple(hh)                                 ! net of tax wage
        pc(hh)                                  ! unit expenditure cost households
        pint(k,kk)$(iof(k,kk)+iofm(k,kk))       ! price of composite intermediate input

        Pmint(k,kk)$(iofm(k,kk))                ! price of imported intermediate input
        Pdint(k,kk)$(iof(k,kk))                 ! price of domestic intermediate input
        pmc(k)$ccm0(k)                          ! consumption price of imports
        pmk(k)$(id0m(k)+stockm(k))              ! investment price of imports
        pmg(k)$gm0(k)                           ! public consumption price of imports
        pu(hh)                                  ! cost of leisure plus composite good
        pinv                                    ! price of investment goods
        pg                                      ! price of public consumption
```

```
$consumers:

        ra(hh)              ! income of private households
        govt                ! revenue account
        invest              ! financing investment

$AUXILIARY:

        TAU_Tk              ! capital tax replacement multiplier
        TAU_Tc              ! consumption tax multiplier
        TAU_Tg              ! public consumption tax multiplier
        TAU_VTk             ! investment tax multiplier
        TAU_IT              ! Labor income tax replacement multiplier
        TAU_InT(k)          ! Labor income tax replacement multiplier
        tau_ls              ! lump sum replacement tax

$prod:y(k) s:0 t:etran(k) va:sigmav(k) L(va):sigmak(k)
        o:pd(k)              q:(y0(k)-expt(k))
        o:px(k)$expt(k)      q:(expt(k))
        i:pint(kk,k)$(iof(kk,k)+iofm(kK,k))       q:ciof(kk,k)
        i:pl                 q:l0(k) va:
        i:rk(j)              q:(k0(j,k)) a:govt N:tau_tk M:(tk(j,k)/(1-tk(j,k))) p:rk0(j,k) L:

$prod:intd(k,kk)$(iof(k,kk)+iofm(k,kk)) a:1.5
        o:pint(k,kk)$(iof(k,kk)+iofm(k,kk))       q:ciof(k,kk)
        i:pdint(k,kk)$(iof(k,kk)) q:iof(k,kk) a:govt N:tau_int(k)
        M:alldint(k,kk) P:Pint0(k,kk) a:
        i:pmint(k,kk)$(iofm(k,kk))      q:(iofm(k,kk)) a:govt N:tau_int(k)
        M:allmint(k,KK) P: Pmint0(k,kk) a:

$prod:Dint(k,kk)$(iof(k,kk))
        o:pdint(k,kk)$(iof(k,kk))      q:iof(k,kk)
        i:pd(k)                        q:iof(k,kk)

$prod:mint(k,kk)$(iofm(k,kk))
        o:pmint(k,kk)$(iofm(k,kk))     q:(iofm(k,kk))
        i:pm(k)$m0(k)                  q:iofm(k,kk)

$prod:x(k)$expt(k)
        o:pfx                          q:(expt(k)+df("expsub",k))
        i:px(k)$expt(k) q:(expt(k))     a:govt T:expsrt(k) P:(1+expsrt0(k))

$prod:im(k)$m0(k)
        o:pm(k)$m0(k)                  q:(m0(k))
        i:pfx                          q:m0(k)

$prod:imf(k)$(ccm0(k)+gm0(k)+id0m(k)+stockm(k))
        o:pmc(k)$ccm0(k)               q:(ccm0(k))
        o:pmk(k)$(id0m(k))             q:(id0m(k))
        o:pmk(k)$(stockm(k))           q:(stockm(k))
        o:pmg(k)$gm0(k)                q:(gm0(k))
        i:pm(k)$(m0(k))                q:(ccm0(k)+gm0(k)+id0m(k)+stockm(k))

$prod:u(hh) a:sigmau(hh)
        o:pu(hh) q:c0(hh)
        i:pc(hh) q:(sum(k, gdc(hh,k)+gmc(hh,k))) a:
        i:ple(hh) q:leisure(hh)        a:
```

```
$prod:c(hh) s:1.5 a:sigmac(hh)
        o:pc(hh)  q:(sum(k, gdc(hh,k)+gmc(hh,k)))
        i:pd(k)   q:(cch0(hh,k))        a:govt N:tau_tc M:vatdc(k) a: P:pdc0(k)
        i:pmc(k)$ccm0(k) q:(cchm0(hh,k))        a:govt N:tau_tc M:vatmc(k) a: P:pmc0(k)

$prod:inv
        o:pinv                 q:gid0
        i:pd(k)                q:(id0(k)+stock(k)) a:govt N:tau_vtk M:vatdk(k) P:pdk0(k)
        i:pmk(k)$(id0m(k)+stockm(k)) q:(id0m(k)+stockm(k)) a:govt N:tau_vtk M:vatmk(k)
P:pmk0(k)

$prod:go s:1.5
        o:pg      q:pub
        i:pd(k)   q:g0(k) a:govt          N:tau_tg M:vatdg(k) P:pdg0(k)
        i:pmg(k)$gm0(k) q:gm0(k) a:govt          N:tau_tg M:vatmg(k) P:pmg0(k)

$prod:ls(hh)
        o:pl q:(wages(hh)) a:govt N:tau_it M:hit(hh)
        i:ple(hh) q:(netwage(hh))

$demand:ra(hh)
        d:pu(hh)  q:c0(hh)
        e:ple(hh) q:(leisure(hh)+netwage(hh))
        e:rk(j)   q:(sum(k,k0(j,k)))
        e:pu(hh)  q:(nettrn(hh))
        e:pfx     q:tbal R:tau_ls

$demand:govt
        d:pg      q:(pub)
        e:pg      q:(grev)
        e:pu(hh)  q:(-gbal)

$demand:invest
        d:pinv    q:(gid0)
        e:pu(hh)  q:saving(hh)

$report:
        V:Y1(k) O:Pd(k) PROD:Y(k)
        V:x1(k) O:Pfx PROD:x(k)
        V:m1(k) O:Pm(k) PROD:im(k)
        V:C1(HH) O:Pc(hh) PROD:C(HH)
        V:tint(kk,k)$(iof(kk,k)+iofm(kK,k)) o:pint(kk,k) PROD:intd(kk,k)
        V:L1(k) I:PL PROD:Y(k)
        V:K1(j,k) I:RK(j) PROD:Y(k)
        V:LS1(HH) i:PLe(hh) PROD:LS(HH)
        V:U1(HH) O:PU(hh) PROD:U(HH)
        V:go1     O:pg       prod:GO
        V:inv1    O:pinv prod:inv
        V:LE(HH) I:PLE(HH) PROD:U(HH)
        V:W1(hh) D:PU(HH) DEMAND:RA(HH)
        V:W(HH) W:RA(HH)

$CONSTRAINT:TAU_Tk
        gsize =E= go;
```

```
$CONSTRAINT:TAU_IT
        go =E= Gsize;

$CONSTRAINT:TAU_tc
        go =E= Gsize;
$CONSTRAINT:TAU_int(k)
        go =E= Gsize;

$CONSTRAINT:TAU_vtk
        go =E= Gsize;

$CONSTRAINT:TAU_tg
        go =E= Gsize;

$CONSTRAINT:TAU_ls
        go =e= Gsize;

$offtext
        $sysinclude mpsgeset uk

        TAU_Tk.l            = 1;
        TAU_Tc.L            = 1;
        TAU_Tg.L            = 1;
        TAU_VTk.L           = 1;
        TAU_InT.L(k)        = 1;
        TAU_IT.L= 1;
        TAU_ls.fx           = 0;
        pfx.fx              = 1;

        option decimals     = 4;
        uk.workspace        =10;
        option mcp          = path;
        uk.iterlim          = 0;
$include uk.gen
solve uk using mcp;

display rk.l;

parameter
        reva                government revenue
        meb                 marginal excess burden of taxes
        va(k)               value added net of tax
        betak(k,J)          share of asset j in capital income
        alpha(hh)           share of composite consumption
        alphal(Hh)          share of leisure
        sumalphc total of consumption share
        alphac              consumption share deaggregated
        VAS                 share in value added
        lifetk              capital income tax rate in new life assumptions
;

parameter welfare change in utility of households
        capital change in capital stock by sector and assets
        output change in output by sector
```

employ change in sectoral employment
export change in exports
Import change in imports
intrd change in intermediate input use
consm change in level of consumption
labsup change in labour supply
ch_leis change in leisure
ktmult capital income tax multiplier
vtmult consumption tax multiplier
htmult labour tax income multiplier
prmult production tax multiplier
trmult tariff rate multiplier
baserev revenue in the base case
newrev revenue in the new case
ktax new capitaltax rate
leiper percentage change in leisure
lsper percentage change in labour supply
emplper percentage change in employment
emplpr percentage change in employment
outper percentage change in output
capper percentage change in assets by sector
basewage baseyear wage
newwage wage in new solution
leiprice price of leisure
mprice domestic price of imported commodity
xprice domestic price of exports
basew
cup composite utility price
ccp composite consumption price
govc

;
parameter

captax new tax rate on capital income
constax new tax rate on consumption
congtax new tax rate on consumption
conitax new tax rate on consumption
prodtax new tax rate on production
ntarif new tariff rate
labtaxn new tax rate on labour income
invch change in investment
goch government size
revindx revenue index
revindx1 revenue index
ubase base utility
ibase base household income
gobase base government consumption
gibase base government income
invbase base inverstor resources
invibase investors baseyear income
xbase level of export in the base case
mbase level of imports in the base case
xvolume volume of eports
mvolume volume of imports

```
cbal current account balance
cbalbase current account balance in the base case
EV              Hicksian moneymetric EV for households
CV              Hicksian moneymetric CV for households
EVg             Hicksian moneymetric EV for government
CVg             Hicksian moneymetric CV for government
EVk             Hicksian moneymetric EV for investors
CVk             Hicksian moneymetric CV for investors
EVT             Total Hicksian moneymetric EV
CVT             Total Hicksian moneymetric EV
evgdp           Hicksian moneymetric EV as % of 1995 UK GDP
cvgdp           Hicksian moneymetric CV as % of 1995 UK GDP
capinflow inflow(+) or outflow(-) of capital
asstallow0      percentage change in inflow of assets by sector
asstallow1      reallocation of assets in uniform capital income tax case
asstinfln  percentage of assets in inflow of assets by sector
kstokk          capital stock
welfr           welfare percentage
chekk           % of error in allocation of assets
swelf0          Aggregate social welfare in the base case
swelf1 New aggregate social welfare
swelf2 change in aggregate social welfare
meb             marginal excess burden of taxes
 evgdp_ Hicksian EV as a percent of GDP
 cvgdp_ Hicksian EV as a percent of GDP
evresult
laborper
outper
tbalk
trade


Option decimals =5;

reva                = govt.L;
va(k)               = PL.L*L1.L(k) +sum(j, RK.L(j)*K1.L(j,k));
betak(k,J) = (rk.L(j)*K1.L(J,K))/va(k);
vas(k, "cap")       = sum(j, betak(k,J));
vas(k, "lab")       = (PL.L*L1.L(k))/va(k) ;
vas(k, "va")        = PL.L*L1.L(k) +sum(j, RK.L(j)*K1.L(j,k));
alpha(hh) =(pc.l(hh)*c1.l(Hh))/(sum(k,gdc(hh,k)+gmc(hh,k))+leisure(hh));
alphac(k,hh)        = (gdc(hh,k)+gmc(hh,k))/SUM(KK,(gdc(hh,kk)+gmc(hh,kk)));
sumalphc            = sum((k,hh), alphac(k,hh));
alphaL(Hh)          = 1-alpha(hh);
alphac(k, "govt")   = ((g0(k)*(1+vatg(k)+dlg(k)+subfg(k)))+gm0(k)*((1+targ(k)
                      +vatg(k)+dlg(k)+subfg(k))))/pub;
alphac(k,"invest")  = ((id0(k)*(1+vatk(k)+subfk(k)))
                      +(id0m(k)*(1+tark(k)+vatk(k)+subfk(k)))
                      +(stock(k)+stockm(k)) )/gid0;
baserev             = grev;
basew               = pl.l;
ubase(hh)           = u1.l(hh);
ibase(hh)           = ra.l(hh);
gobase              = go1.l;
```

```
          gibase      = govt.l;
          invbase     = inv1.l;
          invibase    = invest.l;
          xbase(k)    =x1.l(k);
          mbase(k)    =m1.l(k);
          cbalbase    = sum(k,xbase(k) -mbase(k));

display va,betak,vas,alpha,alphal,alphac, sumalphc;

display ubase, ibase, gobase, gibase, invbase, invibase;
** central elasticities

          etran(k)= etran0(k);
          sigmav(k)= sigmav0(k);
          sigmak(k)= sigmak0(k);
          sigmac(k)= sigmac0(k);
*         sigmau(hh)= 0.75*sigmau0(hh);
*         sigmau(hh)= 0.51;
*         sigmal(hh)= 0.75*sigmal0(hh);

          lselas(hh) = 0.15;
          sigmau(hh) =lselas(hh)*(netwage(hh)/leisure(hh)) +(1-alpha(hh))*(1/(1+(1-
alpha(hh))));

display sigmal;

uk.iterlim =100000;

*uniform tax case
          TAU_Tk.l          =1;
          TAU_Tc.fx         =1;
          TAU_Tg.fx         =1;
          TAU_VTk.fx        =1;
          TAU_InT.fx(k)     =1;
          TAU_IT.fx         =1;
          TAU_ls.l          =1;
          TAU_Tk.lo         =-inf;
          TAU_Tk.up         =inf;
          tk(j,k)           = 0.05;

$include uk.gen
solve uk using mcp;

$include out.gms
$include ev.gms

display "centrl15",sigmav, sigmak, etran,sigmac, sigmau,sigmal,tk0,captax,
vatc0, constax, vatg0, congtax,vatk0, conitax, hit0,labtaxn.tarint0;

display welfare, output,capital, employ, intrd,export, import,consm,ch_leis, pub,
baserev, newrev, leiper, lsper,emplpr, outper, capper,chekk,basewage, newwage,
leiprice,mprice,xprice;
```

```
display "centrl15",lsper,emplpr, outper, capper, tk0;
display "centrl15", xbase, mbase,cbalbase, xvolume, mvolume, cbal;
display "centrl15",ev,cv,evg,evg,evk,cvk,evt,cvt,evgdp_,cvgdp,kstokk,capinflow;

        laborper(k,"centrl15")$l0(k) =100*(L1.l(k)-L0(k))/L0(k);
        outper(k,"centrl15")=100*(y1.l(k)-(y0(k)-expt(k)))/(y0(k)-expt(k));

evresult("centrl15", "ev") =evgdp_;
evresult("centrl15", "cv") =cvgdp_;
sigmak(k)= 0.95*sigmav0(k);
        lselas(hh) = 0.3;
        Sigmau(hh) =lselas(hh)*(netwage(hh)/leisure(hh)) +(1-alpha(hh))*(1/(1+(1-
alpha(hh))));

$include uk.gen
solve uk using mcp;

$include out.gms
$include ev.gms

display "central3",sigmav, sigmak, etran,sigmac, sigmau,sigmal,tk0,captax,
vatc0, constax, vatg0, congtax,vatk0, conitax, hit0,labtaxn,tarint0;

display welfare, output,capital, employ, intrd,export, import,consm,ch_leis, pub,
baserev, newrev, leiper, lsper,emplpr, outper, capper,chekk,basewage, newwage,
leiprice,mprice,xprice;

display "central3",ev,cv,evg,evg,evk,cvk,evt,cvt,evgdp_,cvgdp,kstokk,capinflow;
display "central3",lsper,emplpr, outper, capper, tk0;
display "central3", xbase, mbase,cbalbase, xvolume, mvolume, cbal;

        laborper(k,"centrl3")$l0(k) =100*(L1.l(k)-L0(k))/L0(k);
        outper(k,"centrl3")=100*(y1.l(k)-(y0(k)-expt(k)))/(y0(k)-expt(k));

parameter capper1;
capper1(k,j) = 100*(k1.l(j,k)-k0(j,k))/k0(j,k)$k0(j,k);
evresult("Central3", "ev") =evgdp_;
evresult("Central3", "cv") =cvgdp_;

display laborper, outper;

file ktxt /cap1.txt/; put ktxt;
$libinclude gams2tbl capper1

*$ontext
** unit elasticity case

etran(k)= etran0(k);
sigmav(k)= 1.01;
sigmak(k)= 1.01;
sigmac(k)= 0.5*sigmac0(k);
sigmal(hh)= 0.51*sigmal0(hh);
lselas(hh) = 0.15;
Sigmau(hh) =lselas(hh)*(netwage(hh)/leisure(hh)) +(1-alpha(hh))*(1/(1+(1-alpha(hh))));
```

```
$include uk.gen
solve uk using mcp;

$include out.gms
$include ev.gms

display "unit15",sigmav, sigmak, etran,sigmac, sigmau,sigmal,tk0,captax,
vatc0, constax, vatg0, congtax,vatk0, conitax, hit0,labtaxn,tarint0;

display welfare, output,capital, employ, intrd,export, import,consm,ch_leis, pub,
baserev, newrev, leiper, lsper,emplpr, outper, capper,chekk,basewage, newwage,
leiprice,mprice,xprice;

display "unit15",ev,cv,evg,evg,evk,cvk,evt,cvt,evgdp_,cvgdp,kstokk,capinflow;
display "unit15",lsper,emplpr, outper, capper, tk0;
display "unit15", xbase, mbase,cbalbase, xvolume, mvolume, cbal;

        laborper(k,"unit15")$l0(k) =100*(L1.l(k)-L0(k))/L0(k);
        outper(k,"unit15")=100*(y1.l(k)-(y0(k)-expt(k)))/(y0(k)-expt(k));

evresult("unit15", "ev") =evgdp_;
evresult("unit15", "cv") =cvgdp_;
        sigmak(k)= 0.95*sigmav0(k);
        lselas(hh) = 0.3;
        Sigmau(hh) =lselas(hh)*(netwage(hh)/leisure(hh)) +(1-alpha(hh))*(1/(1+(1-
alpha(hh))));

$include uk.gen
solve uk using mcp;

$include out.gms
$include ev.gms

display "unit15",sigmav, sigmak, etran,sigmac, sigmau,sigmal,tk0,captax,
vatc0, constax, vatg0, congtax,vatk0, conitax, hit0,labtaxn,tarint0;

display welfare, output,capital, employ, intrd,export, import,consm,ch_leis, pub,
baserev, newrev, leiper, lsper,emplpr, outper, capper,chekk,basewage, newwage,
leiprice,mprice,xprice;

display "unit3",ev,cv,evg,evg,evk,cvk,evt,cvt,evgdp_,cvgdp,kstokk,capinflow;
display "unit3",lsper,emplpr, outper, capper, tk0;
display "unit3", xbase, mbase,cbalbase, xvolume, mvolume, cbal;
evresult("unit3", "ev") =evgdp_;
evresult("unit3", "cv") =cvgdp_;

        laborper(k,"unit3")$l0(k) =100*(L1.l(k)-L0(k))/L0(k);
        outper(k,"unit3")=100*(y1.l(k)-(y0(k)-expt(k)))/(y0(k)-expt(k));

evresult("unit3", "ev") =evgdp_;
evresult("unit3", "cv") =cvgdp_;

** central elasticities
etran(k)= 1/2*etran0(k);
```

```
sigmav(k)= 1/2*sigmav0(k);
sigmak(k)= 1/2*sigmak0(k);
sigmac(k)= sigmac0(k);
sigmal(hh)= 0.75*sigmal0(hh);
lselas(hh) = 0.15;
Sigmau(hh) =lselas(hh)*(netwage(hh)/leisure(hh)) +(1-alpha(hh))*(1/(1+(1-alpha(hh))));

$include ptaxl.gms
lifetk(j,k)$cap0(j,k) =trafo(j,k);
tk(j,k)$cap0(j,k) =lifetk(j,k);

$include uk.gen
solve uk using mcp;

$include out.gms
$include ev.gms
captax(j,k,"life") =TAU_Tk.L*tk(j,k);

display "life15",sigmav, sigmak, etran,sigmac, sigmau,sigmal,tk0,captax,
vatc0, constax, vatg0, congtax,vatk0, conitax, hit0,labtaxn,tarint0;
display "life15",lsper,emplpr, outper, capper;
display "life15",tk0, lifetk;
display "life15", welfare, output,capital, employ, intrd,export, import,consm,ch_leis, pub,
baserev, newrev, leiper, lsper,emplpr, outper, capper,chekk,basewage, newwage,
leiprice,mprice,xprice;

display "life15",ev,cv,evg,evg,evk,cvk,evt,cvt,evgdp_,cvgdp,kstokk,capinflow;

display     vatdc0,     vatmc0,   vatdk0 ,vatmk0, vatdg0, vatmg0,alldint0, allmint0;
            laborper(k,"life15")$l0(k) =100*(L1.l(k)-L0(k))/L0(k);
            outper(k,"life15")=100*(y1.l(k)-(y0(k)-expt(k)))/(y0(k)-expt(k));

evresult("life15", "ev") =evgdp_;
evresult("life15", "cv") =cvgdp_;
            sigmak(k)= 0.95*sigmav0(k);
            lselas(hh) = 0.3;
            Sigmau(hh) =lselas(hh)*(netwage(hh)/leisure(hh)) +(1-alpha(hh))*(1/(1+(1-
alpha(hh))));

$include uk.gen
solve uk using mcp;

$include out.gms
$include ev.gms
display "life3",sigmav, sigmak, etran,sigmac, sigmau,sigmal,tk0,captax,
vatc0, constax, vatg0, congtax,vatk0, conitax, hit0,labtaxn,tarint0;
display "life3",lsper,emplpr, outper, capper;
display "life3",tk0, lifetk;
display "life3", welfare, output,capital, employ, intrd,export, import,consm,ch_leis, pub,
baserev, newrev, leiper, lsper,emplpr, outper, capper,chekk,basewage, newwage,
leiprice,mprice,xprice;

display "life3",ev,cv,evg,evg,evk,cvk,evt,cvt,evgdp_,cvgdp,kstokk,capinflow;
            laborper(k,"life3")$l0(k) =100*(L1.l(k)-L0(k))/L0(k);
            outper(k,"life3")=100*(y1.l(k)-(y0(k)-expt(k)))/(y0(k)-expt(k));
```

```
evresult("life3", "ev") =evgdp_;
evresult("life3", "cv") =cvgdp_;

display laborper, outper,capper;
display evresult;

$exit

*household income taxes
** unit elasticity case

etran(k)= etran0(k);
sigmav(k)= 1.01;
sigmak(k)= 1.01;
sigmac(k)= 0.5*sigmac0(k);
sigmal(hh)= 0.51*sigmal0(hh);
lselas(hh) = 0.15;
Sigmau(hh) =lselas(hh)*(netwage(hh)/leisure(hh)) +(1-alpha(hh))*(1/(1+(1-alpha(hh))));

TAU_int.lo(k) =-inf;
TAU_int.up(k) = inf;
TAU_Tk.fx          =1;
TAU_Tc.fx          =1;
TAU_Tg.fx          =1;
TAU_VTk.fx         =1;
TAU_InT.fx(k)      =1;

TAU_it.lo =-inf;
TAU_it.up = inf;
TAU_ls.lo =-inf;
TAU_ls.up = inf;
hit(hh) = 0.2;

$include uk.gen
        solve uk using mcp;
$include out.gms
$include ev.gms

display "hit",sigmav, sigmak, etran,sigmac, sigmau,sigmal,tk0,captax,
vatc0, constax, vatg0, congtax,vatk0, conitax, hit0,labtaxn,tarint0;

display "hit", welfare, output,capital, employ, intrd,export, import,consm,ch_leis, pub,
baserev, newrev, leiper, lsper,emplpr, outper, capper,chekk,basewage, newwage,
leiprice,mprice,xprice;

display "hit",ev,cv,evg,evg,evk,cvk,evt,cvt,evgdp_,cvgdp,kstokk,capinflow;
display "hit",lsper,emplpr, outper, capper, capinflow, capital;

display "hit", xbase, mbase,cbalbase, xvolume, mvolume, cbal;
display tarint0,tarc0,targ0,tark0,vtint0,vatc0,vatg0,vatk0,dlint0, dlc0,dlg0,hit0,tk0;

SET STFLAG /CPU_Time, Model_Stat, Solve_Stat/
PARAMETER STATUS Termination status flags;
```

```
STATUS("CPU_Time") = uk.resusd;
STATUS("Model_Stat") = uK.modelstat;
STATUS("Solve_Stat") = uK.solvestat;

display status;
*$offtext

**capital inflow-outflow case
TAU_Tk.lo =-inf;
TAU_Tk.up =inf;
tk(j,k) = 0.3;
TAU_Tg.lo =-inf;
TAU_Tg.up =inf;
TAU_Tc.lo =-inf;
TAU_Tc.up =inf;
TAU_vtk.lo =-inf;
TAU_vTk.up =inf;
TAU_it.lo =-inf;
TAU_it.up =inf;

sigmav(k) =.5*sigmav0(k);
sigmak(k) =.5*sigmak0(k);
sigmac(k) =.5*sigmac0(k);
sigmak(k) =.51;
sigmav(k) =.51;
sigmak(k) =.5*sigmak0(k);
sigmav(k) =.5*sigmav0(k);
sigmau(hh) =.15;
sigmal(hh) =.25;
lselas(hh) = 0.15;
Sigmau(hh) =lselas(hh)*(netwage(hh)/leisure(hh)) +(1-alpha(hh))*(1/(1+(1-alpha(hh))));
etran(k) = .6*etran0(k);

asstallow0(j,k)$cap0(j,k)        =100*(k1.l(j,k)-k0(j,k))/cap0(j,k);
asstallow1(j,k)$cap0(j,k)        =(k1.l(j,k)-k0(j,k));

*fix the rental rate to base year values

rk.fx(j) =1;

*          TAU_tk.up = inf;
           tk(j,k) =0.3;
           tbal = sum(k, px.l(k)*x1.l(k)-pm.l(k)*m1.l(k))-sum(j,sum(k,k1.l(j,k)-k0(j,k)));

$include uk.gen
           solve uk using mcp;
           tk(j,k) =0.3;

$include uk.gen
           solve uk using mcp;
$include out.gms
$include ev.gms
tbal = sum(k, px.l(k)*x1.l(k)-pm.l(k)*m1.l(k))-sum(j,sum(k,k1.l(j,k)-k0(j,k)));
asstinfln(j,k)$k0(j,k)=(((k1.l(j,k)-k0(j,k))-asstallow1(j,k)))/cap0(j,k);
```

```
trade(k,"export") =xvolume(k);
trade(k,"import") =mvolume(k);
trade(k,"netexp") =xvolume(k)-mvolume(k);
display "capfl15",ev,cv,evg,evg,evk,cvk,evt,cvt,evgdp_,cvgdp;
display "capfl15",tbal,capinflow, asstallow0, asstallow1,asstinfln, trade,emplpr, outper, capper;

$exit
lselas(hh) = 0.3;
        Sigmau(hh) =lselas(hh)*(netwage(hh)/leisure(hh)) +(1-alpha(hh))*(1/(1+(1-
alpha(hh))));
        tk(j,k) =0.3;
        tbal = sum(k, px.l(k)*x1.l(k)-pm.l(k)*m1.l(k))-sum(j,sum(k,k1.l(j,k)-k0(j,k)));

$include uk.gen
        solve uk using mcp;
        tk(j,k) =0.3;

$include uk.gen
        solve uk using mcp;
$include out.gms
$include ev.gms
        tbal = sum(k, px.l(k)*x1.l(k)-pm.l(k)*m1.l(k))-sum(j,sum(k,k1.l(j,k)-k0(j,k)));
        asstinfln(j,k)$k0(j,k)=(((k1.l(j,k)-k0(j,k))-asstallow1(j,k)))/cap0(j,k);

trade(k,"export") =xvolume(k);
trade(k,"import") =mvolume(k);
trade(k,"netexp") =xvolume(k)-mvolume(k);
display "capfl3",ev,cv,evg,evg,evk,cvk,evt,cvt,evgdp_,cvgdp;
display "capfl3", tbal,capinflow, asstallow0, asstallow1,asstinfln, trade;
```

*****Computation of Equivalent variation**

```
        EV(hh, "unif") = ((u1.l(hh)-ubase(hh))/ubase(hh))*ibase(hh);
        CV(hh, "unif") =((ubase(hh)-u1.l(hh))/u1.l(hh))*ra.l(hh);
        EVg("unif") = ((go1.l-gobase)/gobase)*reva;
        CVg("unif") = ((gobase-go1.l)/go1.l)*gibase;

        EVk("unif") = ((inv1.l-invbase)/invbase)*invibase;
        CVk("unif") = ((invbase-inv1.l)/inv1.l)*inv1.l;

        EVT("unif") = sum(hh,((u1.l(hh)-ubase(hh))/ubase(hh))*ibase(hh))
                        +((go1.l-gobase)/gobase)*reva
                        +((inv1.l-invbase)/invbase)*invibase;

        CVT("unif") = sum(hh,((ubase(hh)-u1.l(hh))/u1.l(hh))*ra.l(hh))
                        +((gobase-go1.l)/go1.l)*gibase
                        +((invbase-inv1.l)/inv1.l)*inv1.l;
        evgdp("unif") = 100*(sum(hh,((u1.l(hh)-ubase(hh))/ubase(hh))*ibase(hh))
                        +((go1.l-gobase)/gobase)*reva
                        +((inv1.l-invbase)/invbase)*invibase
                        )/(sum(k,va(k))+grev);
        evgdp_ = 100*(sum(hh,((u1.l(hh)-ubase(hh))/ubase(hh))*ibase(hh))
                        +((go1.l-gobase)/gobase)*reva
                        +((inv1.l-invbase)/invbase)*invibase )/(sum(k,va(k))+grev);
```

```
cvgdp("unif") = 100*(sum(hh,((ubase(hh)-u1.l(hh))/u1.l(hh))*ra.l(hh))
                              +((gobase-go1.l)/go1.l)*gibase
                              +((invbase-inv1.l)/inv1.l)*inv1.l
                              )/(sum(k,va(k))+grev);

cvgdp_ = 100*(sum(hh,((ubase(hh)-u1.l(hh))/u1.l(hh))*ra.l(hh))
                              +((gobase-go1.l)/go1.l)*gibase
                              +((invbase-inv1.l)/inv1.l)*inv1.l
                              )/(sum(k,va(k))+grev);
```

*****Output Handling**

```
output(k, "unif") = y1.l(k)-(y0(k)-expt(k));
employ(k, "unif") = L1.l(k)-L0(k);
export(k, "unif") = x1.l(k)-expt(k);
import(k, "unif") = m1.l(k)-m0(k);
consm(hh, "unif") = c1.l(hh)-(sum(k, (gdc(hh,k)+gmc(hh,k))));
capital(j,k) = k1.l(j,k)-k0(j,k);
capinflow(j,"unif") = sum(k,k1.l(j,k)-k0(j,k));
kstokk(j) = sum(k,cap0(j,k));
intrd(kk,k) = tint.l(kk,k)-(iof(kk,k)+iofm(kk,k));
xvolume(k) = pfx.l*x1.l(k);
mvolume(k) = pfx.l*m1.l(k);
tbalk(k) =xvolume(k) -mvolume(k);
cbal = sum(k,xvolume(k) -mvolume(k));

captax(j,k, "unif") =TAU_Tk.L*tk(j,k);
constax(k, "unif") =TAU_tc.L*vatc(k);
congtax(k, "unif") =TAU_tg.L*vatg0(k);
conitax(k, "unif") =TAU_vtk.L*vatk0(k);
ktax(j,k,"unif") =TAU_Tk.L*tk0(j,k);
newrev("unif") = sum((j,k),k1.l(j,k)*ktax(j,k,"unif"));

ch_leis(hh, "unif") = le.l(hh)-leisure(hh);

labsup(hh, "unif") =ls1.l(hh)- wages(hh);
welfare(hh, "unif") = 1-U.l(hh);
labtaxn(HH,"unif") =TAU_it.L*hit0(hh);

outper(k, "unif") =100*(y1.l(k)-(y0(k)-expt(k)))/(y0(k)-expt(k));
capper("unif",j,k)$k0(j,k) = 100*(k1.l(j,k)-k0(j,k))/k0(j,k);
chekk("unif",j) = sum(k,capper("unif",j,k)$k0(j,k)*k0(j,k));
leiper(hh, "unif") = 100*(le.l(hh)-leisure(hh))/leisure(hh);
lsper(hh, "unif") = 100*(ls1.l(hh)-netwage(hh))/netwage(hh);
emplper(k, "unif")$L0(k) = 100*(L1.l(k)-L0(k))/L0(k);
emplpr(k, "unif") = emplper(k, "unif");

basewage(hh, "unif") =basew;
newwage(hh, "unif") = pl.l;
leiprice(hh, "unif") =ple.l(hh)*(1-hit0(hh));
mprice(k, "unif")$m0(k) =pfx.l;;
xprice(k, "unif")$expt(k) =px.l(k);
```

**** Scenario analysis**

```
$include ukbase.gms
```

***moving to only capital income taxes**

**** central elasticities**

```
        etran(k)= etran0(k);
        sigmav(k)= sigmav0(k);
        sigmak(k)= sigmak0(k);
        sigmac(k)= sigmac0(k);
        sigmal(hh)= 0.75*sigmal0(hh);
lselas(hh) = 0.15;
Sigmau(hh) =lselas(hh)*(netwage(hh)/leisure(hh)) +(1-alpha(hh))*(1/(1+(1-alpha(hh))));

TAU_Tk.l =1;
TAU_Tc.L =1;
TAU_Tg.L =1;
TAU_VTk.L =1;
TAU_InT.L(k) =1;
TAU_IT.L =1;

tk(j,k) =0.25;

$include uk.gen
solve uk using mcp;

$include ev.gms
$include out.gms
parameter
evgdp1 equivalent variation as a fraction of GDP;

evgdp1("bs-bs") =evgdp_;

sigmak(k) =0.75;
$include uk.gen
solve uk using mcp;

$include ev.gms

evgdp1("bs-.75") =evgdp_;

sigmak(k) =1.01;
$include uk.gen
solve uk using mcp;

$include ev.gms

evgdp1("bs-1.01") =evgdp_;

sigmak(k) =3.0;
$include uk.gen
solve uk using mcp;
```

```
$include ev.gms

evgdp1("bs-3.0") =evgdp_;

sigmak(k) =5.0;
$include uk.gen
solve uk using mcp;

$include ev.gms

evgdp1("bs-5.0") =evgdp_;

sigmav(k) =0.75;
sigmak(k) =0.75;

$include uk.gen
solve uk using mcp;

$include ev.gms

evgdp1(".75-.75") =evgdp_;

sigmav(k) =0.75;
sigmak(k) =1.01;

$include uk.gen
solve uk using mcp;
$include ev.gms

evgdp1(".75-1") =evgdp_;

sigmav(k) =0.75;
sigmak(k) =3.0;

$include uk.gen
solve uk using mcp;
$include ev.gms

evgdp1(".75-3") =evgdp_;

sigmav(k) =0.75;
sigmak(k) =5.0;

$include uk.gen
solve uk using mcp;
$include ev.gms

evgdp1(".75-5") =evgdp_;

**
sigmav(k) =1.01;
sigmak(k) =0.75;
```

```
$include uk.gen
solve uk using mcp;

$include ev.gms

evgdp1("1.01-.75") =evgdp_;

sigmav(k) =1.01;
sigmak(k) =1.01;

$include uk.gen
solve uk using mcp;
$include ev.gms

evgdp1("1.01-1") =evgdp_;

sigmav(k) =1.01;
sigmak(k) =3.0;

$include uk.gen
solve uk using mcp;
$include ev.gms

evgdp1("1.01-3") =evgdp_;

sigmav(k) =1.01;
sigmak(k) =5.0;

$include uk.gen
solve uk using mcp;
$include ev.gms

evgdp1("1.01-5") =evgdp_;

**3

sigmav(k) =3.0;
sigmak(k) =0.75;

$include uk.gen
solve uk using mcp;

$include ev.gms

evgdp1("3.0-.75") =evgdp_;

sigmav(k) =3.0;
sigmak(k) =1.01;

$include uk.gen
solve uk using mcp;
$include ev.gms
```

```
evgdp1("3.0-1") =evgdp_;

sigmav(k) =3.0;
sigmak(k) =3.0;

$include uk.gen
solve uk using mcp;
$include ev.gms

evgdp1("3.0-3") =evgdp_;

sigmav(k) =3.0;
sigmak(k) =5.0;

$include uk.gen
solve uk using mcp;
$include ev.gms

evgdp1("3.0-5") =evgdp_;

*5

sigmav(k) =5.0;
sigmak(k) =0.75;

$include uk.gen
solve uk using mcp;

$include ev.gms

evgdp1("5.0-.75") =evgdp_;

sigmav(k) =5.0;
sigmak(k) =1.01;

$include uk.gen
solve uk using mcp;
$include ev.gms

evgdp1("5.0-1") =evgdp_;

sigmav(k) =5.0;
sigmak(k) =3.0;

$include uk.gen
solve uk using mcp;
$include ev.gms

evgdp1("5.0-3") =evgdp_;

sigmav(k) =5.0;
sigmak(k) =5.0;

$include uk.gen
```

```
solve uk using mcp;
$include ev.gms

evgdp1("5.0-5") =evgdp_;

display "els15", evgdp1;
```

***labour supply elasticity of 0.3**

```
lselas(hh) = 0.3;
Sigmau(hh) =lselas(hh)*(netwage(hh)/leisure(hh)) +(1-alpha(hh))*(1/(1+(1-alpha(hh))));

sigmav(k) =0.75;
sigmak(k) =0.75;

$include uk.gen
solve uk using mcp;

$include ev.gms

evgdp1(".75-.75") =evgdp_;

sigmav(k) =0.75;
sigmak(k) =1.01;

$include uk.gen
solve uk using mcp;
$include ev.gms

evgdp1(".75-1") =evgdp_;

sigmav(k) =0.75;
sigmak(k) =3.0;

$include uk.gen
solve uk using mcp;
$include ev.gms

evgdp1(".75-3") =evgdp_;

sigmav(k) =0.75;
sigmak(k) =5.0;

$include uk.gen
solve uk using mcp;
$include ev.gms

evgdp1(".75-5") =evgdp_;

**

sigmav(k) =1.01;
sigmak(k) =0.75;
```

```
$include uk.gen
solve uk using mcp;

$include ev.gms

evgdp1("1.01-.75") =evgdp_;

sigmav(k) =1.01;
sigmak(k) =1.01;

$include uk.gen
solve uk using mcp;
$include ev.gms

evgdp1("1.01-1") =evgdp_;

sigmav(k) =1.01;
sigmak(k) =3.0;

$include uk.gen
solve uk using mcp;
$include ev.gms

evgdp1("1.01-3") =evgdp_;

sigmav(k) =1.01;
sigmak(k) =5.0;

$include uk.gen
solve uk using mcp;
$include ev.gms

evgdp1("1.01-5") =evgdp_;

**3

sigmav(k) =3.0;
sigmak(k) =0.75;

$include uk.gen
solve uk using mcp;

$include ev.gms

evgdp1("3.0-.75") =evgdp_;

sigmav(k) =3.0;
sigmak(k) =1.01;

$include uk.gen
solve uk using mcp;
$include ev.gms

evgdp1("3.0-1") =evgdp_;
```

```
sigmav(k) =3.0;
sigmak(k) =3.0;

$include uk.gen
solve uk using mcp;
$include ev.gms

evgdp1("3.0-3") =evgdp_;

sigmav(k) =3.0;
sigmak(k) =5.0;

$include uk.gen
solve uk using mcp;
$include ev.gms

evgdp1("3.0-5") =evgdp_;

*5

sigmav(k) =5.0;
sigmak(k) =0.75;

$include uk.gen
solve uk using mcp;

$include ev.gms

evgdp1("5.0-.75") =evgdp_;

sigmav(k) =5.0;
sigmak(k) =1.01;

$include uk.gen
solve uk using mcp;
$include ev.gms

evgdp1("5.0-1") =evgdp_;

sigmav(k) =5.0;
sigmak(k) =3.0;

$include uk.gen
solve uk using mcp;
$include ev.gms

evgdp1("5.0-3") =evgdp_;

sigmav(k) =5.0;
sigmak(k) =5.0;

$include uk.gen
solve uk using mcp;
$include ev.gms
```

```
evgdp1("5.0-5") =evgdp_;

display "els3", evgdp1;
```

*****MEB computation**

```
$Title code of compute the marginal excess burden of taxes in the UK model

$include ukbase.gms
option decimals =3;
tk(j,k) =tk0(j,k);

parameter repmeb,reprev,revtw;
```

**** higher elasticities**

```
sigmav(k) =.95*sigmav0(k);
sigmak(k) =sigmak0(k);
sigmac(k) =1.75*sigmac0(k);
sigmau(hh) =1.5;
lselas(hh) = 0.3;
Sigmau(hh) =lselas(hh)*(netwage(hh)/leisure(hh)) +(1-alpha(hh))*(1/(1+(1-alpha(hh))));
etran(k) = 1.2*etran0(k);

display "high",sigmav, sigmak, sigmac, sigmau,sigmal, etran;

PARAMETER
        REVCH   change in revenue
        MEB     marginal excess burden of taxes
        MEVT    change in total welfare
;

set txi tax instruments /ktax, prot, hhtax,vtc,vtg,vatk/,
        tx_ktax(txi) capital income tax                   / ktax/
        tx_int(txi) tax on intermediate input             / prot/
        tx_hhtax(txi) household income tax                / hhtax/
        tx_vatc(txi) value added tax on cons              / vtc/
        tx_vatg(txi) value added tax on gov cons          / vtg/
        tx_vatk(txi) value added tax on capital           / vatk/;
```

***install base year tax rates**

```
        tarint(k,kk)$iofm(k,kk)        = tarint0(k,kk);
        tarc(k)                        = tarc0(k);
        targ(k)                        = targ0(k);
        tark(k)                        = tark0(k);

        dlint(k,kk)$iof(k,kk)          = dlint0(k,kk);
        dlc(k)$cc0(k)                  = dlc0(k);
        dlg(k)$g0(k)                   = dlg0(k);

        vtint(k,kk)$iof(k,kk)          = vtint0(k,kk);
        vatc(k)$(cc0(k)+ccm0(k))       = vatc0(k);
```

```
vatg(k)$(g0(k)+gm0(k))                  = vatg0(k);
vatk(k)$(id0(k)+id0m(k))                = vatk0(k);

subint(k,kk)$(iof(k,kk)+iofm(k,kk))     = subint0(k,kk);
subfc(k)$(cc0(k)+ccm0(k))               = subfc0(k);
subfg(k)$g0(k)                          = subfg0(k);
subfk(k)$id0(k)                         = subfk0(k);
subfe(k)$expt(k)                        = subfe0(k);

tk(j,k)                                 = tk0(j,k);
hit(hh)                                 = hit0(hh) ;

vatdc(k)= vatdc0(k);
vatmc(k)= vatmc0(k);
vatdk(k)= vatdk0(k);
vatmk(k)= vatmk0(k);
vatdg(k)= vatdg0(k);
vatmg(k)= vatmg0(k);


vatdc(k) = (1+subfc(k))*(1+dlc(k))*(1+vatc(k))-1;
vatmc(k) = (1+tarc(k))*(1+dlc(k))*(1+vatc(k))-1;
vatdk(k)= (1+subfk(k))*(1+dlk(k))*(1+vatk(k))-1;
vatmk(k)= (1+tark(k))*(1+dlk(k))*(1+vatk(k))-1;
vatdg(k)= (1+subfg(k))*(1+dlg(k))*(1+vatg(k))-1;
vatmg(k)= (1+targ(k))*(1+dlg(k))*(1+vatg(k))-1;

crevfc = sum(k, (vatdc(k)*cc0(k))+vatmc(k)*ccm0(k));
crevfk = sum(k, (vatdk(k)*(id0(k)+stock(k)))+(vatmk(k)*(id0m(k)+stockm(k))));
crevfg = sum(k, (vatdg(k)*g0(k))+vatmg(k)*gm0(k));
display crevfc, crevfk,crevfg;


alldint(k,Kk) = (1+vtint(k,kk))*(1+dlint(k,kk))*(1+subint(k,kk))-1;
allmint(k,Kk) = (1+tarint(k,kk))*(1+dlint(k,kk))*(1+vtint(k,kk))-1;

alldint0(k,kk) = alldint(k,Kk);
allmint0(k,kk) = allmint(k,Kk);
vatdc0(k)= vatdc(k);
vatmc0(k)= vatmc(k);
vatdk0(k)= vatdk(k);
vatmk0(k)= vatmk(k);
vatdg0(k)= vatdg(k);
vatmg0(k)= vatmg(k);

    Pint0(k,kk)         =(1+alldint0(k,kk));
    pmint0(k,kk)        = (1+allmint0(k,kk));
    pdc0(k)             =(1+vatdc0(k));
    pmc0(k)             =(1+vatmc0(k));
    pdk0(k)             =(1+vatdk0(k));
    pmk0(k)             =(1+vatmk0(k));
    pdg0(k)             =(1+vatdg0(k));
    pmg0(k)             =(1+vatmg0(k));
    uk.iterlim          =100000;
```

```
TAU_Tk.fx           =1;
TAU_int.fx(k)       =1;
TAU_it.fx           =1;
TAU_tc.fx           =1;
TAU_tg.fx           =1;
TAU_vtk.fx          =1;

loop(txi,

        If (tx_ktax(txi),
        tk(j,k) =1.01*tk0(j,k);
$include uk.gen
        solve uk using mcp;
        TAU_tk.fx = 1;
        MEVT(txi) = sum(hh,((ubase(hh)-u1.l(hh))))
                          +((gobase-go1.l))
                          +((invbase-inv1.l));
        REVCH(txi) = (GOVT.L-REVA);
        meb(TXI) =(MEVT(txi)/((pub/grev)*REVCH(txi)));
                tk(j,k) =tk0(j,k);
        repmeb(txi,"meb") =meb(txi);
        repmeb(txi,"revch") =pubshr*revch(txi);
        revmeb(txi,"MEVT") =mevt(txi);
        );
        if (tx_hhtax(txi),
                hit(hh) = 1.01*hit0(hh) ;
$include uk.gen
        solve uk using mcp;
                TAU_it.fx =1;
        MEVT(txi) = sum(hh,((ubase(hh)-u1.l(hh))))
                          +((gobase-go1.l))
                          +((invbase-inv1.l));
        REVCH(txi)        = (GOVT.L-REVA);
        meb(TXI)          = (MEVT(txi)/((pub/grev)*REVCH(txi)));
        hit(hh)           = hit0(hh) ;
        repmeb(txi,"meb")  =meb(txi);
        repmeb(txi,"revch") =pubshr*revch(txi);
        repmeb(txi,"MEVT") =mevt(txi);
        );

        if (tx_vatc(txi),
                vatdc(k)= 1.01*vatdc0(k);
                vatmc(k)= 1.01*vatmc0(k);

$include uk.gen
        solve uk using mcp;
                TAU_tc.fx = 1;
        MEVT(txi) = sum(hh,((ubase(hh)-u1.l(hh))))
                          +((gobase-go1.l))
                          +((invbase-inv1.l));

        REVCH(txi) = (GOVT.L-REVA);
        meb(TXI) =(MEVT(txi)/((pub/grev)*REVCH(txi)));
        vatdc(k)= vatdc0(k);
```

```
                vatmc(k)= vatmc0(k);
        repmeb(txi,"meb") =meb(txi);
        repmeb(txi,"revch") =pubshr*revch(txi);
        repmeb(txi,"MEVT") =mevt(txi);
        );

        if (tx_int(txi),
        alldint(k,Kk) =1.01*alldint0(k,Kk);
        allmint(k,Kk) =1.01*allmint0(k,Kk);
$include uk.gen
        solve uk using mcp;

                TAU_int.fx(k) = 1;
        MEVT(txi) = sum(hh,((ubase(hh)-u1.l(hh))))
                +((gobase-go1.l))
                +((invbase-inv1.l));

                REVCH(txi) = (GOVT.L-REVA);
                meb(TXI) =(MEVT(txi)/((pub/grev)*REVCH(txi)));
        alldint(k,Kk) =alldint0(k,Kk);
        allmint(k,Kk) =allmint0(k,Kk);
        repmeb(txi,"meb") =meb(txi);
        repmeb(txi,"revch") =pubshr*revch(txi);
        repmeb(txi,"MEVT") =mevt(txi);
        );

        if (tx_vatk(txi),
        vatdk(k)= 1.01*vatdk0(k);
        vatmk(k)= 1.01*vatmk0(k);

$include uk.gen
        solve uk using mcp;
                TAU_vtk.fx = 1;
        MEVT(txi) = sum(hh,((ubase(hh)-u1.l(hh))))
                +((gobase-go1.l))
                +((invbase-inv1.l));
                REVCH(txi) = (GOVT.L-REVA);
                meb(TXI) =(MEVT(txi)/((pub/grev)*REVCH(txi)));
                vatdk(k)= vatdk0(k);
                vatmk(k)= vatmk0(k);
        repmeb(txi,"meb") =meb(txi);
        repmeb(txi,"revch") =pubshr*revch(txi);
        repmeb(txi,"MEVT") =mevt(txi);
        );

        if (tx_vatg(txi),

                vatdg(k)= 1.01*vatdg0(k);
                vatmg(k)= 1.01*vatmg0(k);
$include uk.gen
        solve uk using mcp;
                TAU_tg.fx = 1;
        MEVT(txi) = sum(hh,((ubase(hh)-u1.l(hh))))
                +((gobase-go1.l))
```

```
                    +((invbase-inv1.l));
            REVCH(txi) = (GOVT.L-REVA);
            meb(TXI) =(MEVT(txi)/((pub/grev)*REVCH(txi)));
            vatdg(k)= vatdg0(k);
            vatmg(k)= vatmg0(k);
        repmeb(txi,"meb") =meb(txi);
        repmeb(txi,"revch") =pubshr*revch(txi);
        repmeb(txi,"MEVT") =mevt(txi);
        );

);

put "High substitution elasticity case";
display "high",meb, revch, mevt;
*display tk0,prt0,hit0,vtc0,vtk0,vtg0,tarfrt0;
display "high",sigmav, sigmak, sigmac, sigmau, etran,lselas;
display "high",repmeb;

$exit
sigmav(k) =.95*sigmav0(k);
sigmak(k) =.5*sigmak0(k);
sigmac(k) =.5*sigmac0(k);
sigmak(k) =.51;
sigmav(k) =.51;
sigmak(k) =.5*sigmak0(k);
sigmav(k) =.5*sigmav0(k);
sigmau(hh) =.25;
sigmal(hh) =.25;
lselas(hh) = 0.15;
Sigmau(hh) =lselas(hh)*(netwage(hh)/leisure(hh)) +(1-alpha(hh))*(1/(1+(1-alpha(hh))));
etran(k) = .6*etran0(k);

loop(txi,
        If (tx_ktax(txi),
                tk(j,k) =1.1*tk0(j,k);
$include uk.gen
        solve uk using mcp;
        TAU_tk.fx = 1;

        MEVT(txi) = sum(hh,((ubase(hh)-u1.l(hh))))
                    +((gobase-go1.l))
                    +((invbase-inv1.l));

        REVCH(txi) = (GOVT.L-REVA);
        meb(TXI) =(MEVT(txi)/(pubshr*REVCH(txi)));
        tk(j,k) =tk0(j,k);
        repmeb(txi,"meb") =meb(txi);
        repmeb(txi,"revch") =pubshr*revch(txi);
        repmeb(txi,"MEVT") =mevt(txi);
        );

        if (tx_hhtax(txi),

        hit(hh) = 1.01*hit0(hh) ;
```

```
$include uk.gen
        solve uk using mcp;
        TAU_it.fx =1;

        MEVT(txi) = sum(hh,((ubase(hh)-u1.l(hh))))
                      +((gobase-go1.l))
                      +((invbase-inv1.l));

        REVCH(txi) = (GOVT.L-REVA);
        meb(TXI) =(MEVT(txi)/(pubshr*REVCH(txi)));
        hit(hh) = hit0(hh) ;
        repmeb(txi,"meb") =meb(txi);
        repmeb(txi,"revch") =pubshr*revch(txi);
        repmeb(txi,"MEVT") =mevt(txi);
         );

        if (tx_vatc(txi),
        vatdc(k)= 1.01*vatdc0(k);
        vatmc(k)= 1.01*vatmc0(k);

$include uk.gen
        solve uk using mcp;
        TAU_tc.fx = 1;
        MEVT(txi) = sum(hh,((ubase(hh)-u1.l(hh))))
                      +((gobase-go1.l))
                      +((invbase-inv1.l));

        REVCH(txi) = (GOVT.L-REVA);
        meb(TXI) =(MEVT(txi)/(pubshr*REVCH(txi)));
        vatdc(k)= vatdc0(k);
        vatmc(k)= vatmc0(k);
        repmeb(txi,"meb") =meb(txi);
        repmeb(txi,"revch") =pubshr*revch(txi);
        repmeb(txi,"MEVT") =mevt(txi);
         );

        if (tx_int(txi),

        tarint(k,kk)$iofm(k,kk)          = 1.01*tarint0(k,kk);
        vtint(k,kk)$iof(k,kk)            = 1.01*vtint0(k,kk);
        dlint(k,kk)$iof(k,kk)            = 1.01*dlint0(k,kk);
        subint(k,kk)$(iof(k,kk)+iofm(k,kk)) = 1.01*subint0(k,kk);

$include uk.gen
        solve uk using mcp;

        TAU_int.fx(k) = 1;
        MEVT(txi) = sum(hh,((ubase(hh)-u1.l(hh))))
                      +((gobase-go1.l))
                      +((invbase-inv1.l));

        REVCH(txi) = (GOVT.L-REVA);
        meb(TXI) =(MEVT(txi)/(pubshr*REVCH(txi)));
        tarint(k,kk)$iofm(k,kk)          = tarint0(k,kk);
```

```
        vtint(k,kk)$iof(k,kk) = vtint0(k,kk);
        dlint(k,kk)$iof(k,kk) = dlint0(k,kk);
        subint(k,kk)$(iof(k,kk)+iofm(k,kk)) = subint0(k,kk);

        repmeb(txi,"meb") =meb(txi);
        repmeb(txi,"revch") =pubshr*revch(txi);
        repmeb(txi,"MEVT") =mevt(txi);
        );

        if (tx_vatk(txi),
        vatdk(k)= 1.01*vatdk0(k);
        vatmk(k)= 1.01*vatmk0(k);

$include uk.gen
        solve uk using mcp;
        TAU_vtk.fx = 1;
        MEVT(txi) = sum(hh,((ubase(hh)-u1.l(hh))))
                    +((gobase-go1.l))
                    +((invbase-inv1.l));

        REVCH(txi) = (GOVT.L-REVA);
        meb(TXI) =(MEVT(txi)/(pubshr*REVCH(txi)));
                vatdk(k)= vatdk0(k);
        vatmk(k)= vatmk0(k);
        repmeb(txi,"meb") =meb(txi);
        repmeb(txi,"revch") =pubshr*revch(txi);
        repmeb(txi,"MEVT") =mevt(txi);
        );

        if (tx_vatg(txi),
        vatdg(k)= 1.01*vatdg0(k);
        vatmg(k)= 1.01*vatmg0(k);
$include uk.gen
        solve uk using mcp;
        TAU_tg.fx = 1;
        MEVT(txi) = sum(hh,((ubase(hh)-u1.l(hh))))
                    +((gobase-go1.l))
                    +((invbase-inv1.l));

                REVCH(txi) = (GOVT.L-REVA);
        meb(TXI) =(MEVT(txi)/(pubshr*REVCH(txi)));
        vatdg(k)= vatdg0(k);
        vatmg(k)= vatmg0(k);

        repmeb(txi,"meb") =meb(txi);
        repmeb(txi,"revch") =pubshr*revch(txi);
        repmeb(txi,"MEVT") =mevt(txi);
        );
);

put "low substitution elasticity case";
display "low",meb, revch, mevt, pubshr;
*display tk0,prt0,hit0,vtc0,vtk0,vtg0,tarfrt0;
display "low",sigmav, sigmak, sigmac, sigmau, etran,lselas;
display "low",repmeb;
```

INDEX